UNLIMITED INTIMACY

UNLIMITED INTIMACY

REFLECTIONS ON THE SUBCULTURE OF BAREBACKING

TIM DEAN

THE UNIVERSITY OF CHICAGO PRESS • CHICAGO AND LONDON

TIM DEAN is Director of the Humanities Institute at the University of Buffalo (SUNY), where he is also a professor of English. He is the author of *Beyond Sexuality* and editor of *Homosexuality and Psychoanalysis*, both published by the University of Chicago Press.

The University of Chicago Press, Chicago 60637
The University of Chicago Press, Ltd., London
© 2009 by The University of Chicago
All rights reserved. Published 2009
Printed in the United States of America

16 15 14 13 12 11   3 4 5

ISBN-13: 978-0-226-13938-8 (cloth)
ISBN-13: 978-0-226-13939-5 (paper)
ISBN-10: 0-226-13938-7 (cloth)
ISBN-10: 0-226-13939-5 (paper)

Library of Congress Cataloging-in-Publication Data

Dean, Tim, 1964–
    Unlimited intimacy : reflections on the subculture of barebacking / Tim Dean.
        p. cm.
    Includes bibliographical references and index.
    ISBN-13: 978-0-226-13938-8 (cloth : alk. paper)
    ISBN-13: 978-0-226-13939-5 (pbk. : alk. paper)
    ISBN-10: 0-226-13938-7 (cloth : alk. paper)
    ISBN-10: 0-226-13939-5 (pbk. : alk. paper)
    1. Unsafe sex. 2. Gay men—Psychology. 3. Risk-taking (Psychology) 4. Male homosexuality—Psychological aspects. I. Title.
    HQ76.D42 2009
    306.77—dc22

                                                                2008042801

⊗ The paper used in this publication meets the minimum requirements of the American National Standard for Information Sciences—Permanence of Paper for Printed Library Materials, ANSI Z39.48-1992.

In no way am I asking anyone to change his or her behavior on the strength of ways I have or have not behaved. What I am asking is that all of us begin to put forward the monumental analytical effort, in whichever rhetorical mode we choose, needed not to interpret what we say, but to say what we do.

SAMUEL R. DELANY, "STREET TALK/STRAIGHT TALK"

We have learned to cherish different cultures as unique expressions of human inventiveness rather than as the inferior or disgusting habits of savages. We need a similarly anthropological understanding of different sexual cultures.

GAYLE RUBIN, "THINKING SEX"

CONTENTS

PREFACE

This study began when I became aware that the terms in which my previous book had discussed "unsafe sex" among gay men were drastically behind the times. I had been thinking about anal sex without condoms as essentially a mistake, as the sort of lapse that might be amenable to psychoanalytic interpretation, when I discovered that unprotected sex had become the basis for a distinct subculture. After two decades of safe-sex education, erotic risk among gay men has become organized and deliberate, not just accidental. The principled abandonment of condoms has led to scenarios of purposeful HIV transmission and, on that basis, to the creation of new sexual identities and communities. Thus the emergence of what has come to be known as bareback subculture represents not only an unprecedented situation in the history of AIDS but also a new chapter in the history of sexuality.

It is not hard to envisage how this shift in sexual practice has become the subject of intense controversy both inside the gay community and beyond it. My view of the controversy is that, while focusing on an extremely significant phenomenon, it has tended to generate more heat than light. *Unlimited Intimacy* represents an attempt to shed some light on a subculture that, despite what many in the gay community fervently wish, is not likely to disappear anytime soon. It is quite normal, although not very helpful, to imagine that handling the subject with extreme discretion might minimize its importance or even abolish its existence. Gay people don't need this kind of publicity, especially at a moment when the campaign for same-sex marriage looks set to finally win us equal rights. I beg to differ. My thesis is that the emergence of a subculture of bareback sex is not merely coincident with but directly related to the campaign for same-sex marriage that has occupied so much attention in recent years. As I elaborate in chapter 1, gay men have discovered that, on the basis of viral transmission, they can form relations and networks understood in terms of kinship—networks that represent an alternative to, even as they often resemble, normative heterosexual kinship.

Commentary on the bareback phenomenon almost unanimously treats it as pathological behavior; to do otherwise may appear to justify ostensibly indefensible conduct. Given that I make every effort *not* to pathologize the subculture, I would like it to be understood from the outset that *Unlimited Intimacy* is far from an apologia for barebacking. I contend that an unclouded view of this subculture may be gained only by checking the impulse either to criticize or to defend it. New, apparently unintelligible behavior such as the organized sharing of infected semen requires not a rush to judgment but a careful suspension of judgment, before certain actions may become remotely transparent. Since I am aware that a prolonged deferral of judgment in the face of such inflammatory sexual practices might be regarded as disingenuous agnosticism on my part, I respectfully solicit the reader's forbearance as I try, in the pages that follow, to keep open a vital margin between defense and critique.

It is crucial to this book's argument that risky sex has become the basis for a subculture. I suggest that, as a specifically subcultural practice, unprotected sex among gay men might best be approached anthropologically. In other words, bareback subculture should be regarded as a foreign culture by outsiders and approached with due care and respect. Like any culture, this one has its own language, rituals, etiquette, institutions, iconography, and so on. A large part of the current project consists in attempting to describe what subcultural participants are up to and how they seem to understand what they are doing. Barebacking is overdetermined behavior, by which I mean that no single causal explanation—whether in terms of the availability of antiretroviral medications or the popularity of illegal drugs such as crystal methamphetamine—is sufficient to account for it. Purposeful unprotected sex among gay men has become very complex and highly meaningful behavior. It cannot be dismissed simply as pathology or argued away with one-dimensional explanations.

In approaching the subculture in this manner, I have been guided by anthropologist Gayle Rubin's useful principle of benign sexual variation—that is, the idea that different cultural organizations of sexuality should be understood nonhierarchically. The principle of benign sexual variation upholds the quite uncomplicated axiom that no single consensual erotic practice is a priori preferable over any other. There is no best way of having sex. Conceptually this is not difficult to get one's head around; yet, for most North Americans, this principle seems much harder to accept than, for example, the idea of benign racial variation. It often appears unfathomable that others would consent to forms of erotic practice that nothing could persuade me to participate in; but just because I would not be willing to engage in certain sexual acts does not mean that others should not. The element of consent is integral to Rubin's argument: the principle of benign sexual variation applies only to consensual sex. I tried to keep this principle in mind as I investigated a subcultural organization of sexuality that departs from mainstream gay norms, as well as from those of straight society.

My research has been based primarily in San Francisco, where the subculture originated. This book's introduction considers various methodological challenges entailed in the investigation of sexual subcultures, especially for someone with no formal training in the subject. Research for this study has taken me into unfamiliar methodological territory, while also forcing me to confront erotic practices that tested my limits. Intellectual work on sexuality is distinguished by the fact that, when it comes to sex, everyone is an expert and no one is. By this I mean that everyone, even a child, has his or her own theory of sexuality (Freud spoke of children's "sexual theories," for example); yet it is notoriously difficult to get an accurate and complete account from *anyone* about his or her fantasies, desires, and erotic practices. There are various ways of accounting for this difficulty, although fewer means of overcoming it.

My data on the subculture derive from three main sources: informal participant observation, pornography produced by and for the subculture, and bareback Web sites. Readers who imagine that practitioners of such stigmatized activity would be inclined toward reticence about their behavior miss completely the significance of barebacking as the basis for a subculture. Inevitably such a subculture's self-representation takes pornographic forms and, as with other new subcultures, flourishes online. Chapters 2 and 3 examine bareback pornography in the context of broader cultural debates about sexually explicit representation. I argue that this genre of porn emerged in order to document a set of practices that already were quite well established and, therefore, cannot legitimately be blamed for causing behavior that many in the gay community view with dismay. Demonstrating that this porn appeals not to the standard rationale of fantasy for its justification but to the opposite, documentary realism, I consider how hard-core pornographic conventions paradoxically militate against faithful subcultural representation. Bareback porn is compelled to negotiate a particular problem, namely, that the hard-core convention of screening male orgasm conflicts with the subculture's commitment to internal ejaculation. Given the kinds of solutions devised to overcome this representational obstacle, I argue that bareback porn should be understood as not merely a troubling source of entertainment for certain gay men but as a specific experiment in thinking. This pornography merits sustained attention not least because it is engaged in working through fundamental problems of representation.

The book's final chapter assesses the status of online cruising (which is now highly developed) by differentiating it from older forms of cruising in urban spaces such as streets, parks, theaters, bars, clubs, bathhouses, and tearooms. Drawing on a sociological distinction between contact and networking, I suggest that the principal virtue of cruising is to initiate contact with strangers. The distinction between contact and networking makes evident how cruising online reduces contact with strangers to a form of networking. Recasting this sociological distinction in psychoanalytic terms, I argue that avoiding strangers provides a means of shunning contact with *strangeness*, particularly one's own strangeness or otherness. I suggest that, far from being reducible to promiscuity, gay cruising constitutes a philosophy of living whose ethics depends on whether the openness to strangeness is cultivated or, conversely, curtailed. To the extent that unprotected sex represents a disposition of openness to the other, it may be regarded as ethically exemplary. Chapter 4 thus considers more directly the ethics of barebacking and attempts to untangle its ethically admirable implications from those that are less so.

Condoms *feel* anachronistic to many gay men now, and I wanted to know why. Through the investigation of a new sexual subculture—and by drawing on a range of methodological approaches, including feminist anthropology, Freudian psychoanalysis, disability theory, and queer critique—*Unlimited Intimacy* aims to contribute to several well-established and emergent areas of research: the ethnography of subcultures, the anthropology of kinship, cultural studies of pornography, and the philosophy of the stranger. Rapid technological developments in medicine and electronic communication have had as one of their myriad effects what I would call a marked acceleration in the history of sexuality. New erotic practices, identities, communities, and discourses emerge, only to mutate, at a pace hitherto unimaginable. This book tries to capture a moment in that unfolding history so as to reflect on its significance. Conscious that my account of the subculture may be already out of date, I offer these reflections less as a definitive statement than as a provocation to further thinking.

In the research and writing of *Unlimited Intimacy*, I have been aided by a far-flung network of friends, lovers, acquaintances, colleagues, and readers whom it is an unmitigated pleasure to thank. The names of some individuals appear more than once, in recognition of their assistance and support in more than one context; for reasons of anonymity, privacy, or my own forgetfulness, the names of others do not appear here. I am profoundly grateful to them all for their stimulation, support, and good-natured interrogations of my thesis.

Michael Scarce kick-started this book over dinner in San Francisco, in October 2000; his own research on barebacking has been a formative influence on my thinking. Karol Marshall first suggested that I write down my escapades and discoveries in the subculture. Janet Lyon was there from the very beginning of this project, with her expertise in medical matters and disability theory.

I have benefited enormously from opportunities to present my research on this subject at various institutions: Austin College, University of California–Berkeley, Brown University, Buffalo State College, Carnegie Mellon University, Dartmouth College, University College–Dublin, Harvard University, University of Helsinki, University of Leeds, University of London, Northwest Center for Psychoanalysis (Seattle), Old Dominion University, University of Rochester, Slought Foundation (Philadelphia), Syracuse University, Temple University, Texas A&M University, University of Toronto, Trent University, Western Michigan University, York College of Pennsylvania, and York University. For those invitations and their hospitality, I wish to thank Todd Penner, Leo Bersani, Genie Brinkema, Allen Shelton, Jeff Williams, Don Pease, Michael O'Rourke and Noreen O'Connor, Brad Epps, Harri Kalha, Barbara Engh, Lisa Downing, Cynthia Dyess and Karol Marshall, Anita Fellman and David Metzger, Linda Edwards and Susan Gustafson, Aaron Levy and Jean-Michel Rabaté, Michael D. Dwyer, Robert Caserio, Brenda Bethman, John Paul Ricco, Richard Dellamora and Veronica Hollinger, Chris Nagle, Colbey Emmerson Reid, and Tom Loebel.

Although I have not taught a course (or even part of a course) on barebacking, my students have been vital interlocutors on this subject. I particularly wish to acknowledge Kevin Arnold, Lily Cates, Anthony Chase, Richard

Chiavetta, Sara Eddleman, Sue Feldman, Mary Foltz, Nate Gorelick, Ryan Hatch, Alla Ivanchikova, Chris Madson, Amanda Morrison, Matt Pieknik, Steven Ruszczycky, Rebecca Sanchez, Siobhan Scarry, Anthony Siu, Andrea Spain, and Mikko Tuhkanen. Genie Brinkema, who was virtually a coauthor of the chapters on pornography, deserves special thanks.

A number of friends generously read the manuscript and offered bracingly frank feedback. Without the incisive suggestions of Leo Bersani, Matti Bunzl, Robert Caserio, Chip Delany, Cynthia Dyess, Jason Friedman, Lauren Goodlad, Scott Herring, Chris Lane, Tom Loebel, Janet Lyon, Karol Marshall, Don Pease, David Schmid, and Kaja Silverman, this book would be much poorer.

In addition to friendship, the following colleagues in Buffalo have given me ideas that found their way into *Unlimited Intimacy*: Rachel Ablow, Carrie Bramen, Susan Cahn, Diane Christian, Joan Copjec, Robert Lopez, Ruth Mack, Carine Mardorossian, Steven Miller, Gary Nickard, Hershini Young, and Ewa Ziarek. Others whose conversation and wisdom have entered these pages include Colleen Boggs, Billy Brennan, C. L. Cole, Merrill Cole, Mario Corona, Lee Faver, Samantha Frost, Sam Geraci, Octavio Gonzales, David Greven, Hunter Hargraves, Sarah Hill, Donatella Izzo, Kris Jacobson, Vincent Lankewish, Richard Nashwinter, Melissa Orlie, Griselda Pollock, Larson Powell, Jasbir Puar, Jean-Michel Rabaté, Frances Restuccia, Adrian Rifkin, Larry Schehr, Tricia Sheffield, Alfred Thomas, Dan Warner, Kath Weston, Robyn Wiegman, and Sharon Willis. In San Francisco, Jason Friedman and Jeffrey Friedman generously opened their home for my extended visits; their hospitality made a difference.

The pleasure of writing this book has been intensified by those with whom I share daily intimacies. My partner, Ramón Soto-Crespo, provided unconditional support for my research; he knew when to leave me alone to write, and he read every page once I was done. The experience of psychoanalysis with Dr. Alice Jones has redefined intimacy for me. Not only did I begin and end this book while in analysis, I also explored most of its concerns in daily sessions with Dr. Jones, to the extent that *Unlimited Intimacy* feels like a product of my analysis—a product, that is, of psychological as well as intellectual and sexual exploration.

At the University of Chicago Press, Doug Mitchell is my dream-come-true editor. Having encouraged this project from the outset, he steered it with a sure hand—not to mention his characteristic wit and charm—through an unusually stormy review process. Doug's faith in this book has been critical, as has the assistance of his right-hand man, Tim McGovern. Four readers for the Press showed me what needed to be clarified. I am grateful to them all.

INTRODUCTION: CONFESSIONS OF A BAREBACKER

I like to bareback—to fuck without condoms.

Whether gay or straight, who wouldn't admit to preferring intimacy free from the muted sensations and interruptions of rubber or latex? (Even rubber and latex fetishists don't go in much for condoms.) The problem lies in the first half of this opening sentence, in the description of sex without condoms as "barebacking." Queer culture, drawing an analogy from equestrian pursuits and invoking a quintessentially North American cowboy image, has coined the term "barebacking" to describe gay men's deliberate abandonment of prophylaxis during sex. As medical sociologist Michael Scarce noted in an early report on the phenomenon, "some people use barebacking to describe all sex without condoms, but barebackers themselves define it as both the premeditation and eroticization of unprotected anal sex."[1] Although it seems important to differentiate the principled rejection of condoms during high-risk sex from ordinary rubberless fucking in which little risk is involved, I also want to maintain a sense of continuity between barebacking and regular unprotected intercourse, whether gay or straight, in order to consider the implications of regarding *all* condomless sex as barebacking. Thus I shall be using the term in both senses (to describe all sex without condoms and to describe specific subcultural practices), although I'll endeavor to clarify my usage as the argument proceeds.

"Barebacking" is now fully embedded in queer vernacular as the label for a distinct erotic preference. Yet the term barely existed prior to 1997, AIDS

---

1. Michael Scarce, "A Ride on the Wild Side: An HIV-Prevention Activist Goes through the Latex Looking Glass to Discover Who's Doing It Raw, and Why," *POZ*, February 1999, 52.

having rendered inconceivable the idea that gay men would intentionally relinquish protection when fucking. All that changed in the late 1990s with the advent of drug therapies that sharply reduced AIDS-related mortalities in the populations to which they're available. With the threat of death deferred, gay men's erotic practices changed again: now something called the *bareback community*—with its own Web sites, pornography, and subcultural codes—flourishes online and underground in the gay community. This book is about that change and about the profound, though barely acknowledged, cultural transformations that have accompanied it.

By seeking to define (but also to challenge definitions of) barebacking, this introduction attempts to establish how the practice of unprotected sex among men has become thoroughly socialized behavior. In the pages that follow, I explain how, in becoming the basis for a subculture, barebacking merits a less medicalized approach than it hitherto has received; it warrants, in other words, an approach that would anatomize the subculture's demographics, rituals, and underlying fantasies, rather than simply try to devise strategies for stamping it out. My argument takes an additional turn when I suggest that barebacking cannot be understood as restricted to the subculture it has created, since barebacking concerns an experience of unfettered intimacy, of overcoming the boundaries between persons, that is far from exclusive to this subculture or, indeed, to queer sexuality. After establishing the significance of barebacking as a subculture, I suggest that it also may be considered "post-subcultural." Thus I aim to describe the specificity of the subculture and to explore the methodological challenges entailed in researching stigmatized sexual behavior, but I also wish to generalize from the subculture, insofar as the issues it raises exceed those of HIV prevention and the history of North American gay male identity. Strange as it may sound to say so, this book and the subculture that it anatomizes are not principally about AIDS.

Typically the emergence of bareback subculture has been viewed as a case of pathological self-destructiveness or, at best, gross irresponsibility on the part of those who should know better. Gay journalist Charles Kaiser recently declared, "A person who is HIV-positive has no more right to unprotected intercourse than he has the right to put a bullet through another person's head."[2] And the playwright Larry Kramer, indefatigable on this issue, asks rhetorically, "Has it never, ever occurred to you that not using a condom is

---

2. Quoted in Andrew Jacobs, "Gays Debate Radical Steps to Curb Unsafe Sex," *New York Times*, February 15, 2005, A2.

tantamount to murder?"[3] One prominent gender theorist, the author of an incisive critique of antipornography feminism, responded to my research no less hyperbolically by characterizing the subculture as "gay men creating death camps for themselves."

Show demographics of users?

In the face of such reactions (which I have found surprisingly common among otherwise enlightened colleagues), I would like to make explicit from the start that *Unlimited Intimacy* tries to resist the easy comfort of demonizing individuals who bareback, on one hand, or the glib condemnation of the inadequacies of safe-sex education, on the other. Some commentators have tended to explain the return to risky sex as a result of the conflicting social messages that bombard gay men, as if we were essentially victims of a homophobic culture. "They internalize the homophobia of the culture around them, and act it out on their own bodies," suggests one gay journalist in his account of barebacking.[4] Blaming bareback sex on homophobia is as politically and intellectually inadequate as blaming it on barebackers themselves. Rather than either condemning or excusing bareback sex, I would like to defer judgment about it in order to open a space in which real thinking can occur—thinking that is not constrained by assumptions about what barebacking must represent. Having written previously about sexual risk, I thought that I knew what barebacking must be about; on further investigation, I discovered that I did not. Thus my initial claim about the ethics of barebacking is that it is *unethical* to decide whether the practice should be regarded as blameworthy or otherwise before the subculture has been explored.

Not homophobia but normativity

When I began this project, little substantial research existed on the subject. Although many articles and two books on barebacking have appeared subsequently (and, doubtless, there are more in the pipeline), none of this research considers the significance of unprotected sex as the basis for a specific subculture.[5] Although far less pathologizing than journalistic commentary on the

3. Quoted in Johann Hari, "The New HIV Threat," *Independent*, November 7, 2005, available at http://news.independent.co.uk/uk/health__medical/article325335.ece.

4. Hari, "New HIV Threat." Although she makes a more nuanced argument, Cindy Patton also tends to blame the return to risky sex on the inadequacies of heteronormative safe-sex education. See Patton, *Fatal Advice: How Safe-Sex Education Went Wrong* (Durham, NC: Duke University Press, 1996).

5. See Perry N. Halkitis, Leo Wilton, and Jack Drescher, eds., *Barebacking: Psychosocial and Public Health Approaches* (Binghamton, NY: Haworth Medical, 2005); Michael Shernoff, *Without Condoms: Unprotected Sex, Gay Men, and Barebacking* (New York: Routledge, 2006); and David M. Halperin, *What Do Gay Men Want? Sex, Risk, and Subjectivity* (Ann Arbor: University of Michigan Press, 2007). Shernoff's volume and the studies collected in Halkitis, Wilton, and Drescher are based almost exclusively on research in New York, whereas *Unlimited Intimacy* focuses on the development of bareback subculture primarily in San Francisco.

phenomenon, recent academic work on barebacking tends to approach the behavior in individualistic terms by asking what motivates men to bareback and how they might be discouraged from doing so. This research proceeds from the assumption that, if we can understand the forces prompting such risky behavior, then we might be able to curtail it. In other words, it assumes from the outset that barebacking is pathological. Even Michael Shernoff—who at one point suggests that, "in the age of AIDS, male-male sex without condoms is sometimes normal, adaptive, understandable, explainable, and probably unstoppable as well as ethically defensible"—insists on distinguishing between bareback sex that occurs among strangers and that which occurs in a monogamous gay couple.[6] By calling the latter "unprotected anal intercourse (UAI)," a term that no one but a tin-eared social scientist would ever use to describe his or her own erotic life, Shernoff normalizes barebacking within seroconcordant couples by shifting the stigma to casual condomless sex. He thus tacitly reinforces the perception of barebacking as pathological behavior. Media and academic discourse on the subject manifests an almost irresistible tendency toward "othering" bareback sex as deviant or pathological.[7] In this book, by contrast, I am curious about what might be learned if bareback subculture were to be investigated without that assumption.

THE INVENTION OF BAREBACKING

In the first decade of the epidemic, Douglas Crimp wrote, in a landmark article, that sexual conservatives "insist that our promiscuity will destroy us when in fact *it is our promiscuity that will save us.*"[8] Contending that gay men's adoption of safer sex (using condoms with multiple partners) stemmed directly from our history of promiscuity, Crimp argued that the quality and quantity

---

6. Shernoff, *Without Condoms*, 28.

7. A notable exception to this tendency is J. P. Cheuvront, "High-Risk Sexual Behavior in the Treatment of HIV-Negative Patients," *Journal of Gay and Lesbian Psychotherapy* 6, no. 3 (2002): 7–26, which provides a thoughtful critique of how marginalizing the sexual risk taker as a "damaged other" serves primarily to quell our own anxieties about risk and infection. See also Cheuvront, "Attaining Meaning in the Face of Sexual Risk-Taking and Risk-Taking Consequences," *Studies in Gender and Sexuality* 8, no. 1 (2007): 69–85. In a similar vein, Dave Holmes and Dan Warner take a nonpathologizing, psychoanalytic approach to semen exchange among men who have sex with men, arguing that many barebackers "not only desire sex with other men, but something more. It is the desire for this 'something more' that fouls attempts by these men to practise 'safe sex,' for this something more is not possible through what the health establishment has defined as safe sex." From Holmes and Warner, "The Anatomy of a Forbidden Desire: Men, Penetration and Semen Exchange," *Nursing Inquiry* 12, no. 1 (2005): 12–13.

8. Douglas Crimp, "How to Have Promiscuity in an Epidemic," in *AIDS: Cultural Analysis/Cultural Activism*, ed. Douglas Crimp (Cambridge, MA: MIT Press, 1988), 253, emphasis in the original.

of gay erotic experience provided unique resources for devising technologies of protection and thus of mutual care. Rather than being understood as self-destructive behavior, promiscuity could be redescribed as promoting recipro-cal care and self-protection. In this line of thinking, promiscuity is not merely defended in the face of AIDS panic but is actually promoted as the route to something new. Promiscuity, in other words, concerns more than new sex partners: it also concerns new ideas and new ways of doing things. Not so much a compulsive repetition of the same, promiscuity would be a name for discovery of the new, a synonym for creativity.[9] Sexual adventurousness gives birth to other forms of adventurousness—political, cultural, intellectual. I too wish to recommend promiscuity in this broader sense, and I will have more to say later in this introduction about how purity may be considered as an enemy of the intellect.

What might happen if we were a little more promiscuous about promis-cuity itself, if we defined it more broadly, permitting promiscuity to affect all forms of attention, all those moments when our regard approaches and touches something else? That question guides this book's trajectory; I answer it directly only in the final chapter, where I consider cruising less as a localized gay male practice than as an ethical philosophy of living that is available to anyone, irrespective of gender or sexuality. In order to make that argument, however, I first want to consider promiscuity of the unequivocally sexual kind. Barebacking epitomizes promiscuous sex: it mixes bodies and semen and blood without compunction. Barebacking is the next logical step in the enterprise of gay promiscuity. To Crimp's argument we must reply that, in-deed, gay men invented safer sex and risk-reduction guidelines, but now we have invented barebacking. Unprotected anal sex between men has become something different than it once was: barebacking does not represent a "re-lapse" or a misguided return to what gay sex before AIDS used to be. As I elaborate in chapter 2, gay pornography registers this distinction, in that porn produced during the 1970s and early '80s has been marketed for more than a decade as "pre-condom," whereas recent condomless videos are produced and marketed specifically as "bareback." Although it doubtless is true that, throughout the AIDS epidemic, some men have never used condoms for anal sex—that, in other words, safer-sex education, like any kind of education,

9. In his very interesting critique of monogamy, psychoanalyst Adam Phillips suggests, slightly differently, that promiscuity is a synonym for adaptation. See Phillips, *Monogamy* (New York: Pan-theon, 1996), aphorism 100.

has never been 100 percent effective—this fact remains at best marginally relevant to my argument. Only by recognizing barebacking as an invention on the part of contemporary queers does one stand a chance of appreciating what's at stake in the way gay men fuck now.

Unaccountable though it seems at first blush, bareback subculture actually signals profound changes in the social organization of kinship and relationality. The AIDS epidemic has given gay men new opportunities for kinship, because sharing viruses has come to be understood as a mechanism of alliance, a way of forming consanguinity with strangers or friends. Through HIV, gay men have discovered that they can "breed" without women. *Unlimited Intimacy* does not take for granted what might seem obvious, namely, that bareback subculture is all about death. For some of its participants, bareback sex concerns different forms of life, reproduction, and kinship. As will become clear, barebacking isn't merely Russian-roulette sex, that is, fucking with life-and-death stakes; barebacking also raises questions that complicate how we distinguish life-giving activities from those that engender death.

UNCLOSETING HIV

Adjudications of life and death—and of kinship—are closely regulated by law. From a legal perspective, the deliberate transmission of HIV counts as a felony in the majority of states.[10] Hence the tendency is to keep bareback subculture underground, to protect it with a kind of closet. Barebackers have appropriated the military's homophobic "Don't ask, don't tell" policy and applied it to HIV: when online ads for bareback parties use this phrase, they mean that any discussion of serostatus is prohibited, as is condom use. A national study of the sexual etiquette of HIV-positive people found that non-disclosure of serostatus during casual or anonymous sex is more prevalent

10. At last count, thirty-one of the forty-eight contiguous states had criminal statutes on HIV transmission. Remarkably, five states (Illinois, Iowa, Missouri, South Dakota, and Tennessee) explicitly don't require HIV transmission for conviction of the felony of "criminal transmission of HIV." As the Illinois statute puts it, "the actual transmission of HIV is not a required element of the crime" (720 *Illinois Compiled Statutes*, sec. 5/12-16.2). It is sufficient grounds for conviction that the defendant knew he or she was HIV positive and had sex with someone without disclosing his or her serostatus, thereby neglecting to provide opportunity for consent. In all five of these states, as in most others, consenting to sex with an HIV-positive person is deemed an affirmative defense against the charge. However, the state of Missouri is unique in explicitly denying the use of a condom as a defense; according to a 2002 revision of its statute, condom use without serostatus disclosure constitutes a class B felony, "unless the victim contracts HIV from the contact, in which case it is a class A felony" (*Missouri Revised Statutes*, sec. 191.677 [2002]). See "State Criminal Statutes on HIV Transmission," Lambda Legal Web site, available at http://www.thebody.com/lambda/criminal__law.html.

among men fucking men than it is during sex involving women or long-term gay partners.[11] This closeting of HIV status is as double-edged as any closet, since it confers a measure of protection through deniability while incarcerating in silence those it shelters.

Given that, in this book, I draw on some of my own experience with the subculture, I should mention that during casual bareback sex nobody *ever* has inquired about my HIV status. Having been asked about my most intimate fantasies and desires by perfect strangers, and having been solicited to perform all manner of sexual acts by men I'd barely met, I never have been asked whether I'm HIV positive or negative. Only one of the dozen or so readers of this manuscript, the fearless Samuel R. Delany, inquired directly about my HIV status. Evidently the closet around serostatus extends well beyond bareback subculture, making disclosure of this detail seem uniquely intimate. As Eve Kosofsky Sedgwick has shown, closets tend to be structured in order to permit the "open secret" of everyone's knowing, or assuming, personal information that no one is willing to actually acknowledge to the individual whom it most concerns.[12] Let me put it this way: no one (except Delany) ever *asked me* about my HIV status.

At the time of Delany's inquiry, I considered it to be tactical to withhold information about my own HIV status from appearing in these pages. My rationale for doing so stemmed from a desire to stimulate reflection among readers concerning what difference it makes whether the author of this book has HIV inside his body or not. Fully aware that readers might wish to know, I aimed to make that wish to know subject to examination in its own right. By not disclosing my HIV status, I was hoping to avoid the reduction of my argument to that of someone with a particular serostatus. *Unlimited Intimacy* mounts an argument against identification politics, and I wanted it to be read without the reader's being able to either identify or disidentify unequivocally with its author on this basis. In developing this rationale for nondisclosure in the context of an intellectual argument, I had imagined—naively, as it turned

11. Daniel H. Ciccarone, David E. Kanhouse, Rebecca L. Collins, Angela Miu, James L. Chen, Sally C. Morton, and Ron Stall, "Sex without Disclosure of Positive HIV Serostatus in a U.S. Probability Sample of Persons Receiving Medical Care for HIV Infection," *American Journal of Public Health* 93, no. 6 (June 2003): 949–54. A notable exception to this general trend is Geek Slut, a fortysomething HIV-positive barebacker who maintains a fascinating blog (available at http://www.geekslut .org); in "Ethical Behavior for a Poz Faggot" (posted June 27, 2006; accessed June 2007), he emphasizes his commitment to disclosure of HIV status in all sexual encounters.

12. See Eve Kosofsky Sedgwick, *Epistemology of the Closet* (Berkeley: University of California Press, 1990).

out—that my thesis would not be identified with the position of either HIV-positive or -negative men.

Among the many discoveries of *Unlimited Intimacy* is that, when it comes to the matter of unprotected sex, interlocutors and readers constantly make assumptions about HIV status. The fact that nobody asks doesn't mean that the question is not on everyone's mind. As of this moment of revision, in July 2007, I am HIV negative—a fact that I mention now because it has dawned on me that many of the men whom I've barebacked over the past decade, as well as many of this book's readers, have tended to assume, without seeking confirmation, that I must be HIV positive. When I describe engaging in anonymous bareback sex, I would prefer that the reader not imagine that I am potentially infecting other men. The possibility that some have read this book under that assumption helps account for the extremely strong reactions elicited by earlier drafts. It thus seems worth relinquishing the strategic desire to elude a certain positioning, with all the likely consequences of identification and disidentification that this entails, in order to forestall the violence of those particular reactions.[13]

BAREBACKING AS BEHAVIOR AND AS IDENTITY

Andrew Sullivan is one HIV-positive gay man who is very open about his status. But he is less public about his desire to bareback. Midway through 2001, the conservative pundit was "outed" cruising online for bareback sex, using the screen name "RawMuscleGlutes" and soliciting the kind of uninhibited group sex that he has publicly condemned other gay men for practicing and gay culture for sponsoring. When confronted, Sullivan did not deny that he was seeking condomless sex with other HIV-positive men, but he did repudiate the label of barebacker and the outlaw status that it implies. Despite his erotic preferences, Sullivan remains committed to an assimilationist model of homosexuality, publicly advocating the legal recognition and social normalization of lesbians and gays, particularly through marriage.[14]

13. In thinking through these issues of self-disclosure, I have found conversations with Scott Herring especially useful. For a brilliant analysis of the history of cultural efforts to make sexuality legible and the resistance to those efforts, see Herring, *Queering the Underworld: Slumming, Literature, and the Undoing of Lesbian and Gay History* (Chicago: University of Chicago Press, 2007).

14. An excellent analysis of the Sullivan bareback debacle may be found in Richard Kim's "Andrew Sullivan, Overexposed," *Nation*, June 5, 2001, available at http://www.thenation.com/doc/20010618/kim20010605. See also Paul Robinson, *Queer Wars: The New Gay Right and Its Critics* (Chicago: University of Chicago Press, 2005), chap. 2. Sullivan's assimilationist thesis is expounded in his book *Virtually Normal: An Argument about Homosexuality* (New York: Knopf, 1995).

What interests me about Sullivan's case is its illustrating how the determined pursuit of bareback sex can remain so easily at odds with a bareback identity. Many gay men, both HIV positive and HIV negative, who enjoy fucking without condoms do not consider themselves barebackers. As recently as June 2006, one young gay man in San Francisco avowed that, although he does not use condoms with his boyfriend, he believes that barebackers "are an urban legend." Not only do some men who bareback fail to regard themselves as barebackers, they don't believe that such people even exist. Moralizing labels such as *hypocrite* or psychologizing diagnoses such as *in denial* do not adequately account for what's going on with men like Sullivan or this anonymous San Franciscan. There is something about barebacking that prompts its distancing as an identity category. This tendency helps explain the difficulty of specifying how widespread barebacking has become or how many participants the subculture currently enlists.

Self-identified barebackers, although now constituted as a visible and vocal minority, appear to be uninterested in the rights-based discourses that serve to consolidate other minority populations. Unlike others experimenting with same-sex kinship arrangements, such as lesbian and gay parents, barebackers are not looking to have their relationships legally recognized. They are happy to consider themselves outlaws, claiming only the right to fuck whom and how they wish. If the category *queer* is defined in opposition not to heterosexuality but to heteronormativity, then bareback subculture pushes the envelope by positioning itself in opposition to gay norms as well: we might say that barebacking is antihomonormative.[15] The outlaw rhetoric helps to explain why the gay community is so reluctant to talk openly about barebacking: it jeopardizes public acceptance of homosexuality and represents astonishingly bad PR.

15. In the course of distinguishing heteronormativity from heterosexuality, Lauren Berlant and Michael Warner argue that heteronormativity "has no parallel, unlike heterosexuality, which organizes homosexuality as its opposite. Because homosexuality can never have the invisible, tacit, society-founding rightness that heterosexuality has, it would not be possible to speak of 'homonormativity' in the same sense." From Berlant and Warner, "Sex in Public," *Intimacy*, ed. Lauren Berlant (Chicago: University of Chicago Press, 2000), 312n2. Although my understanding of heteronormativity as a concept relies on Berlant and Warner's work (here and elsewhere), I disagree that there is no context in which it would be legitimate to speak of *homonormativity*. One of the explanations for bareback subculture is that a certain social organization of homosexuality—manifested in the mainstream gay life with which, in places such as San Francisco, everybody is so familiar that it lends itself to virtually "invisible, tacit, society-founding rightness"—has become normalizing to such an extent that a new kind of social organization of queer sexuality seems necessary. That emergent form of queer social organization is bareback subculture. Although she does not rationalize it in these terms, Lisa Duggan also employs the concept of homonormativity in *The Twilight of Equality? Neoliberalism, Cultural Politics, and the Attack on Democracy* (Boston: Beacon, 2003).

The very existence of bareback subculture potentially legitimates discrimination against those who are (or are perceived to be) HIV positive. Needless to say, the bareback phenomenon endangers public funding for AIDS research, treatment, and education.

Given these considerations, it is not easy to establish what kind of minority barebackers compose—whether, in terms of numbers, barebackers are statistically significant or whether they qualify as a sexual minority that democratic pluralism should take into account. "This site is for those who feel that they don't fit into the 'safe-sex world,'" announce the founders of barebackcity.com, invoking the standard rhetoric of marginalization as a basis for community formation.[16] In some respects, barebackers have constituted themselves as a sexual minority on the model of the SM community or the leather community (with both of which they overlap and exist in tension). This identity as a minority community organized around the abandonment of condoms—or, to put it more positively, organized around the giving and receiving of semen—is something new. The subculture of what is colloquially known as "cum swapping" needs to be distinguished from gay sex practices that, before AIDS, never gave rise to subcultural communities. In the 1970s, one might be known as a guy who enjoyed eating semen out of another guy's ass, but the preference (or fetish) for felching was not regarded as either a necessary or a sufficient condition of communal identity.

On one hand, barebackers represent a new minority constituency; on the other, any gay man may have unprotected anal sex without adopting the identity of barebacker—just as some married men and other ostensibly straight guys regularly participate in casual same-sex erotic activity without regarding themselves as gay. It is easy enough to maintain a conscious belief in the importance and necessity of safer sex while not using condoms; barebackers may be understood as those who have relinquished that mental prophylactic along with latex. But their discourse—that is, the rhetoric of barebacking—makes it harder to sustain the disavowal that characterizes this typical disjunction between believing in safe sex while failing to use protection. Barebackers say that they've abandoned not just physical barriers but also the false comfort of hypocrisy. For openly gay men who have had the courage to defy society's heteronormative expectations, there is something appealing in the idea of piercing through another layer of bad faith—of saying, in effect, that not only

The handwritten word "Identity" appears in the left margin with a bracket.

16. From http://www.misc.barebackcity.com/aboutus.asp (accessed June 2003). This Web site has been moved to http://ubb1.ultimatebareback.com/aboutus.asp (accessed August 2006).

am I not the good heterosexual that I was supposed to be but I'm also not the good homosexual who always practices safe sex that I'm assumed to be. Having disappointed one normative expectation about masculinity, it is easier to disappoint others.

In the face of a persistent desire to dismiss barebacking as negligible—"just a bunch of really vocal guys who want to continue this image of being reckless, hedonistic gay men who will do anything to get laid...relatively minor acting-out"—the figure of the barebacker, far from representing a tiny minority, offers an image and an identity with which any gay man may flirt.[17] Bareback sex looks especially alluring when coupled with images of hypermasculinity, as in the bareback pornography that I discuss in chapters 2 and 3. This new porn style pictures the risks involved in unprotected sex as cognate with other physical tests that are necessary to constitute a heroic masculinity of almost mythical dimensions. As long as masculinity remains a source of fascination and desire for gay men, bareback iconography will constitute a potent fantasy object for the silent majority as well as for the vocal minority. A gay man might not identify as a barebacker, even as he is aroused by images of barebacking. In this way, I suggest, barebacking gives rise to a distinctly permeable subculture. It is not only their bodies' vaunted permeability but also the paradoxical permeability of the subculture erected on this basis that accounts for the boundary-enforcing, often hysterically distancing reactions provoked by discussions of barebacking.

THINKING AND NOT THINKING ABOUT A VIRUS

Considering the dimension of fantasy challenges the distinction between barebacking as a behavior and barebacking as an identity. I find it striking that, when bareback sex is approached from an epidemiological perspective, the dimension of fantasy disappears completely. In other words, when sex between men is reduced to issues of viral transmission, it is no longer treated as sexuality: the overwhelming focus on prophylaxis suppresses considerations of fantasy, of intimacy, and of pleasure. Bareback subculture reclaims gay sex *as sexuality* by relegating epidemiological concerns to secondary status. In

17. Shana Krochmal, public relations spokeswoman for the San Francisco Stop AIDS Project, quoted in Gregory A. Freeman, "In Search of Death," *Rolling Stone*, February 6, 2003, 47. In an angry response to the *Rolling Stone* article, Andrew Sullivan dismisses those who chase after HIV as a "sub-subculture," suggesting that such people are mentally ill and hardly worth taking into account as statistically significant. See Sullivan, "Sex- and Death-Crazed Gays Play Viral Russian Roulette!" *Salon*, January 24, 2003, available at http://www.salon.com/opinion/sullivan/2003/01/24/rolling/print.html.

order to clarify the range of responses to more than two decades' worth of defining sex between men in terms of disease prevention, I want to differentiate three provisional categories of barebacking, based on attitudes toward HIV. These three categories may be summarized as barebacking with the desire or intention to *not* transmit HIV, barebacking with indifference to HIV, and barebacking with a desire or intention for viral transmission. Participants in the subculture may fall into any one of these three categories and may shift among them (these are categories of intention and practice, not of identity). Since HIV remains invisible to the naked eye and may lie undetected inside the body for many years, gay men have developed a range of ideas, beliefs, and fantasies about it, only some of which coincide with current scientific knowledge about the virus.[18]

It needs to be acknowledged that a substantial proportion and perhaps the majority of instances of barebacking combine a desire for unprotected sex with a desire to contain HIV. Plenty of HIV-negative men practice unprotected sex while nonetheless wishing to remain uninfected; correlatively, most HIV-positive men who bareback have no wish to infect others. Yet only recently have statements such as these become intelligible as anything other than paradoxes or contradictions. Despite a widespread desire to contain the AIDS epidemic, barebacking has emerged as the willingness to take sexual risks has increased. The willingness to take risks has been accompanied by the development of various strategies of risk reduction; abandoning condoms does not mean abandoning all caution or sense of responsibility. Common strategies of risk reduction among barebackers include what health professionals call "serosorting," "negotiated safety," and "strategic positioning." Gay men have been employing these strategies for many years, even decades, but health experts have dignified them with names only recently, in reluctant acknowledgement of the widespread rejection of condoms.

Serosorting describes the tendency to pursue unprotected sex only with those who share one's HIV status. At the beginning of the AIDS epidemic, a common axiom of safe-sex education urged gay men to assume that everybody with whom they had sex was HIV positive, and therefore they should always use condoms. From the perspective of an HIV-positive man, however, if all one's sex partners are positive too, then it makes as much sense to dis-

---

18. For a very interesting discussion of how we know what we know about HIV-transmission risks, see Samuel R. Delany, "The Gamble," *Corpus* 3, no. 1 (2005): 140–69. In addition to analyzing what counts as scientific knowledge on this issue, Delany describes his own sexual risks—his "gamble"—but without using the term barebacking.

pense with condoms as to use them religiously. This, at least, is what most HIV-positive barebackers have concluded.[19] For those positive men who have decided to forgo prophylactics, the possibility of reinfection with a different strain of the virus or a drug-resistant strain seems too remote to affect their sexual decisions.[20] When a gay man is already HIV positive, he may feel that there is little left to lose. This assumption is, in part, a result of the "virus-centered" approach to gay men's health—as if, medically and sexually speaking, concerns about HIV overrode all other considerations.

Andrew Sullivan, the conservative gay pundit, and Michael Shernoff, a gay therapist who published the first book on barebacking, both explicitly advocate serosorting, albeit from different points on the political spectrum. Sullivan suggests that "the incentive of intimacy"—less euphemistically, the freedom to bareback—might be more effective than the disincentive of fear as

19. Research indicates that HIV-positive men bareback more frequently than their HIV-negative counterparts and that they are more likely to bareback with those whom they believe to be likewise positive. See, for example, Perry N. Halkitis, Leo Wilton, Jeffrey T. Parsons, and C. Hoff, "Correlates of Sexual Risk-Taking Behavior among HIV-Positive Gay Men in Seroconcordant Primary Partner Relationships," *Psychology, Health, and Medicine* 19 (2004): 99–113; and Leo Wilton, Perry N. Halkitis, Gary English, and Michael Roberson, "An Exploratory Study of Barebacking, Club Drug Use, and Meanings of Sex in Black and Latino Gay and Bisexual Men in the Age of AIDS," in Halkitis, Wilton, and Drescher, *Barebacking*, 67.

20. Thus far, scientific evidence about the risk of reinfection (or "superinfection") remains inconclusive, with only a handful of cases documented over the past decade. Periodically, the media generate alarms about a "supervirus," one or another drug-resistant strain of HIV that appears poised to unleash a virulent new epidemic; these alarms have been proved false repeatedly. See Jeff Hoover, "Big, Bad Media Bugout," *POZ*, May 2005, 6–7, and the accompanying sidebar on super-viruses, superinfections, and supertransmissions, by Walter Armstrong. The latest supervirus scare came in February 2005, when the New York City health commissioner, Thomas R. Frieden, MD, held a press conference to announce that a 46-year-old gay man in New York had been diagnosed with a multidrug-resistant, rapidly progressing viral strain that led to AIDS in a matter of months. Having tested negative for HIV in May 2003, the unnamed man had hundreds of bareback sex partners during the fall of 2004, while high on crystal methamphetamine, and tested positive for HIV in December 2004. By January 2005, he was hospitalized with AIDS. The hitherto unseen coincidence of rapid progression to AIDS and multidrug resistance prompted the scare, along with the belief that this man had transmitted the "supervirus" to possibly hundreds of partners. See Marc Santora and Lawrence K. Altman, "Rare and Aggressive HIV Reported in New York," *New York Times*, February 12, 2005, A3. Yet despite weeks of elaborate contact tracing, extraordinary publicity, and genetic sequencing of hundreds of HIV-positive blood samples, two months later the New York City Department of Health had failed to locate *any* additional cases of infection with the hastily announced supervirus. See Marc Santora, "Tests Pending in Cases Tied to Fierce HIV," *New York Times*, March 30, 2005, B5. From the beginning, prominent HIV/AIDS scientists such as Robert Gallo, co-discoverer of HIV, were highly critical of the alarmist handling of this case. In retrospect, the health commissioner's ballyhooed announcement looks similar to the federal government's elevation of the color-coded terrorist threat at strategic moments, in order to inspire anxiety, if not terror, in the population for purposes of social control.

a motive for stopping the spread of HIV.[21] As a strategy of disease prevention, however, serosorting has multiple limitations: it does not prevent the transmission of other diseases, and, on a pragmatic basis, it cannot work among the many men who do not know their HIV status. For those who *do* know their status, disclosure remains peculiarly difficult (though less so online). Rather than raising this potentially awkward issue in casual sexual encounters, many men quietly make contextual assumptions about their partners' HIV status. In other words, serosorting often occurs tacitly rather than explicitly. It is easy to assume that a willingness to bareback means that the other guy must have the same status as oneself. An HIV-positive man may think, "If he's letting me fuck him without a rubber, he must be poz too"; at the same time, his HIV-negative partner may be thinking, "If he's fucking me without a rubber, he must be neg." As a strategy of disease prevention, then, serosorting tends to work better in principle than in practice.[22]

The practice of serosorting has drawn criticism from another angle: some gays lament that it promotes "viral segregation" or "viral apartheid." Politically, it is much more acceptable for HIV-positive men to reject sex with HIV-negative men than the reverse, since any exclusion of positive partners on the basis of their serostatus threatens to reinforce mainstream society's stigmatization of HIV-positive people—a stigmatization that the queer community has resisted since the dawn of the epidemic. Doubtless our resistance to stigmatizing people with AIDS and HIV-positive people laid the groundwork for the emergence of bareback subculture. My point, though, is that, as a form of "viral apartheid," the strategy of serosorting introduced an ostensibly impermeable barrier into the sexual community at precisely the moment when gay men were wearying of sexual barriers. To substitute the barrier of "viral segregation" for that of latex eliminates one limit only by imposing another.

Similarly, the risk-reduction strategy of *negotiated safety* substitutes the limit of monogamy for that of latex. Given that this strategy rationalizes the abandonment of condoms in strictly controlled circumstances, it is not surprising that the doctrine of negotiated safety originated outside the United States. A central element of Australian and European safe-sex education, negotiated safety involves gay men in a committed couple going bareback only

21. Andrew Sullivan, "Poz4Poz Saves Lives," *Advocate*, October 11, 2005, 112. See also Shernoff, *Without Condoms*.

22. For a vivid example of the misrecognitions involved in tacit serosorting, see Glenn Gaylord, "Interview with a Barebacker," *Positive Living* (AIDS Project Los Angeles), May 2000, available at http://www.thebody.com/apla/may00/barebacker.html.

when both repeatedly test negative for HIV. As Shernoff correctly observes, "negotiated safety makes AIDS prevention professionals in the United States nervous," because they do not wish to be seen as condoning the abandonment of condoms.[23] Although the doctrine of negotiated safety preceded the emergence of bareback subculture by several years, it should be regarded as a fully rationalized, supremely safe version of barebacking—and therefore, some would say, it hardly qualifies as barebacking at all. Negotiated safety enables unlimited intimacy with a single partner, while simultaneously imposing stringent limits on extramarital liaisons. With this approach—in which condom use remains the norm relative to which a single exception may be carefully elaborated—the investment lies in safety rather than in risk.

By contrast, the technique of *strategic positioning* is employed during bareback sex between serodiscordant partners. Here a high-risk situation may be ameliorated by the HIV-positive man's taking the role of "bottom," while his HIV-negative partner takes that of "top." This configuration reduces (although it certainly does not eliminate) the risk of infection, since viral transmission occurs most readily when a positive man ejaculates inside a negative man's rectum. As a term, *strategic positioning*, like *negotiated safety*, is derived from Australian research; as a practice, it does not qualify as safer sex (the only sanctioned goal of HIV prevention in the United States) but as a harm-reduction technique.[24] It is a strategy that I regularly adopt when barebacking with strangers. In addition to its obvious limitations, however, strategic positioning works best when the parties involved already prefer the "strategic" sexual role that the technique prescribes; it does not work for HIV-negative men who love getting fucked in the ass.

The various strategies and techniques that I have described are predicated on an acknowledgment that the condom code has fallen into desuetude, together with a desire to bareback without becoming infected or infecting others. However, a second category of barebacking places no such emphasis on

23. Shernoff, *Without Condoms*, 201. He continues: "This nervousness is reflected in an unwillingness on the part of U.S. AIDS service organizations to address honestly the issue that increasing numbers of gay men are not using condoms for anal sex, and if both men are uninfected and only having sex with each other this is not a high-risk behavior. U.S. AIDS service organizations and prevention messages reflect a timidity in avoiding the kind of honest harm reduction information about barebacking that appears in England and Australia out of fear that if they were to do so it would be construed as an endorsement of barebacking, just as conservative politicians accuse needle exchange programs of being an endorsement of intravenous drug use" (ibid.).

24. See P. Van de Ven et al., "In a Minority of Gay Men, Sexual Risk Practice Indicates Strategic Positioning for Perceived Risk Reduction Rather than Unbridled Sex," *AIDS Care* 14, no. 4 (2002): 471–80.

avoiding HIV transmission. Two recent studies of barebackers who cruise online have noted a significant distinction between *indifferent* and *deliberate* transmission of the virus.[25] Many barebackers do not know (or do not care to know) either their own or their partners' serostatus. One man who lists his status as "unknown" writes in his online profile, "You can hide your status until AFTER YOU CUM INSIDE ME if you wish. I'll take any load from hot guys that is offered to me."[26] This surprisingly common attitude is quite distinct from that of serosorting, on one hand, and actively seeking HIV transmission, on the other.

Different Web sites cater to these different categories of barebacking. For example, barebackjack.com takes an explicit harm-reduction approach and furnishes advice on how to minimize transmission risks without resorting to condoms. By contrast, ultimatebareback.com (formerly barebackcity.com) announces its indifference to HIV transmission and other medical issues associated with barebacking. Both of the studies referred to above (by Tewksbury and by Dawson et al.) are based on analysis of data from ultimatebareback.com; the quotation about concealing HIV status until it is too late comes from this Web site too. We might conclude that barebackers who remain indifferent to transmission risks have chosen, for whatever reason, to dissociate their sex from concerns about the virus. They want to have sex without thinking about HIV one way or the other. Their intention is for "raw" sex but not for viral transmission or epidemic amplification. Yet indifference is not usually understood as a category of intention or of fantasy; it remains hard to assess. Indifference appears to represent not a particular desire, however strange, but the absence of desire. From an epidemiological perspective, barebacking with indifference to HIV may yield results similar to those of barebacking with an active desire for viral transmission; yet there is an important distinction between the attitudes underlying these different categories of the practice.

25. See Richard Tewksbury, "Bareback Sex and the Quest for HIV: Assessing the Relationship in Internet Personal Advertisements of Men Who Have Sex with Men," *Deviant Behavior* 24 (2003): 477; and Alvin G. Dawson, Michael W. Ross, Doug Henry, and Anne Freeman, "Evidence of HIV Transmission Risk in Barebacking Men-Who-Have-Sex-With-Men: Cases from the Internet," in Halkitis, Wilton, and Drescher, *Barebacking*, 82.

26. In the course of elaborating his erotic preferences, this man explains: "If it's wild[,] kinky[,] and not supposed to be done, I'm probably into it. I have a big cum fetish and I love it when guys use me as a cum hole. Call me what you will, just breed me after you do it. GANG BANGS, anonymous scenes, much more, just ask. I'll back up to glory holes or get naked and bend over in a dark room or back alley."

The third category of barebacking, in which a desire for unprotected sex coexists with an active desire for viral transmission or viral exchange, interests me the most in this book, partly because it appears to be the least explicable from a rational point of view. It is easy to understand why a sero-concordant gay couple would choose to dispense with condoms, and, furthermore, it is comprehensible, if not necessarily justifiable, that men might wish to fuck bareback without thinking about the consequences of their doing so. It is much harder to comprehend why an elaborate subculture has developed around men who fuck without protection precisely in order to become infected. Let me be clear: the third category of barebacking concerns less irresponsible HIV-positive men who wish to penetrate others without bothering with condoms than men who are clamoring to be penetrated and explicitly consenting to have infected semen ejaculated inside their mouths and rectums. Some of these men are HIV positive already, whether or not they know it and whether or not they claim otherwise in their online solicitations for bareback "breeding." Some of the men who solicit infected semen, however, are HIV negative. Indeed, Tewksbury's study of 880 advertisements posted on barebackcity.com during January 2003 found that nearly three-quarters (70.6 percent) of those soliciting unprotected sex identified as HIV negative.[27]

Even if many of these barebackers were mistaken about or misrepresenting their HIV status—indeed, even if we assume that the majority of barebacking occurs between seroconcordant couples, thereby minimizing potential infection—these practices nevertheless reveal a fantasy of risk that warrants consideration. Far from being indifferent to HIV, those who identify as bug chasers have made the virus central to their erotic lives. They are having sex not only with other men but also with a virus. To the extent that these barebackers deliberately have incorporated an invisible microbe into their sexual practices and relationships, these practices and relationships deserve to be considered through the psychoanalytic category of fantasy. Categories of intention, behavior, and identity remain fundamentally inadequate for grasping what motivates this subculture. Chapter 1 is devoted to exploring the multiple and contradictory fantasies that animate the practice known as "bug chasing." Chapters 2 and 3 examine the subculture's extensive corpus of pornography as a staging of these fantasies. Although porn appears as an obvious site for the investigation of a culture's fantasies, the now voluminous literature on barebacking includes virtually no consideration of its distinctive

27. Tewksbury, "Bareback Sex," 475.

pornography—as if the fantasies that motivate a new sexual practice some-how were inconsequential.

POSITIVE VERSUS NEGATIVE IMAGES OF GAY MEN

I have the impression that in certain sexual contexts—when cruising in parks, back rooms, video arcades, or sex clubs—barebacking has established itself as a new norm and that using or mentioning condoms has become anomalous, a breach of sexual etiquette. This impression derives from my own experience: with only rare exceptions, men in these public sex venues announce, when they say anything at all, that they wish to be penetrated and have semen ejaculated inside them ("I want you to cum in my ass"). In such contexts, as I have indicated, nobody has ever asked about my HIV status or volunteered information about his own. At Blow Buddies, a popular gay sex club in San Francisco that emphasizes safer sex, fucking was explicitly prohibited until ownership of the club changed hands in 2002; now fucking with a condom is permitted, but barebacking is forbidden. In my experience, however, most of the fucking at Buddies is bareback; in only one instance did the other guy slip a condom on me, after watching me fuck his friend without one. Once, upstairs at Buddies, a man encouraged me to fuck him bareback, but, clearly anxious about what we were doing, he kept repeating, "don't cum inside me" (I didn't). Even this memorable exception seems to suggest that bareback sex with internal ejaculation has become a new unspoken norm.[28]

The gay community is reluctant to acknowledge the demographic and epidemiological significance of bareback sex, because it threatens our public image. In view of the fact that this book is appearing with a university press, I would like to take a moment to consider how the damage threatened by full acknowledgment of barebacking carries somewhat different implications within the public space of the university than it does in the public spheres outside. Since the late 1960s, the gradual academic institutionalization of civil rights movements—in women's studies, African American studies, ethnic American studies, lesbian and gay studies, disability studies—has relied on a commitment to correcting erroneous images of minorities. We are in the business of critiquing negative images of women, nonwhites, and

---

28. This impression is confirmed by a recent ethnographic study of sex in two bathhouses, which found that, although condoms are readily available, "across all sexual activities and all men in the bathhouses, there are virtually no condoms used." See Richard Tewksbury, "Bathhouse Intercourse: Structural and Behavioral Aspects of an Erotic Oasis," in *Sexual Deviance: A Reader*, ed. Christopher Hensley and Richard Tewksbury (Boulder: Lynne Rienner, 2003), 223.

queers; in so doing, we produce more-accurate representations of the comparatively disenfranchised and thereby contribute to multicultural society's self-knowledge. Since the production of knowledge and the production of affirmative images often coincide, controversy attends any intellectual investigation that produces the kind of "negative image" of gays represented by barebackers.

For decades we have battled stereotypes of queers as homicidal or suicidal, only to have articulate proponents of deliberate HIV transmission emerge from within our own ranks. We have argued that homosexuals are not doomed, not unreproductive, not sick, not serial killers, and no more violent than heterosexuals.[29] We have assumed that gains in civil rights for queers, such as the passage of antidiscrimination laws, depended on making such arguments persuasively—that, in other words, the kind of intellectual critique one might make of media representations of gays could contribute to concrete reforms outside the academy. The fact that the 2003 Supreme Court decision invalidating sodomy statutes invoked lesbian and gay scholarship in support of its argument seemed to confirm this assumption.[30] Now the emergence of an organized and articulate subculture of barebacking compromises such arguments by bringing to light images of gay men that are wildly divergent from the ones we've been promoting.

But exactly whose public image is represented by the institutionalized gay movement anyway? How important is an ideal image of homosexuality and for whom? These questions concern not merely inclusion (do barebackers get their own float in the next gay pride parade?) but the broader issue of how homosexuality's social acceptance is being won by the sanitizing of queer people's image. And what sanitizes better than desexualizing gayness, downplaying kinkiness, and pathologizing the sexual subcultures, including barebacking, that queers have invented? A suspicion that the mainstream gay movement had achieved considerable institutional success only by desexualizing queers crystallized in Michael Warner's thesis that the stigma on

29. For a representative sampling of work that makes this argument in lesbian and gay studies, see Diana Fuss, "Monsters of Perversion: Jeffrey Dahmer and *The Silence of the Lambs*," in *Media Spectacles*, ed. Marjorie Garber, Jann Matlock, and Rebecca L. Walkowitz (New York: Routledge, 1993), 181–205; Lynda Hart, *Fatal Women: Lesbian Sexuality and the Mark of Aggression* (Princeton, NJ: Princeton University Press, 1994); and Jeff Nunokawa, "'All the Sad Young Men': AIDS and the Work of Mourning," in *Inside/Out: Lesbian Theories, Gay Theories*, ed. Diana Fuss (New York: Routledge, 1991), 311–23. For an especially nuanced account of this problematic, see David Schmid, *Natural Born Celebrities: Serial Killers in American Culture* (Chicago: University of Chicago Press, 2005), esp. chap. 6.

30. See *Lawrence v. Texas*, 539 U.S. 558 (2003).

homosexual identity was being expunged by the intensification of sexual shame.[31] You could feel better about being gay as long as you felt worse about being a slut. In other words, you could be openly and proudly gay at the office, but the dozen guys you sucked off last weekend at Blow Buddies must remain a dirty secret. Those encounters could not count as sociability or intimacy, only as extreme acting out or freakish behavior.

An ideal image of homosexuals as perfectly normal and thus unthreatening has been produced in order to justify granting us the rights and protections enjoyed by heterosexuals. But such a strategy disenfranchises even further those who don't conform to the ideal image—"queers, sluts, prostitutes, trannies, club crawlers, and other lowlifes," in Warner's words.[32] People closely associated with sex compromise the ideal image and mess things up; they menace our boundaries, auguring disruptions of integrity, by threatening to draw us out of ourselves into promiscuous contact and mixing. Unregulated sex defines nonrespectability precisely because it disrespects the boundaries that separate persons, classes, races, and generations from each other. Socially unsanctioned sex or promiscuous mixing jeopardizes ideal images because it muddles identification, contaminating one thing with another. After all, an ideal image (whether of homosexuality or any other category) is nothing but an image ripe for identification—something in which one wishes to recognize him- or herself.

Here I'm trying to redescribe Warner's critique in psychoanalytic terms because I think that *The Trouble with Normal* is hampered by the psychologizing of subjectivity implicit in its model of shame.[33] It is always possible to convert shame into pride, to "resignify" sexual shame by making the abject and the repugnant into objects of identification. In construing unprotected anal sex as the basis for an identity category, barebackers already have done so. For example, the Web site bareback.com, appropriating the logic of gay pride, pro-

31. See Michael Warner, *The Trouble with Normal: Sex, Politics, and the Ethics of Queer Life* (New York: Free Press, 1999).

32. Warner, *Trouble with Normal*, ix.

33. I have long been concerned with how queer theorists' tendency to reject psychoanalysis leaves us with only psychological descriptions of subjectivity, that is, individualizing, ego-based theories that cannot account for the unconscious and thus cannot explain the transindividual dimensions of subjectivity. See Tim Dean, *Beyond Sexuality* (Chicago: University of Chicago Press, 2000). This problem becomes especially acute when the conversation turns to shame, as otherwise-sophisticated theorists appeal for inspiration to figures such as Erving Goffman and Silvan Tomkins. In addition to Warner's reliance on Goffman, see Eve Kosofsky Sedgwick, *Touching Feeling: Affect, Pedagogy, Performativity* (Durham, NC: Duke University Press, 2003), for an attempt to revive Tomkins.

vides opportunities not only to connect with other men for bareback sex but also to purchase (along with your bareback porn) fetching "bareback.com" T-shirts and tank tops. For a more daring sartorial image, you may choose black T-shirts and tanks emblazoned in red with the international symbol for biohazard. In accordance with the commercialization of gay pride, you can now proudly market your body as a biological weapon, embracing the fears that many HIV-negative people harbor about those who are HIV positive, while advertising your dangerous availability to fellow barebackers.

Shame can be endlessly "resignified" as pride (or dignity) because the two exist in an imaginary dialectic. Any imaginary dialectic locks us into a struggle over identification, a perpetual fight to distinguish desirable images with which one wishes to identify from those in which one refuses to recognize him- or herself. Doubtless this dialectical struggle entails a social battle, involving multiple power relations that condition what counts as desirable, what an ideal image is, and what's recognizable as beautiful, as sexy, as a relationship, as a social good. My claim, however, is that the struggle over images and identification—which also gets rehearsed in academic work debating the cultural representation of minorities ("Is this movie conveying a positive image of gays?")—constrains politics to the imaginary domain and that the time has come to dispel this constraint on our political thinking. I wish to make a critique not of identity politics (that has been done plenty of times already) but of identification politics. By "identification politics," I mean any politics grounded in recognition, namely, the politics of the ideal image. In order to make this critique, I need to reprise some psychoanalytic ideas about identification and its incommensurability with sexuality.[34]

THE TROUBLE WITH IDENTIFICATION POLITICS

The very possibility of identification with an ideal image implies a gap between the one who identifies and the ideal. We are not born with a sense

---

34. One locus classicus for this critique would be Charles Taylor's *Multiculturalism and "The Politics of Recognition": An Essay*, ed. Amy Gutmann (Princeton, NJ: Princeton University Press, 1992). For a very useful critique of identification politics from a Lacanian perspective, see Parveen Adams, *The Emptiness of the Image: Psychoanalysis and Sexual Differences* (London: Routledge, 1996). For a different, though nonetheless illuminating, critique of identification politics in the canon debate, see John Guillory, *Cultural Capital: The Problem of Literary Canon Formation* (Chicago: University of Chicago Press, 1993), which tackles problems of identification and representation from the perspective of Bourdieuian sociology. An excellent anthropological critique of identification politics may be found in Elizabeth A. Povinelli, *The Cunning of Recognition: Indigenous Alterities and the Making of Australian Multiculturalism* (Durham, NC: Duke University Press, 2002).

of self but must compose one from images outside ourselves. Initially one is an organism without a self and without much sense of where one's own body ends and another's begins. In psychoanalytic terms, one begins, paradoxically, as an organism without a body and subsequently achieves a sense of self—a sense, that is, of one's own borders and, correlatively, of what's inside and what's outside the self—only through identification with an image, classically a mirror image. Identification with an image involves a moment of recognition, of saying to oneself, "that's me"—even though that "me," having no prior existence, comes into being only at this epiphanic moment. The delight of this moment lends all identificatory images an ideal quality, irrespective of their particular content, since an image ostensibly resolves boundary uncertainty.

That uncertainty can be reactivated by sex, often in the form of anxiety, insofar as sex confuses the separateness and hence the distinguishability of bodies, thereby shattering (or threatening to shatter) our sense of corporeal integrity. But thanks to the logic of psychic division, what generates anxiety also can generate something akin to pleasure. There is a different kind of pleasure involved in violating one's self-image (what Leo Bersani calls "self-shattering"), a pleasure in tension with that of secure boundaries and self-recognition. Since the pleasure of self-shattering or self-loss tends to be experienced as more intense than that of self-recognition or security, we refer to the former as *jouissance*; *jouissance* isn't merely a stronger pleasure but exists in tension with it. In standard psychoanalytic terms, we could say that the tension between the pleasure of recognition and the *jouissance* of self-shattering is figured by the conflict between the ego and the unconscious, or, in other words, between identity and desire. There is something about sex that troubles identification, rendering a politics of identification malapropos when it comes to sexual matters.[35]

The implicit gap between an ideal image and the one who identifies with it presents a problem in its own right, since it is through this gap that the superego emerges, along with the discomfort of subjective guilt or bad conscience.

---

35. Here I am schematizing a psychoanalytic argument about the relation between sex and identity that is encapsulated in Leo Bersani's notion of self-shattering, a concept he develops from Laplanche's discussion of *ébranlement*, which in turn is derived from Freud's account of infantile sexuality. See Sigmund Freud, *Three Essays on the Theory of Sexuality*, in vol. 7 of *The Standard Edition of the Complete Psychological Works of Sigmund Freud*, ed. and trans. James Strachey (London: Hogarth, 1953–74), 123–243; Jean Laplanche, *Life and Death in Psychoanalysis*, trans. Jeffrey Mehlman (Baltimore: Johns Hopkins University Press, 1976); and Leo Bersani, *The Freudian Body: Psychoanalysis and Art* (New York: Columbia University Press, 1986), esp. chap. 2.

We identify with an ideal image, only to be plagued by a nagging sense of failing to live up to the ideal. Identification, in the subjective form that I'm considering, never produces identity (in the sense of complete indistinguishability between two or more terms) but only an approximation; full adequation with the image remains forever out of reach. Identification is not psychic cloning. This helps explain why dramas of identification do not end with the ego's initial formation but continue throughout life.[36]

For Freud, in *Civilization and Its Discontents*, the failure to live up to an identificatory image (or ego-ideal) is the source of our unhappiness: the gap between an ideal image and the subject who identifies with it can be shrugged off no more easily than the sadistic torments of the superego, whose genesis lies in the ego-ideal. Although Freud points out that the impossibly exacting demands of the superego may be understood in terms of *cultural* ideals—when he speaks of the "cultural superego," we cannot help thinking of just how inadequate Madison Avenue's ideal images tend to make us feel—we mustn't lose hold of the psychoanalytic insight that the *mechanism of identification itself* constitutes the problem. No solution is to be found in new imaginaries or less exclusionary identificatory images, since the gap that motivates identification provides the superego with its opening. As soon as there's an ideal, no matter how progressive, there's an aperture into which the superego insinuates itself and starts making us miserable.[37] Ideals—whether of queerness, negritude, or feminist subjectivity—instill a living-up-to-them dynamic that quickly becomes painful. Most gay men, even the buffest and most handsome, worry that they are not buff or handsome enough. By definition, the politics of identification cannot be anything but a politics of ideals. For this reason, a solution to imaginary antagonism is not to be found at the imaginary level; the quest for "alternative imaginaries" is doomed from the start.[38]

36. On identification and cloning, see Adam Phillips, "Sameness Is All," in *Promises, Promises: Essays on Literature and Psychoanalysis* (London: Faber, 2000), 334–41.

37. Étienne Balibar develops this point in a very interesting essay in which he argues that all ideals, including that of nonviolence, entail violence and, indeed, superegoistic cruelty. See Balibar, "Violence, Ideality and Cruelty," in *Politics and the Other Scene*, trans. Christine Jones, James Swenson, and Chris Turner (London: Verso, 2002), 129–45.

38. The quest for "alternative imaginaries" is part of Judith Butler's project. See Butler, *Bodies That Matter: On the Discursive Limits of "Sex"* (New York: Routledge, 1993), esp. 91. For his account of the "cultural superego" and an argument that the ethics of psychoanalysis opposes (rather than tries to reinforce) superegoistic injunctions, see Sigmund Freud, *Civilization and Its Discontents*, in vol. 21 of *Standard Edition*, 57–145, esp. 141–43. The psychoanalytic concept of the superego differs considerably from the psychological construction that goes under its name. My understanding of this difference has been enhanced by Bersani, *Freudian Body*, esp. chap. 1 (reformulated in Leo Bersani,

Michael Warner registers a version of this point when he begins *The Trouble with Normal* by noting how the inevitable failure to live up to sexual ideals generates not only dissatisfaction but also sexual oppression:

> Sooner or later, happily or unhappily, almost everyone fails to control his or her sex life. Perhaps as compensation, almost everyone sooner or later also succumbs to the temptation to control *someone else's* sex life. Most people cannot quite rid themselves of the sense that controlling the sex of others, far from being unethical, is where morality begins.[39]

It is as if the sexual behavior of people you don't care for were obscurely understood to be part of your own sex life—as if we're all involved erotically not only with those we love and find desirable but also with those we hate and find abhorrent. If this is the case—and Warner seems to think so without benefit of the psychoanalytic logic that characterizes desire and disgust as two sides of the same coin—then the bareback phenomenon might be less distant from mainstream gay and straight sexualities than many prefer to imagine. Not only may any gay man bareback without adopting the identity of barebacker, but heterosexuals also regularly have sex without condoms; indeed, I hardly ever come across a straight man or woman who actually prefers sex with condoms over sex without them. Let's face it: at some level we all enjoy barebacking, even if we consistently use prophylactics. I think that most heterosexuals would find it hard to commit themselves to a life in which sex *always* involved condoms. These days virtually everyone imagines that the safe-sex maxim "Use a condom every time" does not apply to him or her but to those whose pleasure seems less significant or legitimate than his or her own. Fucking without a condom is often regarded as a privilege of the normatively coupled in the age of AIDS. The right to bareback seems to come only with monogamy.[40]

In making what may look like an appeal to mainstream empathy for barebackers, I want to suggest that disidentification from the bareback phenomenon is not quite as easy as one might wish. At the same time, however, I want to insist that taking bareback subculture seriously need not depend on identification with it. While challenging the violent disidentifications that tend to accompany discussions of barebacking, *Unlimited Intimacy* tries to elaborate something other than a politics of empathy, identification, or recognition. It

---

"Can Sex Make Us Happy?" *Raritan* 21, no. 4 [2002], 15–30); and Joan Copjec, *Imagine There's No Woman: Ethics and Sublimation* (Cambridge, MA: MIT Press, 2002).

39. Warner, *Trouble with Normal*, 1, emphasis in the original.

40. In *Without Condoms*, Shernoff comes dangerously close to advancing exactly this argument.

is possible to care about something without recognizing oneself (or an aspect of oneself) in it. Barebackers might not be as different from you as they first appear to be; yet it would be a mistake to understand barebacking by simply identifying with it. One limitation of those accounts of risky sex that explain it as a response to homophobia lies in their tacit assumption that we care about those who are different from ourselves only by empathizing or identifying with them. Rather than feeling outraged by barebackers' irresponsibility and destructiveness, we believe that we can understand their behavior as generated by a culture whose lethal homophobia makes gay men the agents of their own elimination. Thus rather than feeling outrage or disgust, we empathize with the plight of these men; we feel for them as we would feel for ourselves in a culture that wishes us dead.

This kind of political appeal relies on my capacity to imagine myself in the other's place. The alternative to what I'm calling the politics of identification is an impersonal ethics in which one cares about others even when one *cannot* see anything of oneself in them. I describe this ethics as "impersonal" because it entails regarding the other as more than another person: it is not a question of discerning that "sex-crazed killers" are people too but of basing ethics on the *failure* to identify others as persons and of seeing how otherness remains irreducible to other persons, as well as to social categories of difference. Learning to appreciate others as complex subjective beings like oneself, rather than regarding others as types or as appropriable objects, is challenging but, as an ethical approach, quite inadequate. Enlarging my estimation of others until they seem as worthy of consideration as I seem to myself represents, in fact, a diminishment of otherness. Thus in contradistinction to the politics of identification, we have the ethics of alterity.[41] I'm suggesting that, precisely because bareback subculture seems foreign to everything one knows and believes, it demands an ethical approach, rather than a cogent demystification in the name of politics. While calming the impulse to identify with or violently disidentify

---

41. My argument draws on a continental tradition of ethical thought that combines two principal strands, one philosophical and the other psychoanalytic: the first is that of Levinas, particularly as read by Derrida; the second is that of Lacan, particularly his reading of Kant in Seminar 7. For some of this ethical tradition's coordinates, see Emmanuel Levinas, *Entre Nous: Thinking-of-the-Other*, trans. Michael B. Smith and Barbara Harshav (New York: Columbia University Press, 1998); Jacques Derrida and Pierre-Jean Labarrière, *Altérités* (Paris: Osiris, 1986); and Jacques Lacan, *The Seminar of Jacques Lacan*, book 7, *The Ethics of Psychoanalysis, 1959–1960*, ed. Jacques-Alain Miller, trans. Dennis Porter (New York: Norton, 1992). I first attempted to outline an impersonalist ethics of alterity with respect to homosexuality in "Homosexuality and the Problem of Otherness," in *Homosexuality and Psychoanalysis*, ed. Tim Dean and Christopher Lane (Chicago: University of Chicago Press, 2001), 120–43.

from bareback subculture, this ethical approach also remains distinct from the know-nothing relativism that would claim that whatever others do sexually is fine by me, as long as they're not harming anyone. A significant aspect of bareback subculture entails HIV transmission, thereby disqualifying from the outset a merely relativist approach to sexual behavior.

Not only does bareback subculture rely on forms of publicness—public sex institutions, such as bathhouses and back rooms, as well as the virtual publics created by bareback Web sites—but, insofar as it raises public health issues, barebacking cannot be considered a wholly private matter. It is not a question of tolerance for what other people do in the privacy of their own homes. This book represents an attempt to think publicly about bareback sex without resorting to the moralism of trying to legislate others' sex lives. I'm claiming that thinking about bareback subculture happens most productively when judgments concerning whether it is good or bad are deferred. I'm arguing that intellectual and political work involves more than adjudication among positive and negative images of others or of ourselves. And I'm suggesting that, just as there is a crucial ethical space that may be accessed once we suspend questions of identification with the other, there is a vital margin between condemning and condoning bareback subculture.

On several occasions when I've lectured on barebacking, audience members have interpreted my refusal to indict bareback subculture as a defense of barebacking. I run the risk of glamorizing it by not unequivocally condemning it, I'm warned, and of leading impressionable listeners astray. To the extent that this is true, I hope that the considerations outlined above help explain why I find it ethically imperative to take that particular risk. Far too often our desire to identify the politics of a phenomenon such as barebacking serves as a cover for deciding very quickly whether we approve or disapprove of it, thereby locating ourselves securely in relation to what may seem difficult or disturbing. Adjudicating the politics of bareback subculture can be a way of reassuring ourselves that we're on the right side of it, uncontaminated by it, when what I'm trying to suggest is that seeing how we're implicated in this phenomenon may be tougher than we readily acknowledge. It is not only "the other" who barebacks.

Following Warner, I contend that sexual ethics begins not with making judgments about (or trying to regulate) others' sex lives but with establishing others' freedom from interference, even as we recognize our mutual sexual interdependence. This ethics is especially challenging in the case of bareback subculture, because the prospect of intentional HIV transmission tends to elicit a visceral response. A man's desire to ingest not merely another man's semen but semen that he knows contains the virus can be particularly hard to countenance. Our secret disgust at what turns other people on readily transmutes into horror at this prospect. Partly because the desire for incorporating infected semen remains so hard to recognize as anything but pathological, I wish to speak about bareback subculture outside the framework provided by the dialectics of identification and disidentification.

One consequence of this approach is some measure of uncertainty about where one stands in relation to acts and desires that might occasionally seem so disturbing as to be inadmissible to consciousness. This book tries to make that uncertainty the subject of reflection, rather than resolving it, because uncertainty is integral to the phenomenon I'm describing. It is difficult to be certain about the moment of HIV transmission; indeed, the very notion of risk, whether sexual or otherwise, has uncertainty built into it. If barebacking is defined not as intentional unprotected anal intercourse between men who remain unaware of each other's HIV status but, more broadly, as fucking without condoms, then few adults remain wholly unimplicated in it. When subjected to philosophical or psychoanalytic scrutiny, the emphasis that social scientists and public health researchers place on *intentional* unprotected anal sex in their definitions of barebacking provides a fairly shaky basis for demarcating one erotic practice from others. In addition, the capacity for erotic experience to dissolve, as well as to enhance, one's sense of self means that sex readily breeds uncertainty about one's standing relative to it.

Tolerance for other sexualities depends on not having to contemplate the gory details of what other people like to do with their bodies. It is not simply a case of preferring not to participate in certain kinds of sexual activity but also of preferring not to even have to think about them—as if to think too hard about certain sexual acts were virtually tantamount to doing them. By this logic, if I can't bear to think about certain sexual acts, then nobody should be doing them. Or, in other words, if somebody else is doing what I cannot countenance, then there must be something wrong with him or her. This logic leads seamlessly to the pernicious notion that I won't have to think about certain sexual acts if others can be prevented from doing them. My libidinous thoughts may be controlled by regulating how others are permitted to exercise their bodily freedoms. The integrity of my consciousness demands that others' liberty be curtailed.

If witnessing two guys holding hands in public generates the impression, as it does for some people, that "they're shoving their sexuality down my throat," then we can begin to see how the inviolability of consciousness is connected to a sense of corporeal integrity. Thus perhaps we can see the relation between freedom of thought and a willingness to have one's consciousness disturbed, even violated. Thinking about sex in ethical terms requires some tolerance for boundary insecurity—tolerance, that is, for uncertainty about one's position relative to disturbing graphic material. What I'm trying to get at here is the deep connection between sexual ethics and intellectual labor, a connection encapsulated in the notion of broadmindedness. Opening one's mind to ideas, images, and scenarios that seem rebarbative enlarges one's mental capacity in a way that suggests some interdependence between sexual ethics and intellectual ethics, or between erotic permissiveness and the liberty to think.[42] Pressure to adjudicate the rightness or wrongness of sexual behavior revokes those permissions. This is partly what I meant when I observed earlier that purity is the enemy of the intellect. Anything that curtails your capacity to think has to be a problem—an ethical as well as an intellectual problem. As I elaborate in chapter 4, opening one's mind to difficult or foreign subject matter forms part of the general ethical enterprise of opening oneself to alterity.

NEVER SAY NO

Another way of describing the paradoxical discipline entailed in allowing oneself to think hard about potentially intolerable subjects would be to call it psychoanalysis. In my thinking about bareback subculture, I have found the disposition of psychoanalytic neutrality particularly helpful, despite the fact that psychoanalysis, generally regarded as a body of thought inhospitable to queers, seldom is associated today with sexual permissiveness. The psychoanalytic rule of free association—"that whatever comes into one's head must be reported without criticizing it"—requires a suspension of judgment that permits different forms of thinking to emerge.[43] Once you commit to following a train of thought irrespective of where it leads or how risky it seems, then you may find yourself thinking new thoughts and discovering spaces that you would not have come across otherwise. We might say that psychoanalysis, like cocksucking, involves taking risks with one's mouth. Thus although psychoanalysis has an appalling institutional history of pathologizing nonnormative

42. On the distinction between erotic permissiveness and erotic transgression, see Catherine Millet, *The Sexual Life of Catherine M.*, trans. Adriana Hunter (New York: Grove, 2002), esp. 223–24.

43. Sigmund Freud, "The Dynamics of Transference," in *Papers on Technique*, vol. 12 of *Standard Edition*, 107.

sexual behavior and forms of desire, the clinical practice of analysis depends on not pathologizing *any* desire, in order to discover where its logic takes you. Rather than the conservative moralism of "Just say no," psychoanalysis involves the permissive ethic of "Never say no," because the unconscious never says no.[44] This practical refusal to pathologize desire amplifies thought.

One of the strongest objections provoked by earlier drafts of this book had to do with the apparent contradiction between my argument on behalf of suspending judgment and my allusions to participating in the subculture. Am I not being disingenuous—indeed, self-serving—in advocating a suspension of judgment about erotic practices that I admit to pursuing? Doesn't my argument boil down to a case of special pleading, and doesn't *Unlimited Intimacy* covertly endorse barebacking even as it claims otherwise? To describe analytically one's participation in a subculture is not to recommend that others get involved with it; no account of experience necessarily constitutes a recommendation, a justification, or, conversely, an expression of regret concerning that experience. Neither does such an account necessarily imply that the experience is representative or exemplary. As this book's epigraph suggests, *in no way am I asking anyone to change his or her behavior on the strength of ways I have or have not behaved.*

When writing about an underground sexual subculture that, by its nature, tends to resist conventional research methods, I consider it disingenuous to pretend that I don't understand the subculture's appeal or that I haven't learned about it through personal involvement. All I'm advocating is that the practice of bareback sex and the new subculture to which it has given rise be taken as occasions for sustained reflection. In a book published by a university press, it should not be regarded as controversial to advocate thinking. My suggestion is that thinking ranges most freely among its objects when judgments about good or bad—about whether one can identify with the practices and desires in question—are put on hold. To those who contend that suspension of judgment is impossible, I would point out that the practice of free association assumes otherwise; to argue that judgment cannot be suspended or deferred is, in my view, tantamount to declaring that psychoanalysis cannot exist. Thus my understanding of the act or process of thinking, in roughly psychoanalytic terms, is as a practice of opening one's

---

44. "There are in [the unconscious] no negation, no doubt, no degrees of certainty." From Sigmund Freud, "The Unconscious," in *Papers on Metapsychology*, vol. 14 of *Standard Edition*, 186. From this we might deduce that there is no *neg* in the unconscious, no way of figuring unconsciously what it means to be HIV negative.

mind to what might appear as dangerously "other." In advocating an ethic of openness to alterity, *Unlimited Intimacy* suggests that barebacking allegorizes such openness through its acceptance of risk and its willingness to dispense with barriers; therefore, in a sense, the subculture models how we might approach it. This book advocates barebacking less as a sexual practice than as a figure for an ethical disposition. In so doing, it infers a homology between barebacking and psychoanalysis that I would like to elaborate, in order to clarify the role and status of the category of the unconscious in my argument.

When I first began researching sexual risk more than a decade ago, I was guided by the assumption (as were most investigators in the field) that unprotected anal sex was essentially a mistake, a slip-up, a kind of accident. As reports began emerging in the mid-1990s of an increase in unsafe sex among gay men—the very population that pioneered safe-sex practices during the epidemic's first decade—everyone wondered why those who knew better were increasingly "slipping up."[45] My initial answer to this question was that sexual slip-ups could be understood like slips of the tongue or other bungled actions—what Freud's English translator rather grandly called *parapraxes*. The intention to say or do one thing is interrupted by an intention to say or do something else, and these competing intentions signal a subjective conflict that Freud took as mundane, though nonetheless compelling, evidence of our struggle with the unconscious. Drawing on this elementary psychoanalytic idea, I argued that unsafe sex cannot be considered independently of the unconscious, when the category of the unconscious is conceived as social and therefore transindividual, rather than as simply a psychological attribute of individual persons.[46]

I do not wish to retract either that claim or my previous argument, but sexual risk is no longer what it was in the mid-'90s. A thesis about the unconscious cannot explain gay men's deliberate abandonment of condoms in the same way that it explained sexual slip-ups. Whereas I previously employed a psychoanalytic hermeneutic to interpret the phenomenon of "slipping up," now I wish to employ psychoanalysis as a framework that enables the more disturbing aspects of bareback subculture to be approached without judgment. In this way, psychoanalysis offers a methodological approach consistent with that of cultural ethnography—an approach that refuses to censor

---

45. See John Gallagher, "Slipping Up," *Advocate*, July 8, 1997, 33–34.
46. See Dean, "Safe-Sex Education and the Death Drive," in *Beyond Sexuality*, 134–73.

bareback subculture's own accounts of itself in the service of more familiar personal or political positions. The newness and foreignness of deliberate, organized risk demands a mental flexibility and openness that I associate with psychoanalytic listening—the kind of permissive listening that correlates with the practice of saying whatever comes to mind, no matter how apparently outrageous or nonsensical.

In the process of depathologizing barebacking, I argue nonetheless that the subculture cannot be understood in purely rationalist terms—that, in other words, one still needs an account of the unconscious to explain what's at stake. Previous attempts to depathologize barebacking have framed the issue in terms of rational risk assessment, claiming that protease inhibitors usher in "altered realities" that alter gay men's sexual decision making. In my view, such arguments too readily overlook those nonrational motives that lead men to act against what may be regarded as their own best interests. For example, in a widely circulated article, the late Eric Rofes characterized barebacking in purely rationalist terms:

> If HIV-prevention efforts are less effective today than they were a decade ago, it may be because much of the current work refuses to fully accept the altered realities in which today's gay men operate. Those who are having sex without condoms are not lacking in self-esteem or filled with internalized homophobia that triggers them to self-destruct. Nor are they necessarily naive or delusional, believing they are invulnerable to harm or disease.[47]

Although I don't disagree with Rofes—and would second his claim that barebacking has little to do with homophobia or self-hatred—his analysis doesn't penetrate far enough beyond the superficial psychology of rational motivation to explain how queer sex may involve maximizing risk rather than minimizing it.

Well before antiretroviral medication ushered in "altered realities," two distinguished psychologists argued that risky sex could be considered rational if the perceived benefits of sexual fulfillment outweigh the threat of death from AIDS. In a very interesting article that precedes the era of barebacking, Pinkerton and Abramson show how, "in certain cases, behaviors that might appear from without to be foolhardy, even suicidal, may in fact confer sufficient (subjective) benefits to the participants to be psychologically

---

47. Eric Rofes, "Barebacking and the New AIDS Hysteria," *Stranger* (Seattle), April 8, 1999, 17.

justifiable."[48] This is an important point. Sometimes, however, such behaviors may appear to the participants as unjustifiable in strictly rational terms. An early proponent of what was then called simply "unsafe sex" reports that "over and over, I asked myself why it was so appealing for me to get fucked without a condom. I'm a bottom, and I honestly can't tell whether someone is fucking me with or without a condom. It feels the same to me. Yet I still didn't want the barrier, and it really disturbed me that I didn't know why."[49]

In suggesting that sexual conduct is permeated by the nonrational, I'm not arguing that barebacking should be considered necessarily irrational behavior, only that it cannot be understood without taking seriously the fantasies that animate it. Psychoanalysis originates with a fundamental distinction between the irrational and the nonrational, a distinction that exempts the nonrational from the taint of pathology. Freud's value lies in his insistence that all sexuality, even its most routine and vanilla expressions, involves nonrational logics that we may bracket under the rubric *unconscious*. On those odd occasions when sex is undertaken primarily for reproductive purposes, it still isn't exempt from fantasies about reproduction—fantasies that also inform nonreproductive sex. By tracing subjectivity's nonrational logics, Freud revealed gender and sexuality as particularly dense sites for the elaboration of fantasy; gender and sexuality provoke our most wildly counterintuitive stories about ourselves. With respect to the pernicious hierarchy of normal and perverse, Freud leveled the playing field by showing how nobody has a gender—or a fuck—free from the baroque complications of fantasy, whether they're aware of it or not. Thus in addition to complicating the standard distinction between identity and behavior, the category of unconscious fantasy undermines the distinction between normal and pathological. It also necessitates a special kind of listening or attention.

FUCKING AS RESEARCH

When men gather together in groups to fuck without condoms, with virtually every inhibition checked at the door, one can learn a lot about masculinity and nonnormative sexualities by just listening to what's being said and

48. Steven D. Pinkerton and Paul R. Abramson, "Is Risky Sex Rational?" *Journal of Sex Research* 29, no. 4 (1992): 561–62. For a useful, nonpsychoanalytic critique of the rationalist risk-assessment approach to understanding bareback sex, see Mark Davis, "HIV Prevention Rationalities and Serostatus in the Risk Narratives of Gay Men," *Sexualities* 5, no. 3 (2002): 281–99.

49. Stephen Gendin, "I Was a Teenage HIV Prevention Activist," in *Policing Public Sex: Queer Politics and the Future of AIDS Activism*, ed. Ephen Glenn Colter, Wayne Hoffman, Eva Pendleton, Alison Redick, and David Serlin (Boston: South End, 1996), 106.

paying attention to what's being done. One may glean as much from casual participant observation as from official surveys about such behavior or formal interviews with the men involved. The stigma that still adheres to public sex and to barebacking militates against obtaining a thorough account of these activities when the inquiry is posed in more formal terms. Indeed, the report of one community-based cross-sectional study of "men-who-have-sex-with-men (MSM)" in New York admits that, "as is the case with any questionnaire data, the self-reported indices may be undermined by the sensitive nature of the data being collected. To this end, the impact of socially desirable responses may have yielded behavioral indices which are underestimates of the practice of barebacking within the MSM community."[50] Despite the interest of this quantitative study and others like it, their sophisticated statistical analyses decline precipitously in significance when the numbers on which the analyses are based are skewed from the outset. It seems more like wishful thinking than like science to assume that "men-who-have-sex-with-men" will report accurately to authority figures the incidence of potentially felonious activity in which they have engaged.[51]

Since 1997, when I first moved to California for a year, I've been interacting with men—primarily in San Francisco but also in cyberspace—who bareback. I have not conducted any formal interviews or attempted any statistical analyses, and, until recently, I didn't think of going to sex clubs as "research." This book makes no claim to objectivity or ethnographic validity but only to a discipline of listening to and thinking seriously about the subculture. Despite popular assumptions, anonymous sex frequently is punctuated by interesting conversation. After uninhibited, multipartner sex, men tend to speak more freely, as sex researchers and writers such as Samuel R. Delany, Eric Rofes, and Steven Zeeland have shown.[52] There is some truth to the gay academic's

50. Perry N. Halkitis, Leo Wilton, and Paul Galatowitsch, "What's in a Term? How Gay and Bisexual Men Understand Barebacking," in Halkitis, Wilton, and Drescher, *Barebacking*, 45.

51. The incidence of self-reported barebacking in this New York study ran as follows: "While 50% of the men who reported being HIV+ or believed they were HIV+ practiced barebacking, only 29.9% of those who reported being HIV– or believed that they were HIV– practiced this behavior. Thus, HIV+ men were about two times more likely to practice barebacking than HIV– men.... No differences in self-reported barebacking were indicated across race/ethnicity or sexual identity." From Halkitis, Wilton, and Galatowitsch, "What's in a Term?" 42. Although this incidence of self-reported barebacking may appear to be surprisingly high, it strikes me as an underestimation of the prevalence of the practice.

52. See Samuel R. Delany, *Times Square Red, Times Square Blue* (New York: New York University Press, 1999); Eric Rofes, *Dry Bones Breathe: Gay Men Creating Post-AIDS Identities and Cultures* (New York: Harrington Park, 1998); and a quartet of books by Steven Zeeland: *Barrack Buddies and Soldier Lovers: Dialogues with Gay Young Men in the U.S. Military* (New York: Harrington Park, 1993); *Sailors and*

joke that oral history can be conducted better on one's knees. Yet in the inaugural issue of *Instigator Magazine*, a glossy new periodical serving the gay sexual underground (including barebackers), at least one writer aligns anonymous casual sex with an absence of conversation. Complaining that "most [safer-sex] campaigns are designed for guys who *actually know the names of people they fuck*," he asserts that "this is not the real world of gayboy sex, or at least not the one you and I live in. My world of fucking is through holes in plywood walls, back alleys and in crowded cubicles. I don't want to know a guy's name, much less have a conversation with him."[53] In fact, this is only a partially accurate representation of the contemporary world of gay cruising: after glory-hole fucking and crowded cubicle sex, names and numbers are often exchanged in order to arrange a repeat performance. Even when the sex remains completely anonymous, men take breaks for a cigarette or a drink, and conversation begins. It may take several desultory conversations over a period of months before you learn an interlocutor's name, but, as Delany's *Times Square Red, Times Square Blue* amply documents, engaging conversations occur and intimate friendships develop in the transitional spaces that punctuate sex institutions.

As discussed further in chapter 4, I have found the conversation to be better in gay bars with back rooms than in gay bars without them, perhaps because the proximity of the overtly sexual space helps dissolve some of the barriers and pretensions that constrain verbal exchanges elsewhere. One of my most memorable conversations occurred in the cooling-off room at Blow Buddies, a space near the San Francisco club's entrance that screens porn but is off limits to genital activity among the patrons. It's an open room where you can get a free cup of coffee, buy a soda or snack, and munch on the free peanuts while watching porn or cruising the guys wandering about beyond the room's perimeter. If you feel so inclined, you also may have a conversation with the guy seated further down the bench. Interactions in that room, at the play space's margins, are social rather than directly sexual, freer than the more calculated exchanges taking place elsewhere in the club. Since I'm not a novelist, I won't attempt to reproduce the dialogue that occurred in the cooling-off

---

Sexual Identity: Crossing the Line Between "Straight" and "Gay" in the U.S. Navy (New York: Harrington Park, 1995); *The Masculine Marine: Homoeroticism in the U.S. Marine Corps* (New York: Harrington Park, 1996); and *Military Trade* (New York: Harrington Park, 1999). Delany's autoethnography is based in Manhattan, Rofes's in San Francisco, and Zeeland's primarily in San Diego.

53. Jayson Marston, "Fucking in the Real World," *Instigator Magazine*, January 2003, 32, emphasis in the original.

room with a man named Bill on a Wednesday night in October 2001. Yet that casual conversation was one of this book's primary inspirations.

The conversation with Bill did not follow or lead to sex with him, although it could have. Much of what goes on in a sex club is silent, because, unlike elsewhere, verbal language is not required for seduction. Communication in such spaces is primarily visual and tactile. As a result, the conversations that transpire tend to be somewhat more desultory, playful, nonpurposive. I'm interested in how the vernacular description of casual group sex as "play" applies also to some of the verbal exchanges that occur in gay sex institutions and in how these kinds of nonpurposive activities might be understood, by way of Winnicott, as creative—as analogous to aesthetic experience—and as symptoms of psychic health. "Playing," says Winnicott, "facilitates growth and therefore health; playing leads into group relationships; playing can be a form of communication."[54] Winnicott also identifies playing with intimacy and creativity.

It would be a mistake to idealize gay sex institutions as utopian spaces liberated from the conflicts that permeate the world outside their walls, just as it would be misleading to characterize the subcultures that these institutions foster as necessarily transgressive or subversive.[55] A debate over whether bareback sex is subversive or reactionary precludes the argument that I wish to make in this book. In speaking of erotic "play" as a sign of psychic health, I want to suggest that institutions sponsoring such play should not be considered automatically as pathological spaces, regardless of their particular limitations. Those who frequent such institutions have had disappointing as well as delightful experiences in their precincts; one might even have contracted HIV at such a place. But the kind of comparatively nonpurposive interactions permitted by such spaces are, from a psychoanalytic perspective, healthy and beneficent.

In endorsing the structure of certain commercial sex institutions, I'm thinking partly of their architectural layout but also of the configuration of verbal and corporeal exchanges that are encouraged by these spatial designs. As New York artist John Lindell has observed, in an illuminating essay on sex-club architecture, "the notion of drift is essential to the experience of a sex club, where fluidity facilitates passing to an aimless, 'let's see what happens'

54. D. W. Winnicott, *Playing and Reality* (1971; repr., London: Routledge, 1991), 41.
55. See Leo Bersani, "Is the Rectum a Grave?" in Crimp, *AIDS*, 206: "Anyone who has ever spent one night in a gay bathhouse knows that it is (or was) one of the most ruthlessly ranked, hierarchized, and competitive environments imaginable. Your looks, muscles, hair distribution, size of cock, and shape of ass determined exactly how happy you were going to be during those few hours, and rejection, generally accompanied by two or three words at most, could be swift and brutal, with none of the civilizing hypocrisies with which we get rid of undesirables in the outside world."

frame of mind."[56] One goes to such places with the paradoxical aim of aimlessness; unpredictability is part of the pleasure. The sex-club patron resembles Baudelaire's *flâneur*, who readily loses himself in a stream of bodies and whose individuality thus consists in the disappearance of individuality.[57] It is less that the *flâneur* represents the *kind of person* who goes to a sex club than that a cruising ethos conduces to this impersonalizing effect; in other words, a sex club creates the *kind of space* that militates against self-consolidation. Therein lies one of its greatest pleasures and the source of its relief.

A site intended to abet nonpurposive erotic activity, the sex club often is assembled from structures that resemble those that gay men have adapted from their original purposes. The nonpurposive is stimulated by reminders of adapted or perverted purposes. For example, sex clubs regularly dedicate space to glory holes, often in mazelike arrangements that provide partial privacy (one is enclosed on two or three sides) while intensifying anonymity (one sees only what's visible through the hole). As Allan Bérubé has noted in his history of bathhouses, this architecture reconstitutes in safe space the riskier spaces outside the club that, for decades, men have appropriated for their own purposes:

> In the 1970s, fantasy environments were installed which recreated the erotic situations that were still illegal and dangerous outside the walls of the baths. Glory holes recreated the toilets. Mazes recreated park bushes and undergrowth. Steam rooms and gyms recreated the YMCAs. Video rooms recreated the balconies and back rows of movie theaters. Indoor trailer trucks recreated "the trucks," a cruising area of trailer trucks parked along the waterfront at the end of Christopher Street in Greenwich Village. Cells recreated and transformed the environment of prisons and jails, where generations of gay men had ended up for having sex in toilets, parks, and the YMCA.[58]

In quoting sexual risk, such "minor architecture" consolidates the association between gay sex and physical danger, while also retaining the sense of

---

56. John Lindell, "Public Space for Public Sex," in Colter et al., *Policing Public Sex*, 75. What Lindell describes as an ideal architectural layout for a sex club approximates quite closely to that of Blow Buddies, in contrast to the Manhattan clubs that he's criticizing.

57. See Charles Baudelaire, *The Painter of Modern Life, and Other Essays*, trans. Jonathan Mayne (London: Phaidon, 1964). My thinking about the *flâneur* has been stimulated by Alla Ivanchikova, whose "Sidewalks of Desire: Paradoxes of *Flâneurie* in Contemporary Queer Fiction" (PhD diss., University at Buffalo [State University of New York], 2007) brilliantly rehabilitates this modernist figure for contemporary sex-gender politics.

58. Allan Bérubé, "The History of Gay Bathhouses," in Colter et al., *Policing Public Sex*, 201–2.

unpredictability that otherwise might be absent in a place where you're pretty sure that everyone present is a gay man with sex on his mind.[59] Yet by recreating a sense of contingency and risk, sex-club architecture also invokes the sense of inventiveness necessary for adapting urban, often public spaces to unintended purposes.

I have attempted to describe the layout of a sex club such as Blow Buddies, suggesting how its architecture helps to organize a rhythm and flow of interaction among the patrons, because I'm conscious that many of this book's readers (including some of its gay readers) may be comparatively unfamiliar with the secret public institutions of contemporary queer culture.[60] Even men who frequent such institutions often don't notice much about the architecture. Yet I've always regarded walking into a gay bar, let alone a sex club, as tantamount to an anthropological expedition. Warner reminds us that "the sexual cultures of gay men and lesbians are, after all, *cultures* in ways that are often forgotten, especially when they are treated simply as a mass of deviants looking for hormonally driven release. They recognize themselves as cultures, with their own knowledges, places, practices, languages, and learned modes of feeling."[61] To apprehend queer sexual institutions and practices as cultures is to acknowledge that they may warrant our respect even—or especially—when we do not immediately understand them. But it also entails acknowledging that, unlike other cultures, nobody is born into or inherits queer culture: it becomes one's "own" culture only through modes of invention and appropriation. A young homosexual always has to play the role of amateur anthropologist, piecing together the beliefs, practices, and texts of his or her erotic culture adventitiously, often without much formal guidance. In this sense, rather than in conventional disciplinary terms, *Unlimited Intimacy* may be read as partly ethnographic.

SUBCULTURAL DEMOGRAPHICS

Although Warner is right to characterize queer sexual institutions and practices as cultures, it is crucial to my account that we appreciate how bareback sex has given rise to a distinct subculture, one defined by its distance from

59. On the "minor architecture" of sex clubs and other transient spaces, see John Paul Ricco, *The Logic of the Lure* (Chicago: University of Chicago Press, 2002).

60. For a description of Blow Buddies in its early days, see Eric Rofes, *Reviving the Tribe: Regenerating Gay Men's Sexuality and Culture in the Ongoing Epidemic* (New York: Harrington Park, 1996), 191–95.

61. Warner, *Trouble with Normal*, 177, emphasis in the original.

not only heteronormative society but also gay society. Derived from the sociology of deviance, the theory of subcultures offers a template for describing male-dominated, yet comparatively disenfranchised, urban communities whose codes of behavior depart significantly from social norms. Viewing as subcultures those social groups that are organized around popular music, for example (or skateboarding or other "nonproductive," high-risk activities), permits them to be seen as instances of more than mere hoodlumism or social dysfunction. In other words, viewing such groups as subcultures depathologizes their deviance. Some barebackers explicitly have connected what they're doing to the kind of life pursued by Californian skateboarders, seeing in skate subculture an ethic of organized risk that helps rationalize risky sex.[62] Such connections transform those who depart from mainstream norms: no longer mere outlaws, they become members of outlaw communities.

The study of subcultures raises questions about the relationship between a subculture and the dominant culture or society against which it defines itself—a relationship that writers on the subject historically have regarded as oppositional, that is, as politically progressive. Traditionally associated with blue-collar communities, the subcultures investigated by the Birmingham School, for example, have been understood primarily through the lens of class analyses derived from Marx, Gramsci, and most recently Bourdieu.[63] In light of this methodological tradition, it is worth noting that participants in bareback subculture are not drawn predominantly from any particular social class: self-identified barebackers range from upper-middle-class professionals, such as lawyers and bankers, to students, the unemployed, and the homeless.[64] Although not factored by class in any conventional sense, bareback subculture prizes an ethos of hypermasculinity and erotic transgressiveness that tends to be imagined in terms of working-class sexuality, with its military para-

---

62. See http://www.treasureislandmedia.com for stories about, as well as links to, skateboarders and surfers.

63. See, for example, Dick Hebdige, *Subculture: The Meaning of Style* (London: Methuen, 1979), and the canonical essays collected in Stuart Hall and Tony Jefferson, eds., *Resistance through Rituals* (London: Routledge, 1993). The best Bourdieuian analysis of music subcultures is given in Sarah Thornton, *Club Cultures: Music, Media, and Subcultural Capital* (Cambridge: Polity, 1995). An excellent introduction to the field of subcultural studies may be found in Ken Gelder and Sarah Thornton, eds., *The Subcultures Reader* (London: Routledge, 1997). My thinking about subcultures has been enhanced considerably by discussions with Lauren Goodlad and by her own work in this area. See Lauren M. E. Goodlad and Michael Bibby, eds., *Goth: Undead Subculture* (Durham, NC: Duke University Press, 2007).

64. See "Why Barebacking?" introduction in Halkitis, Wilton, and Drescher, *Barebacking*, 3: "research has confirmed that barebacking is a phenomenon that cuts across demographics and serostatus."

phernalia, skinhead haircuts, tattoos, and muscular physiques designed to suggest a life of manual labor. What's necessary to perfect this image is often the kind of leisure and material resources enjoyed by more-affluent classes. The case of a man who flew every weekend from Denver, where he worked, to Atlanta in order to fuck at Fort Troff (a sex club notorious for barebacking and no-holds-barred SM) suggests how expensive full participation in bareback subculture can get.[65] Given the subculture's reliance on the Internet, full participation also requires access to the latest technologies. More than material resources, however, bareback subculture involves modes of aesthetic self-fashioning that, as Foucault has shown, are traditionally available only to social elites.[66] Although barebackers cultivate an image of democratic, rough-and-ready sexuality—they'll fuck anything that moves and, if it doesn't move, they'll fuck it until it does—often they also understand themselves as sexual elites, in a manner akin to some professional athletes. For example, Michael Thorn's editorial in the premiere issue of *Instigator Magazine* describes it as "a magazine for Alpha Males by . . . *Alpha Males.*"[67] Far from being a sexual underclass, then, self-identified barebackers represent themselves as *über-men*—as sexual professionals, experts in eros, and as outlaws, pioneers of the erotic avant-garde.

Whereas the Birmingham School developed its theory of subcultures by examining primarily youth cultures, research indicates that bareback subculture is not factored by age, even as it eroticizes generational categories such as "Daddy," "Boy," "Pup," "Brother," and so on. Perusal of any bareback Web site confirms that participants range in age from twentysomethings to men in their sixties and older. Men who were sexually active before AIDS emerged and who witnessed the devastations of the epidemic's first decade are as likely to identify as barebackers as are those whose sex lives have always been shadowed by viral anxiety. Barebacking mixes generational cohorts, as well as bodily fluids. Although not factored strictly by age, bareback subculture does overlap with specific youth subcultures, such as club culture, skate culture, punk culture, and body-modification culture. Paradoxical though it sounds, barebacking may be, in part, about staying youthful. In her recent

65. As reported by Michael Thorn, "Fort Troff," *Instigator Magazine*, January 2003, 17.

66. See Michel Foucault, *The History of Sexuality*, vol. 2, *The Use of Pleasure*, trans. Robert Hurley (New York: Random House, 1985), and vol. 3, *The Care of the Self*, trans. Robert Hurley (New York: Random House, 1986).

67. Thorn, "Fucking Deep into the Core of Reality," *Instigator Magazine*, January 2003, 2, emphasis in the original.

book on subcultures, Judith Halberstam points out that, insofar as they tend to "resist the heteronormative imperatives of home and family, [queers] also prolong the periods of their life devoted to subcultural participation."[68] What differentiates queer subcultures from other such groupings is, in part, their nonrestriction to any particular age group.

One of the most insistent questions that I have encountered when lecturing on barebacking concerns the subculture's racial demographics. Given how studies of AIDS epidemiology have shown that the incidence of HIV infection in the United States has been rising most significantly in nonwhite populations, such questions are highly apropos. However, other questions lurk behind the ostensibly innocent request for more information about subcultural demographics. One question involves trying to ascertain the participation of African American men in the subculture and its overlap with DL subculture— or men who have sex with other men "on the down low," that is, in secret, without assuming a gay identity. Wondering whether black men are as "bad" as white gay men may be a way of wondering whether bareback subculture is a product of privilege—all those financially comfortable white guys with good medical insurance who can afford the latest drugs and who boast the means to cultivate new forms of hedonism—or whether it is a subculture of the disenfranchised and desperate, those who see no future for themselves in a society whose democratic principles of equality and opportunity are pitilessly ironized by its accelerating material inequities. All the evidence suggests that participants in bareback subculture are as racially diverse as one would expect in a multiracial society such as the United States.[69] Subcultural membership

68. Judith Halberstam, *In a Queer Time and Place: Transgender Bodies, Subcultural Lives* (New York: New York University Press, 2005), 161. Although I have learned much from Halberstam's account of queer subcultures, her claims on behalf of their political radicalism overstate what seem to me to be the much more equivocal political implications of subcultural groupings (early in her book, Halberstam includes "HIV-positive barebackers" in a catalogue of "queer subjects" with considerable subversive potential [10]). Either she is laboring under the misapprehension that HIV-negative men do not bareback or she is making an essentialist assumption about the political potential of HIV-positive, as opposed to HIV-negative, barebackers.

69. Two recent New York–based studies of barebacking conclude that, as one research team put it, "barebacking practices did not significantly differ by race/ethnicity, indicating that in our sample of gay men, the practice is one that transgresses race and culture." From Halkitis, Wilton, and Galatowitsch, "What's in a Term?" 44. The other study drew a more nuanced conclusion: "We found that HIV-positive men, regardless of race/ethnicity, engaged in bareback sex more than HIV-negative men, particularly with other HIV-positive sexual partners. This finding is significant because it indicates similar patterns of bareback sexual behavior across racial/ethnic groups in MSM. However, the qualitative findings from this study suggest that the act of bareback sex holds differential cultural and phenomenological meanings for Black and Latino men." From Wilton et al., "Exploratory Study," 67. The race/ethnicity findings of these studies may be confirmed by consulting

does not depend on race, class, age, serostatus, or even sexuality but simply on one's willingness to embrace risk, to give and to take semen. In this respect, bareback subculture is unusually democratic.

More striking than the subculture's demographics is how bareback discourse sexualizes racial categories, appropriating stereotypes of racial hierarchy as part of a strategy for intensifying eroticism via images of dominance and submission. Particularly in the United States, the sexual roles of "master" and "slave" bear racial connotations whose significance may be exploited to heighten a sense of transgressiveness.[70] Racial difference offers one way of polarizing the top and bottom in a sexual encounter, thereby intensifying the exchange of power between positions, similar to the way that serodiscordance can exaggerate a relationship of dominance and submission. Figuring it in terms of the visible differences of skin color, say, or generational disparity may eroticize the invisible difference between an HIV-positive man and his HIV-negative partner. Although these sexualizations of racial categories have been part of SM culture for some time, barebackers seem especially keen to emphasize racial difference as a way of symbolizing—coloring in, we might say—visually imperceptible disparities between ostensible equals. I elaborate more fully this racializing strategy in chapter 3, where I consider *Niggas' Revenge*, one of the most provocative bareback-porn movies produced in what from the beginning has been an extremely controversial genre. For now I would note that one welcome result of this eroticization of racial difference is the comparative absence of normative whiteness in bareback subculture: as with any other distinguishing feature, whiteness is regarded as a potential fetish item and therefore is advertised.

Although the subculture has fewer membership criteria than most, any individual attribute is amenable to sexualization; once the virus has been counterphobically eroticized, it seems that anything is libidinal fair game. Thus even as the practice of barebacking has created new sexual identities,

---

any of the myriad bareback Web sites, most of which include personal photographs in their online profiles and some of which specify cruisers' racial or ethnic self-identifications. My own experience in San Francisco suggests that white, black, Latino, and Asian men all are barebacking and that bareback gang bangs take pride in their multiracial openness. I discuss further the multiracial openness of these gang bangs in chapter 2, when analyzing the documentary porn film *Fucking Crazy*, dir. Erich Lange (Treasure Island Media, 2003).

70. See, for example, Jayson Marston, "White Skinhead Seeks Black Submissives," in *Strategic Sex: Why They Won't Keep It in the Bedroom*, ed. D. Travers Scott (New York: Harrington Park, 1999), 93–95. Although this story may be characterized as interracial SM porn, it is not bareback pornography, since it includes explicit description of condom use.

it may be corroding gayness as an overarching identity category. Being gay is not a prerequisite for enjoying unprotected anal sex or, indeed, for subcultural membership. Just as some gay men pursue bareback sex without regarding themselves as barebackers, some nonwhite men pursue sex with other men without considering themselves as gay. To a certain extent, bareback subculture is "on the down low" even when nonwhites aren't participating. The social stigma that "homo sex" and, specifically, unprotected anal sex share in common encourages overlap between bareback and DL subcultures; both are often kept secret, which contributes to the excitement of—and thus motivates—subcultural participation.

Straight-identified African American men who pursue sex with other men "on the down low" may eschew condoms because they regard AIDS as a "gay disease": they reject condoms along with gay identity. This disidentification from gay identity and culture says as much about the normative whiteness and racism of mainstream U.S. gay culture as it does about African American homophobia and black masculinity. To the degree that bareback subculture maintains a defiant distance from mainstream gay culture and its commitment to "safe sex," it will continue to attract nonwhite men who wish to fuck other men without seeing themselves as gay. Conversely, to the extent that barebacking is recognized as a specifically gay subcultural practice, DL networks are likely to maintain their own distance from its identities and institutions, with only men of color who already identify as gay participating in it.[71]

The public spotlight recently aimed at men of color "on the down low" has been motivated by a fear that these men act as transmission bridges between gay men and straight women. The ostensibly heterosexual man with a wife or girlfriend who fucks around with other guys on the side risks bringing home to the domestic sphere sexually transmitted diseases (STDs) that are supposed to remain elsewhere.[72] Considerable research indicates, however, that the stereotype of the promiscuous black bisexual man—the man "on the down low"—has been scapegoated for a host of other factors that contribute

71. This ambiguous overlap is exemplified on http://www.machofucker.com, which bills itself as an amateur interracial bareback site and emphasizes above all its participants' unimpeachable masculinity, while downplaying the question of gay identity. The implication is that condom use would compromise these men's masculinity.

72. This paradigmatic narrative and its duplicitous protagonist was given currency by J. L. King, *On the Down Low: A Journey into the Lives of "Straight" Black Men Who Sleep with Men* (New York: Broadway Books, 2004); this book began as a *New York Times Magazine* cover story. The best critique of King's account is Keith Boykin, *Beyond the Down Low: Sex, Lies, and Denial in Black America* (New York: Carroll and Graf, 2005).

to increasing rates of HIV infection in minority populations.[73] Behind the epidemiological concern with transmission vectors lie broader cultural anxieties about how masculine nonwhite men's sexuality remains insufficiently identifiable or locatable. Insofar as these men refuse to conform to the hetero/homo binary that structures sexual intelligibility, their "down low" practices thwart disciplinary efforts to render all bodies, especially nonwhite bodies, fully legible. As with white barebackers, the attempt to identify these men in order to intervene in their sexual behavior is frustrated by the practices' inconsistent and only partial crystallization into recognizable identities.[74] "Down low" erotic practices, like those associated with barebacking, generate quintessentially permeable subcultures that thereby resist surveillance and discipline. In this respect, they might be described more accurately as "post-subcultures," social groupings that are not characterized by the epistemologically reassuring coherence, homogeneity, or boundedness that the term *subculture* often implies.[75]

Allow me to recapitulate my argument on this point before bringing the introduction to a close. *Unlimited Intimacy* adds to the research on barebacking not only by describing its practices, institutions, fantasies, and self-representations in greater detail but also by treating it as fully socialized behavior, that is, as the basis for a new subculture. The book then complicates this approach by showing how the subculture offers a uniquely permeable form of social organization, thus suggesting its participants' resistance to identification. Having anatomized the subculture's demographics, I wish to emphasize that its commitment to overcoming boundaries renders bareback subculture oddly unlocatable. The difficulty of circumscribing it helps account for both the excitement and the anxiety that the subculture elicits. Finally, having characterized bareback subculture as strangely unlocatable, I want to suggest that, although bareback networks flourish in European cities such

---

73. See Wilton et al., "Exploratory Study," 67: "While current epidemiological data demonstrates that heterosexual transmission of HIV has increased, especially for women of color, empirical evidence indicates that a multitude of risk factors relate to these disproportionate rates for Black women including but not limited to cultural factors (i.e., condom use beliefs), behavioral factors (i.e., heterosexual contact, bisexuality, injection drug use), structural factors (i.e., poverty, health disparities), and social factors (i.e., race- and gender-related stress). Nonetheless, with the insurgence of the 'Down Low' phenomenon, Black men's same-gender identities and behavior have been pejoratively constructed and ascribed as the predominant vector of HIV transmission for Black women."

74. I take this insight from the epilogue to Scott Herring's *Queering the Underworld*, 193–210.

75. On the de-essentialization of subcultural theory, see David Muggleton and Rupert Weinzierl, eds., *The Post-Subcultures Reader* (Oxford: Berg, 2003).

as Berlin and London, there is something quintessentially North American about this subculture.

GLOBAL AIDS, LOCAL NETWORKS

Originating in San Francisco in the mid-to-late '90s, bareback networks quickly propagated in virtual space, taking advantage of the medium in which new subcultures flourish. Bareback Web sites—whose dual function as purveyors of pornography and hook-up message boards renders them two-dimensional versions of both the old-time porn cinemas described in Delany's *Times Square Red, Times Square Blue* and the cruise bars, parks, and public toilets where, for generations, men have gathered for anonymous sex—make the subculture both more visible and more accessible. Reserving my principal discussion of online cruising for chapter 4, I wish to note here that the subculture's migration into virtual space lends it translocal possibilities. Indeed, extensive bareback networks have developed in cities such as Berlin that already had substantial leather and SM subcultures. Yet although it is certainly the case that AIDS is a global pandemic, it would not be correct to characterize bareback subculture as a globalized subculture, partly because HIV disease in Kinshasa, for example, is not the same as HIV disease in San Francisco. The AIDS pandemic comprises many microepidemics with different histories, transmission routes, demographics, and viral subtypes. Even as globalization and geographic mobility enabled the emergence of a worldwide pandemic, HIV disease has such vastly different cultural contexts and meanings that it does not make much sense to conceive of bareback subculture in terms of "African AIDS."

To be sure, as a quintessentially North American phenomenon, the subculture partakes of both the general parochialism and a particular disregard for the African subcontinent that typifies U.S. society as a whole. It would be easy, as well as morally reassuring, to condemn barebackers for their fetishization of HIV when, around the globe, numerous people die from AIDS every day. From my perspective, however, this fetishization of HIV marks the subculture's North American origins somewhat differently, signaling its emergence within a national context that tends to understand gay sexuality in terms of communicable pathologies. From the moment that researchers identified the etiologic agent of AIDS as a sexually transmitted virus, the U.S. scientific community has focused on HIV to an unprecedented degree. In other words, before gay men in San Francisco or New York started fetishizing the virus, U.S. scientists and public health experts did so—whether as the ultimate object of high-prestige research or as the phobic object of sex-education campaigns. Focusing so intensively on the virus—rather than on, say, sexual health and erotic pleasure more broadly—enabled an invisible microbe to function as the flash point for all manner of discourses, mythologies, and fantasies. Before it became an object of desire for some gay men, HIV was constituted in the United States as an object of scientific desire. As discussed further in chapter 3, the virus is not only a subcultural but also, more pervasively, a North American cultural fetish.[76] Thus even as it transcends national borders, the subculture remains indelibly marked by its origins in U.S. culture.

Overcoming borders or limits is at the heart of barebacking as a practice and a subculture. This study's title, *Unlimited Intimacy*, comes from a self-identified barebacker's description of his erotic preference; I wanted something that came out of a barebacker's mouth on the cover of my book. More than as a good fuck, it is as "unlimited intimacy" that this man imagines the practice of unprotected anal sex. Commenting on this phrase, documentary pornographer Paul Morris observes that "you can take unlimited intimacy to mean either something that is in itself unsafe, or something that's just basically psychologically and emotionally open, so it turned out for him, skin against skin was a kind of physical metaphor for the emotional experience that he wanted."[77] Behind the characterization of unprotected anal sex as unlimited intimacy, there is a distinctive account of relationality, of what it means to be in contact with other human beings. The term *intimacy* sometimes stands as a euphemism for fucking, but it also signals the emotional experiences that accompany sex. Barebackers' abandonment of condoms is motivated not only by a lust for enhanced physical sensation but also by a desire for certain emotional sensations, particularly the symbolic significance attached to experiences of vulnerability or risk. Rather than mindless fucking, bareback sex is an activity deeply invested with meaning. Despite the emphasis on raw, unmediated contact, barebacking often works most powerfully for

76. On the history of U.S. culture's fetishization of HIV, see Paula A. Treichler, *How to Have Theory in an Epidemic: Cultural Chronicles of AIDS* (Durham, NC: Duke University Press, 1999), esp. chap. 5. On the national specificity of bareback subculture, see Michael Scarce, "Ride on the Wild Side," 55: "extensive barebacking subcultures do not exist in other countries such as Australia where sex-positive harm-reduction models were instituted early on."

77. Comments made at "Visual AIDS: Gay Male Porn and Safer Sex Pedagogy" (roundtable discussion, org. and ed. Nicolas Sheon, Center for AIDS Prevention Studies, University of California, San Francisco, May 28, 1999), 3, available at http://hivinsite.ucsf.edu/prevention/prev__contro/2098.4218.html (accessed September 2000).

its practitioners as a metaphor. Physical contact becomes a way of achieving less tangible forms of contact.

Although the phrase "unlimited intimacy" was coined by one particular man, the desire to erase limits permeates all aspects of the subculture. "No Limits!"—a phrase found repeatedly in online sex ads—may be this subculture's rallying cry. "No Limits!" means that a man takes pride in his readiness to try any erotic activity or position, that the protective limit of latex is unnecessary or unwelcome, that the numerical limit of a single partner has been dissolved by the polymorphous pleasures of group sex, and that the limits of corporeal integrity exist only to be transgressed. A fine example of the implications of exploding bodily limits may be found in a fictional representation of bareback fisting, which describes how one partner dominates the other by sliding his arm ever deeper into the narrator's bowels, until, "for an instant, we shared the feeling of occupying the same place at the same time."[78] The sexual act of fisting brings one man so far inside another as to temporarily obliterate the boundaries that conventionally separate persons. By occupying exactly the same physical space simultaneously, the men in this fantasy have become in some sense identical, beyond individuation. Here sexual contact shades into communion.[79]

Repudiating limits entails a discipline of challenging to the point of dissolution an individual's boundaries, in order to achieve boundlessness. In such a practice, contact or intimacy is desired not only with other persons but also with something more impersonal. The impersonality of anonymous group sex facilitates access to an impersonal intimacy that barebackers often characterize as sacred, rather than profane. In light of this understanding, I would suggest that impersonal intimacy disentangles intimacy from personhood and

78. Toy, "Biker Bitch Fantasy," *Instigator Magazine*, January 2003, 54. Fisting offers "a way to go to a place in my head that I simply can't get to any other way," confirms one aficionado. From Bud Hole, "Fisting: Needing a Hand and Getting One," *Instigator Magazine*, April 2003, 16. "Fisting is the most intense interpersonal relationship you can have with another person, both giving and getting," says Cole Tucker, in an interview in the documentary film *Beyond Vanilla*, dir. Claes Lilja (Strand, 2003).

79. The term "communion" crops up often in discourse around barebacking. One self-identified barebacker comments, "Condoms are not just a question of sensitivity, they are a barrier to physical, emotional, and spiritual communion." Quoted in DeAnn K. Gauthier and Craig J. Forsyth, "Bareback Sex, Bug Chasers, and the Gift of Death," *Deviant Behavior* 20, no. 1 (1999): 90. See also Shernoff, who asks rhetorically, "Is [barebacking], as paradoxical as this may seem, actually an attempt to take care of oneself and to forge a deeper intimacy, closeness, and even spiritual communion?" From *Without Condoms*, 68. Robert E. Goss argues that "gay men are willing to risk their health for the sake of a viral communion that encompasses elements of a transcendent spirituality of sexuality." From Goss, *Queering Christ: Beyond Jesus Acted Up* (Cleveland: Pilgrim, 2002), 78.

from the epistemological imperative to know the other, just as impersonalist ethics separates ethics from the imaginary requirement to empathize with the other. When committed barebackers describe their most intense erotic experiences in these terms, they are not merely rationalizing what most folks regard as deviant behavior but attributing their highest value to certain bodily activities. Although from one perspective fucking without condoms represents sex at its most mundane, from another perspective the history of AIDS has made gay sex without condoms extraordinary, endowing bareback sex with enormous significance. The next chapter examines in greater detail the complex and contradictory meanings that barebackers attribute to their sexual practice, focusing especially on the use of HIV to establish kinship networks. Bareback subculture is an arena of invention that involves experiments in how to *do* things with viruses.

ONE: BREEDING CULTURE

What do bug chasers want?

At the most basic level, bug chasers are men who want the human immuno-deficiency virus inside their bodies. They rarely characterize that desire in such clinical terms, though. The nomenclature generated in bareback subculture employs a more colorful vernacular, as this passage from the home page of a bareback Web site vividly illustrates:

> Who's afraid of the big, bad bug? Not our little piggies. We'll huff and we'll puff and we'll blow your Dick Down! Chase those bugs all over town like the horny toad you are. Get dangerous and seek out new perversions and new fetishes. No matter what you promised, never, ever pull out of Dodge. Breed, get seed and get on your knees to feed. Everybody needs protein, right?[1]

Although devoid of four-letter words (unless you count "Dick"), these jingly sentences may appear as obscene—or at least surreal—to many readers. Their surreality consists in the disjunction between an imperative to seek viral transmission through man-on-man sex and the innocent fairy-tale rhymes in which a very adult advocacy is couched. The style of this passage makes bug chasing seem like harmless cartoon fun. Euphemizing HIV as "the bug" puts seroconversion into the category of relatively innocuous infection. "Bug" is also a term for a fashion or a craze; hence the suggestion that bug chasing is simply the latest fetish, a way of staying erotically au courant. Not only a vital component of gay sexual hipness, the bug—by analogy with the insects that

1. From http://www.bareback.com/images/mid-title-01.gif (accessed June 2003).

toads eat—is also a source of nourishment. It is both glamorous and nutri-
tious. HIV thus is pictured as a source of life rather than of death.

In this through-the-looking-glass world, which blends Disney cartoon imagery with Madison Avenue advertising lingo, men are pigs and wolves and
horny toads, gaily cavorting, feeding, and breeding. The image of "little piggies" alludes to the fable "The Three Little Pigs" (in which the "big bad wolf"
blows down the houses made by the pigs), as well as conjuring a genealogy
of gay sexual types: *wolf* is an outmoded term for male sexual aggressor (this
meaning survives in the phrase "wolf whistle"), whereas *pig* is a term of more
recent derivation that designates a gay man whose motto is "No Limits!" In
the first decades of the twentieth century, *wolf* was the term for a conventionally masculine man who preferred sex with other males; historian George
Chauncey explains that "wolves generally did not seek sexual encounters with
other 'men,' in which they might have been forced into sexual roles that would
have compromised their own masculine identification, but only with punks
or fairies, males ascribed lower status because of their youth or effeminacy."[2]
Chauncey documents the survival of this term into the postwar period, while
other sources indicate that *wolf* had vanished from gay vernacular by the early
1970s, suggesting that this sexual type was a casualty of gay liberation.[3]

Or perhaps wolves metamorphosed into pigs. A term of approbation in
bareback subculture, *pig* refers to a man who wants as much sex as he can
get with as many different men as possible, often in the form of group sex
that includes barebacking, water sports, fisting, and SM ("pig pile" is a long-
established term for a gay orgy or gang bang). There is really no such thing
as a vanilla pig or a safe-sex pig, since the erotic identity of *pig* defies normative constructions of sexual behavior. Being a pig entails committing oneself
to sexual excess, to pushing beyond boundaries of propriety and corporeal
integrity; being a pig thus positions a man for membership in a sexual avant-
garde, and, unsurprisingly, some men advertise their pig status with tattoos,
T-shirts, and various forms of braggadocio. Some bareback-porn actors have
P-I-G tattooed on their knuckles to announce their vocation, and the term
features regularly in the titles of bareback movies, such as *Pigs at the Troff*
(Dick Wadd Productions, 2000) and *Some Pigs* (Dick Wadd Productions,

2. George Chauncey, *Gay New York: Gender, Urban Culture, and the Making of the Gay Male World,
1890–1940* (New York: Basic Books, 1994), 89.

3. Chauncey, *Gay New York*, 397n52. Bruce Rodgers's comprehensive *Gay Talk: A (Sometimes
Outrageous) Dictionary of Gay Slang* (1972; repr., New York: Paragon, 1979) contains no reference to
wolves, thus suggesting the category's dissolution in the wake of Stonewall.

1998). One popular bareback-porn performer, Steve Hurley, has achieved cult status under the name TitPig, a reference to his hugely distended nipples, which tend to provide the focus of any scene in which he appears.[4]

For generations, feminists have charged that men are pigs; barebackers have transformed this reproach into a badge of pride, elevating it into a subcultural identity. They also have masculinized a previously feminine term, since around midcentury "pig" referred, in gay vernacular, to a woman with whom men competed for another man's affections. In glossing this misogynistic usage, one lexicographer notes that a Greek word for the female genitals was *choiros*, "which also means 'pig.'"[5] The hypermasculine actor known as TitPig thus has effected a double gender switch in transforming the feminine connotations of both halves of his screen name. If being regarded as a pig in the world of gay masculinity is equivalent to being considered a stud in the world of straight masculinity, then the principal difference between the two lies in the fact that a gay-sex pig usually acquires his status through voracious bottoming—by taking as many penises and as much semen inside him as he can. As one young man put it:

> To me, it seems being a real man is often at odds with being a *gay man* because of social clichés and sexual limitations imposed upon us by ourselves and society-at-large. I never feel ashamed or less than anyone else when I *suck cock like a whore, get pissed on*, or *take many dicks up my ass*.... I'm just a man alongside other men who all enjoy playing like nasty (sometimes even *violent*) pigs![6]

Hypermasculinity accrues to the man who assumes what used to be thought of as the female role in homosexual relations. The more men by whom one is penetrated, the more of a man he becomes.

Clearly piggery represents a different construction of male-male sexuality than we know from either the classical era or the modern organization of homosexuality under the rule of heteronormativity. The persistent *fin-de-siècle* understanding of male homosexuality as gender inversion—a female soul trapped in a male body—has been expunged from bareback subculture, which concedes only degrees of masculinity. It is not that all men are equal (far from it) but that all are treated as *men* no matter how often they take it up

---

4. See http://www.titpig.net.

5. Alan Richter, *Sexual Slang: A Compendium of Offbeat Words and Colorful Phrases from Shakespeare to Today*, 3rd ed. (New York: HarperCollins, 1995), 166.

6. François Sagat, quoted in *Instigator Magazine*, Featured Fucko, 2006, 51, emphases in the original.

the butt; this may be part of bareback subculture's appeal. An initial answer to the chapter's opening question thus would be that bug chasers want not just semen but to *be men*. Although the sexual bottom regularly is addressed by his tops in the most derogatory feminine terms (such as "bitch," "pussy," and "cunt"), this misogynist rhetoric does not seem to impugn his masculinity; indeed, masculinity may be bolstered rhetorically by the use of terms that refer pejoratively to the female genitals. No matter how one interprets such language, in bareback subculture being sexually penetrated is a matter of "taking it like a man," enduring without complaint any discomfort or temporary loss of status, in order to prove one's masculinity. It is as if what Chauncey identifies as the early twentieth-century organization of working-class erotic culture independently of heterosexuality had reasserted itself a century later—as if, in other words, heterosexuality's hegemony were merely an aberration of the last century, a delusion from which we already are starting to recover.[7]

This chapter explores in greater detail what motivates men to bareback, especially those men who identify as bug chasers. Having suggested that barebacking is overdetermined behavior, I want to anatomize its multiple determinants while also bearing in mind their inconsistency; complex behavior often is motivated by mutually exclusive impulses. Referring to subcultural overdetermination, one Birmingham School ethnographer maintains that "the latent function of subculture is this: to express and resolve, albeit 'magically,' the contradictions which remain hidden or unresolved in the parent culture."[8] In what follows, I pursue the contradictory determinants of barebacking and bug chasing by examining several rationales: embracing risk as a test of masculinity, counterphobically reinterpreting the pathogen as desirable, diminishing fear of HIV/AIDS, increasing doubts about HIV as the cause of AIDS, eliminating anxiety by purposefully arranging seroconversion, and resisting mainstream health norms. These determinants are all related but not mutually compatible. The determinant that interests me most, however, is the one that is inventive rather than primarily reactive—the attempt to use viral exchange to create kinship networks. By treating HIV as a

---

7. See Chauncey, *Gay New York*, 97: "Heterosexuality had not become a precondition of gender normativity in early twentieth-century working-class culture. Men had to be many things in order to achieve the status of normal men, but being 'heterosexual' was not one of them." This characterization applies equally well to early twenty-first-century bareback subculture.

8. Phil Cohen, "Subcultural Conflict and Working-Class Community," in *Culture, Media, Language*, ed. Stuart Hall, Dorothy Hobson, Andrew Lowe, and Paul Willis (London: Hutchinson, 1980), 82.

"gift" whose donation creates consanguineous relations among subcultural members, barebackers are participating, almost invisibly, in the broader cultural enterprise of redefining kinship. Even as they resist mainstream culture, subcultural participants illuminate some of its deepest and unresolved contradictions.

PROVING MASCULINITY

In bareback subculture, as in the military or college fraternities, masculine status is achieved by surviving a set of physical ordeals, including multiple penetrations, humiliations, piercings, tattooings, brandings, and infections. The prophylaxis afforded by condoms is reserved for those who can't handle the real thing. Rather than offering protection, condoms make a man and his masculinity vulnerable to doubt or derision. Latex compromises not only sensation and intimacy but also masculine identity. From this perspective, HIV becomes simply another trial, the endurance of which proves one's mettle. Being HIV positive is like having a war wound or a battle scar. Of course, the fact that HIV-positive North American gay men are living far longer than they did in the 1980s is partly what allows this view of the disease to exist. The introduction of highly active antiretroviral therapies and the emergence of a class of long-term "nonprogressors" (those whose HIV infection shows no signs of developing into AIDS after more than a decade) represent just two of bareback subculture's many enabling conditions.

I'm suggesting that shifts in the cultural construction of masculinity represent an equally significant condition of barebacking. The practice of bug chasing, which at first blush appears unaccountable except as pathology, may be the subculture's response to a particular problem that can be stated in the following way. Although gangbanging, body piercing, and tattooing all can be repeated (thereby providing multiple occasions for authenticating masculine prowess), seroconversion is something that happens only once. It holds a unique status, somewhat akin to losing one's virginity. The "endurance test" of seroconversion acquires additional significance because it occurs internally and therefore remains invisible to the witnesses of one's other feats of fortitude. Pornographic representation is central to bareback subculture because it offers a form of witnessing; yet the permanent alteration effected by seroconversion cannot be witnessed directly. It is the kind of undetectable mark that, historically, has been associated with sexual inversion and that the florid insignia of bareback subculture—tattoos, piercings, and cultivated body types—attempt to counterbalance through their visibility.

I will have more to say about how HIV marks the body's interior, just as tattooing marks the exterior. For now, I want to emphasize how bug chasing represents a way to repeat the unrepeatable, to make seroconversion something you can practice. Bug chasing fosters an illusion that one is the master of, rather than completely subjected to, his erotic destiny. A variant of this technique consists in refusing to take an HIV test, so that each unprotected encounter may be imagined as the one that transmits the virus. In this way, risk can be perpetually renewed, and one's masculine capacity for tolerating risk ever more enhanced. This conceit rationalizes the unprotected sex pursued by Carlos, the pseudonymous Manhattan bug chaser profiled in a controversial *Rolling Stone* article, who allegedly thinks that "every date is potentially The One."[9] Likewise Steve, one of the two founders of barebackcity.com (now ultimatebareback.com), notes in his online profile that he has never been tested for HIV. Needless to say, self-identified barebackers who never have submitted to an HIV test are unlikely to be taking antiretroviral medication.

By "chas[ing] those bugs all over town like the horny toad you are," a man may collect other men's bugs inside his body and transform himself into a sort of terrarium. Bug chasing should be understood as one of the more extreme forms of body modification. One may become not only a bug chaser but also a bug collector, since seropositive semen leaves a trace that ordinary cum does not. Whereas some barebackers want simply as much semen as they can get, bug chasers are less interested in having an HIV-negative man ejaculate inside them: they prefer semen that contains the virus—"poz-cum" or "poz," as it is colloquially known. The slang term "poz" (also the title of a long-established U.S. magazine for HIV-positive readers) functions as both noun and verb: to "poz" another guy is to ejaculate HIV-infected semen inside him. Hundreds of online profiles represent men who are clamoring to enact the fantasy of "getting pozzed."[10] Semen containing HIV signifies much more than ordinary spunk; it is radioactive with meaning. The term "poz" implies that infected semen has developed a positive rather than negative connotation in the subculture's argot; HIV has been transvalued from a bad into a good object, something to be incorporated inside one's body rather than kept outside.

9. Freeman, "In Search of Death," 48.

10. A random quantitative check of the Web site http://www.ultimatebareback.com, on July 25, 2006, indicated 41,626 active members; a search under the category "bug chaser" yielded 726 profiles—that is, 726 members who, when creating their online cruising profile, clicked an icon to indicate that they were interested in giving or receiving "the bug."

Commenting on this transvaluation in his illuminating Web log, HIV-positive bareback blogger Geek Slut (who elsewhere goes by the name Raw Ranger) suggests that a natural desire for semen has been perverted by the exigencies of safe-sex education:

> **The need for seed.** Once a natural part of queer culture has become a sleazy kink. We glorify it. We enjoy it. I guess it's payback, you know. After spending years, our cocks wrapped in plastic marching to the "Safe Sex" rhythm. That didn't work. It was doomed from the start. **We're human beings.** Men. We're not above nature, we ARE nature.
>
> **Seed is** a gift, it's love, it's acceptance. Taking a man's cum—in your ass, down your throat, rubbed into your skin, whatever—even if you don't know his name, is *closeness*. It's an act of love and trust. Even if yawl just met! Both the bottom and the top walk away smiling . . . and content. Now it's a sleazy affair that boys get cracked out of their minds for. Like it's an embarrassing nasty secret thing to want. This is so fucked.[11]

Geek Slut sees the fetish for poz-cum as a regrettable yet nonetheless predictable response to the hysterical rejection of semen earlier in the epidemic. We might extend his point by acknowledging how, partly in reaction to the excessive pathologizing of persons with AIDS, the pathogen has been reinterpreted as desirable.

Or if not desirable, then much less anxiety inducing than it once was. "Who's afraid of the big, bad bug?" testifies to a widespread diminishing of gay men's fear of HIV, a shift documented by Stephen Morin, director of the University of California, San Francisco, AIDS Policy Research Center, in a study showing that San Francisco gay men generally regard HIV as less threatening and thus unprotected sex as less unacceptable.[12] This abatement of terror, which doubtless is a good thing in itself, represents part of the so-called normalization of AIDS and owes much to a growing recognition that the epidemic's crisis mode cannot be sustained indefinitely. Although HIV may persist forever in human populations around the globe, nobody can live permanently under conditions of siege. Barebackers are saying, in effect, that

---

11. Geek Slut, "What Boys Do for Seed," posted October 22, 2004, available at http://www.geekslut.org (accessed November 10, 2004), emphases in the original.

12. Stephen F. Morin et al., "Why HIV Infections Have Increased among Men Who Have Sex with Men and What to Do about It: Findings from California Focus Groups," *AIDS and Behavior* 7, no. 4 (2003): 353–62. My thanks to Dr. Morin for sharing the results of his research with me before its publication.

it seems more unhealthy to live in a state of permanent terror than to live a life that treats HIV as a sort of occupational hazard: HIV comes with the territory of being gay and sexually alive. In other words, barebackers infer that HIV is something of which one is cognizant, without permitting it to determine completely one's most significant choices in the sphere of intimacy. As we have grown accustomed to the presence of HIV, some men have gone from accepting to embracing the possibility of infection. Bug chasing transforms seroconversion into a matter over which one exercises choice and thereby demonstrates one's sexual freedom.

More than as a choice, however, the question "Who's afraid of the big, bad bug?" frames seroconversion as a *challenge* to gay men's masculinity. It pointedly asks whether you're still terrified of HIV and implies that, by contrast, "our little piggies" are man enough to take it. The mode of address on this Web site's home page, though playful, is also defiant and imperative; it issues a series of instructions—"get dangerous and seek out new perversions," "never, ever pull out of Dodge," "breed, get seed and get on your knees to feed"—that could be heard as masterful commands and therefore might be erotically satisfying to fulfill simply because of their authoritative enunciation. One need not identify as a masochist to gain sexual satisfaction from obeying orders; it's just a matter of those imperatives being issued in the right tone of voice. Although the tone of this Web site's home page is not entirely consistent, it persists in the imperative mode:

> Don't tell your mommy, but it's just about time to meet the boy toy of your dreams. Pull out your crank and prepare to get covered and filled with hot cum. Bend over and let some tube snake fill your hot buns! No glove? Good, then get ready for hot love.

This last phrase inverts the popular safe-sex rhyme "No glove, no love" (that is, no sex without a condom), which itself plays on the contemporary rhyme "No pain, no gain." What I find fascinating, beyond these vernacular appropriations, is how the passage's mode of address frames bug chasing as an index of masculinity (by overcoming your fear of HIV, you become master of your sexual destiny and prove your manhood), at the same time that its second-person imperative voice appeals to the desire to be mastered by someone more masculine. According to this paradoxical logic, one is masculinized rather than feminized by submitting to masculine domination. Thus rather than as an index of vulnerability, HIV infection is imagined as the opposite— as the ultimate sign of strength.

SACRIFICIAL EROS

Bareback subculture's hypermasculinization of bottoming, its picturing erotic submission as a proof of manhood, could be seen as a compensatory response to modern society's feminization of male homosexuality—a response, that is, to the gender-inversion model of same-sex desire. But it also could be seen as a response to the feminizing potential of sex itself, namely, the way that intense pleasure overwhelms self-control, threatening the ego's coherence. Here I am thinking of Leo Bersani's contention that what people dislike about sex is its capacity to make them temporarily helpless: there comes a point in the pursuit of pleasure when even the most dominant partner must submit to something more powerful than himself.[13] Submitting to a loss of control, one consequence of which is to undermine the self-mastery associated with masculinity, intensifies erotic pleasure; our culture thus understands that submission as potentially feminizing. This is one implication of Bersani's extrapolation, via Laplanche's reading of Freud, that sexuality is a tautology for masochism. Through its commitment to no-excuses submission and no-limits endurance, however, bareback subculture conversely embraces masochism as proof positive of masculinity. That is to say, by remasculinizing masochism, barebackers have made self-loss into a confirmation rather than an effacement of manhood.

This logic helps explain why bareback subculture regards its most committed participants as heroes. By displaying such fortitude and executing so many feats of endurance in the pursuit of erotic pleasure, these men achieve an ethical status quite distinct from that attributed to them by mainstream culture. Rather than as irresponsible, destructive, or hedonistic, they are seen as heroic warriors and gay patriots; rather than as self-indulgent, their sex is viewed as altruistic, in the sense that barebackers fuck without protection on behalf of those too timid to do so. The position that understands barebacking as a heroic sacrifice on behalf of the gay community has been articulated most cogently by Paul Morris, a remarkable documentary pornographer, who argues that "'unsafe sex' is not only insane, it is also essential":

> For a subculture to be sustained, there must be those who engage in its central and defining activities with little regard for anything else, including life itself.... At the heart of every culture is a set of experiences which members hold not only to be worth practicing, but also necessary to maintain and trans-

13. Bersani, "Is the Rectum a Grave?" 197–222.

mit to those who follow. In the case of a sexual subculture, one often has only one way to do this: by embodying the traditions. Within the complex system of beliefs and practices of an American male sexual subculture, there can be little that is more defining than the communion and connections that are made possible through these central practices. The everyday identity evanesces and the individual becomes an agent through which a darker and more fragile tradition is enabled to continue. Irresponsibility to the everyday persona and to the general culture is necessary for allegiance to the sexual subculture, and this allegiance takes the gay male directly to the hot and central point where what is at stake isn't the survival of the individual, but the survival of the practices and patterns which are the discoveries and properties of the subculture.... The subculture and the virus require the same processes for transmission.[14]

In order to sustain a culture, some of its members must represent the culture in and through their own bodies, no matter how painful or even fatal that embodied representation may be. According to this logic, barebackers sacrifice themselves on behalf of gay culture in the same way that, for example, soldiers sacrifice themselves on behalf of their country during war. If the analogy with wartime patriotism seems farfetched, we might recall that the gay community's loss of men in the 1980s and early '90s was comparable to wartime losses in terms of sheer numbers. Gay men who survived AIDS often have been regarded as survivors of war, and the trauma inflicted by the witnessing of such losses has been invoked to explain gay men's sexual behavior, as if barebacking were a symptom of posttraumatic stress disorder.[15]

What intrigues me most about Morris's risk manifesto is his contention that gay culture and HIV "require the same processes for transmission." Albeit from a very different perspective, Gabriel Rotello argued something similar in his critique of gay sexual ecology.[16] Whereas Rotello suggests that HIV

---

14. Paul Morris, "No Limits: Necessary Danger in Male Porn" (paper presented at the World Pornography Conference, Los Angeles, August 8, 1998), available at http://www.treasureislandmedia.com/TreasureIslandMedia_2007/paulsPapers.php?article=noLimits (accessed August 2001).

15. See Walt Odets, *In the Shadow of the Epidemic: Being HIV-Negative in the Age of AIDS* (Durham, NC: Duke University Press, 1995). It is not just that sex may be one response to shell shock but also that militarism has been heavily eroticized by barebackers, in the form of fetishizing gas masks, combat gear, and camouflage paraphernalia. In the midst of Bush's war on Iraq, Michael Thorn wrote, in an editorial to a military-themed issue of *Instigator Magazine*, that "at least our TVs have been filled with images of HOT fuckers in camo and gasmasks, and everyone now seems to have an adequate supply of duct tape [for bondage]!" From Thorn, Letter from Our Editor, *Instigator Magazine*, April 2003, 2.

16. Gabriel Rotello, *Sexual Ecology: AIDS and the Destiny of Gay Men* (New York: Dutton, 1997).

makes the continuing organization of gay culture around multipartner sex institutions untenable, Morris understands viral transmission as a regrettable byproduct of cultural transmission. The life of the culture depends on the death of its members, or, more precisely, the culture can be perpetuated only by certain members risking their lives. Whereas Rotello argues that the price of a sustainable gay culture is our sacrifice of certain cherished activities (namely, promiscuous unprotected butt fucking and semen exchange), Morris contends that it is preferable to risk lives in order to protect those activities that define the culture. From Morris's perspective, gay culture ceases to exist once we relinquish our sexual freedom; from Rotello's point of view, gay culture will cease to exist *unless* we relinquish some sexual freedom. To put the matter bluntly, one views gay promiscuity as genocidal, while the other views abandoning that promiscuity as genocidal.

Morris and Rotello agree that we need to sacrifice something in order to preserve gay culture, but they disagree on what that something is. Although they subscribe to quite different values, both remain committed to the idea that something about gay culture should be preserved at all costs. Yet just how much should be sacrificed in order to preserve a cultural ideal remains debatable, and, as this study progresses, I shall put some pressure on the assumptions underlying the sacrificial ethic. For now, though, I want to emphasize that diametrically opposed voices in today's queer culture promote a sacrificial ethic and that this ethic remains homologous with the logic of patriotism that we hear invoked so persistently in the United States at present. To the extent that bareback subculture promotes an ethic homologous with that of patriotism (and barebackers embrace the erotics of militarism), it may be defensible in sadly familiar terms. But to the extent that this sacrificial logic is vulnerable to ethical critique, bareback subculture must be subject to the same criticisms as mainstream U.S. cultural values. In other words, bareback subculture may be ethically troubling less for its radical departure from mainstream values than for its perpetuation of them.[17]

The sacrificial logic through which Morris rationalizes barebacking raises a question that reverberates far beyond gay culture, namely, whether physically harmful or constraining practices that are deemed fundamental to a culture's self-definition should be protected or, conversely, extirpated. The question of a culture's right to enact consensual harm on some of its members

---

17. For a strong critique of this kind of sacrificial logic, see Leo Bersani, *The Culture of Redemption* (Cambridge, MA: Harvard University Press, 1990).

is complicated by the question of whether one culture has the right to impose its values on another. When representatives of a more powerful culture intervene to prevent the violence entailed in a subaltern culture's performance of what may be regarded as a sacred ritual, the intervention commits symbolic violence in order to forestall physical violence. Ethically it is necessary to acknowledge that, in such circumstances, one form of violence substitutes for another—in other words, that the well-intentioned abolition of dangerous practices nonetheless perpetrates a kind of symbolic harm on cultures organized around those practices.

This problem is complicated further when the clash of values occurs not between cultures but within a culture—for instance, between the dominant culture and its internal subcultures. In this case, it is less a question of weighing the rights of the individual against those of the collective than of calibrating what rights to self-determination may be exercised by a smaller collective within a larger one. Rather than controversial practices in non-Western cultures, perhaps a better point of comparison for barebacking would be issues in U.S. culture (such as those around hearing impairment and American Sign Language) that pit the self-definition of smaller collectivities against the norms of mainstream society. Since the Deaf community embraces its cultural identity as Deaf more readily than it embraces mainstream bodily norms that treat deafness principally as a medical condition to be overcome, members of that community often resist technological palliatives for hearing impairment, arguing that mainstream society should provide equal access and participatory parity for deaf people rather than seeking to normalize or cure them.[18] More so than the gay community, the disability community has developed a strong critique of bodily norms by arguing against treating physiological, cognitive, or aesthetic impairment as a valid basis for disenfranchisement. Of course, this is a huge area of debate, and I don't want to imply that the gay and disability communities do not overlap (the popularity of certain gay bars among the Deaf quickly dispels that misconception).[19] My point is that, given the currency of sexual puritanism in the United States, it may be via disability

---

18. See Douglas Baynton, *Forbidden Signs: American Culture and the Campaign against Sign Language* (Chicago: University of Chicago Press, 1996); and Carol Padden and Tom Humphries, *Inside Deaf Culture* (Cambridge, MA: Harvard University Press, 2005).

19. For an interesting article on Deaf leather culture, see Dave Hughes, "Falling on Deaf Ears," *Instigator Magazine*, 2006: 27–29. In a groundbreaking critique of what he terms "compulsory able-bodiedness," Robert McRuer makes apparent the connection between mainstream culture's attitude toward deafness and its attitude toward the HIV positive. See McRuer, *Crip Theory: Cultural Signs of Queerness and Disability* (New York: New York University Press, 2006), 8–9.

theory as much as via theories of sexuality that HIV-positive people can argue most cogently the question of their self-determination.

THE IMPERATIVE OF HEALTH

The conflict between bareback subculture and mainstream U.S. culture may be grasped as a contest between two secular ideals—that of sexual pleasure and that of health—with barebackers embracing the former as the greater good. This isn't simply a question of individual versus collective rights, because the pursuit of erotic pleasure defines the subculture; that is, the pursuit of pleasure defines a collective entity rather than defining merely certain individuals. In contrast to our customary understanding of how collectivities demand that their members renounce some portion of individual pleasure, bareback subculture functions as a collectivity by virtue of its members refusing to renounce pleasure. Fucking without protection concerns less selfish gratification than "allegiance to the subculture," as Morris puts it—allegiance, that is, to an entity beyond the self. In bareback subculture, promiscuous sex thus entails a particular kind of fidelity.

Fidelity to the subcultural ideal of erotic pleasure necessitates betrayal of the mainstream cultural ideal of health—or, more precisely, betrayal of a distinctly medicalized understanding of what counts as health. Increasingly, Western societies promote images of an intact human body that can be sustained into advanced age as desirable for not simply the biological organism but also the ethical subject. Sociologists such as Robert Crawford and Nikolas Rose argue that, since the nineteenth century, the pursuit of health has been understood as the pursuit of moral personhood, even though the emergence of germ theory ostensibly recast moralistic conceptions of disease etiology.[20] With the rise of bacteriology and the consequent emergence of a biomedical model of disease at the end of the nineteenth century, illness came to be understood as caused by microbes, and thus medicine developed as a repertoire of techniques for destroying those microbes or inhibiting their spread. Thanks to the germ theory of disease, some of the moral associations of illness were displaced.

The triumph of bacteriology and immunology in the twentieth century threw into relief the significance of noncommunicable chronic illnesses—

20. Nikolas Rose, *The Politics of Life Itself: Biomedicine, Power, and Subjectivity in the Twenty-First Century* (Princeton, NJ: Princeton University Press, 2007); and Robert Crawford, "The Boundaries of the Self and the Unhealthy Other: Reflections on Health, Culture and AIDS," *Social Science and Medicine* 38, no. 10 (1994): 1347–65. See also Crawford, "Healthism and the Medicalization of Everyday Life," *International Journal of Health Services* 10, no. 3 (1980): 365–88.

such as hypertension, cancer, and heart disease—for which there is no single etiologic agent. As medical historian Allan Brandt suggests, "in the postwar era the limits of the germ theory to address systemic chronic disease led to a new recognition of environmental and behavioral forces as determinants of disease."[21] Epidemiological theories of disease prevalence complemented and to some extent superseded the germ theory, with increasingly sophisticated statistical measurements furnishing the opportunity to conceptualize health as a calculus of risk. The emergence of modern epidemiology thus laid the ground for a remoralization of illness, based on a renewed sense that susceptibility to disease could be controlled by the stringent regulation of diet and exercise, as well as by avoidance of the risks associated with smoking, alcohol, illegal drugs, and sexual promiscuity. Rather than sources of pleasure, the latter were redefined as sources of danger, and the new emphasis on behavioral determinants of disease reinforced a sense that the pursuit of health was the individual's moral responsibility.

Once again you can be held morally accountable for the state of your physical well-being. According to Foucault, eighteenth-century European society generated an "imperative of health" that made the active pursuit of health "at once the duty of each and the objective of all."[22] Although the ancients elaborated complex regimens of diet and exercise for elite citizens, their regimens were not understood in terms of a universal mandate for health and were not deemed applicable to the populace. Those assumptions changed in the eighteenth century, as the concept of health became attached to modern institutions of power and thus to the regulatory unit of biopower, namely, identity. "The concept of health is absolutely central to modern identity," particularly class identity, argues Crawford.[23] In an especially penetrating recent study,

21. Allan M. Brandt, "Behavior, Disease, and Health in the Twentieth-Century United States: The Moral Valence of Individual Risk," in *Morality and Health*, ed. Allan M. Brandt and Paul Rozin (New York: Routledge, 1997), 59.

22. Michel Foucault, "The Politics of Health in the Eighteenth Century," in *Essential Works of Foucault, 1954–1984*, vol. 3, *Power*, ed. James D. Faubion, trans. Robert Hurley et al. (New York: New Press, 2000), 94. On the circle recently drawn between eighteenth-century and late-twentieth-century conceptions of health, see Charles Rosenberg, "Banishing Risk: Continuity and Change in the Moral Management of Disease," in Brandt and Rozin, *Morality and Health*, 35–51: "'Psycho-somatic medicine' and 'holistic medicine' are concepts that have become fashionable in the second half of the twentieth century. Both can be seen as reactions against the categorical claims of the mechanistic reductionist style of medical explanation that dominated the first half of the century. And both are often seen as new and advanced ways of thinking about health and disease. Both, however, would have been seen as orthodox—if not as truisms—by any eighteenth- or early-nineteenth-century physician" (45).

23. Crawford, "Boundaries of the Self," 1348.

Nikolas Rose explains how "health, understood as an imperative, for the self and for others, to maximize the vital forces and potentialities of the living body, has become a key element in contemporary ethical regimes."[24] Health is now a disciplinary rubric, offering a rationale for the institutional control of whole populations, as well as a matrix for self-understanding and self-discipline. Modern epidemiology's redescription of health in terms of risk has transformed health into a precarious state that needs constant monitoring and assessment. Being a middle-class U.S. citizen today entails perpetual self-surveillance regarding diet, exercise, and medication; bourgeois identity requires the vigilant practice of a kind of corporate risk management with respect to one's body and its pleasures. Every meal is a potential minefield for health maintenance, since daily nutrition has become larded with risks unknown to previous generations. Our increased knowledge about nutrition, disease, and medicine has not produced a greater sense of security but, on the contrary, a heightened sense of risk.[25]

Working from a different methodological approach, the German sociologist Ulrich Beck has identified risk as the defining feature of postmodernity. His account of the "risk society" emphasizes how environmental damage, terrorism, and other instances of "manufactured risk" have saturated everyday life during the past several decades. Because the risks of nuclear catastrophe or global warming exceed temporal, geographic, and institutional boundaries, we now live in a world where risk cannot be contained. This characteristic of contemporary life reorients social theory from its preoccupation with the distribution of social goods to a new focus on the distributed effects of social "bads." More than a decade before 9/11, Beck was arguing that the engine of the risk society was fear or anxiety:

> The dream of class society is that everyone wants and ought to have a *share* of the pie. The utopia of the risk society is that everyone should be *spared* from poisoning.... The driving force in the class society can be summarized in the

24. Rose, *Politics of Life Itself*, 23. Rose's point is that the politics of health (which took hold in the eighteenth century and intensified throughout the nineteenth and early twentieth centuries) has been superseded by a politics of "life itself" (in the twenty-first century) that seeks to regulate our vital capacities primarily at the level of neither the individual nor the population but, rather, at the molecular level.

25. For a strong critique of the contemporary promotion of "wellness," see Howard M. Leichter, "Lifestyle Correctness and the New Secular Morality," in Brandt and Rozin, *Morality and Health*, 359–78, which argues that wellness ideology is less concerned with health than with social status. The ostentatious pursuit of health represents U.S. culture's latest version of conspicuous consumption.

phrase: *I am hungry!* The movement set in motion by the risk society, on the other hand, is expressed in the statement: *I am afraid!*[26]

Fear, anxiety, aversion: psychoanalytically speaking, these all involve different psychic mechanisms; yet one or another of these affects increasingly seems to motivate social responses to a wide range of phenomena. Although Beck's diagnosis of the risk society, originally made in 1986, seems ever more prescient two decades later, he has less to say about the implications of eroticizing risk or about how the reactionary mobilization of the rhetoric of risk might be resisted. Indeed, to a large extent, he appears to believe that, given the proliferation of risk, we *should* be afraid.

Considered from the perspective of both Beck's critique of the risk society and Foucault's critique of normalization, it is not difficult to see how "health" represents an instrument of power that might be questioned. Versions of these perspectives inform some barebackers' tendency to characterize proponents of HIV prevention as "condom Nazis." What Foucault called "the imperative of health" has been infiltrated by superegoistic ideals to such an extent that one's physical condition rarely can be regarded as wholly satisfactory. Demands for a better body and for more stringent risk avoidance have intensified relentlessly. Although defined as the body's normal state, health also has been idealized as something for which one must strive; it is no longer something one simply possesses.[27] When framed in terms of "lifestyle," everyday living is transformed into an interminable exercise in risk management—a situation exacerbated by the weaving of contemporary ideas about health with aesthetic criteria. The way in which physical well-being increasingly concerns not only the body's internal functions but also its external appearance reinforces the normative idealization of health. We want to be healthy because we want to be normal. Taking some critical distance on the social apparatus of normalization and its mobilization of the rhetoric of risk thus makes room for skepticism about health imperatives.

26. Ulrich Beck, *Risk Society: Towards a New Modernity* (London: Sage, 1992; first published in German in 1986 by Suhrkamp Verlag), 49, emphases in the original. See also Beck, *World Risk Society* (Cambridge: Polity, 1999).

27. Hans-Georg Gadamer makes a similar point in *The Enigma of Health: The Art of Healing in a Scientific Age*, trans. Jason Gaiger and Nicholas Walker (Stanford: Stanford University Press, 1996), where he argues that the standardizing principles and practices of modern medicine are inappropriate for determining health (see esp. chap. 8).

DON'T BUY THE HIV LIE

Such skepticism sometimes extends to questioning the causal relation between HIV and AIDS. In a previously quoted essay, the late gay activist and writer Eric Rofes remarked that "we now believe many HIV-positive men will never develop AIDS."[28] Although this conviction has been generated by the success of antiretroviral drug therapies and the emergence of long-term nonprogressors, Rofes's statement is barely distinguishable from more eccentric claims that dismiss HIV as the cause of AIDS altogether. "ACT-UP San Francisco does not believe AIDS is caused by a virus," contends activist David Pasquarelli, speaking on behalf of an especially controversial chapter of the direct-action group AIDS Coalition to Unleash Power. Once the province of maverick researchers such as Peter Duesberg, doubts about HIV's causal status have spread in the gay community and beyond, as HIV-positive people live longer and longer. There now exists a burgeoning International AIDS Dissidence Movement, composed of scientists and activists dedicated to questioning the causal link between HIV and AIDS, as well as the enormous profits that pharmaceutical companies make on HIV medications.[29]

During the early stages of work on this book, I was living in San Francisco, where every day I walked down Market Street, one of the city's principal thoroughfares. At the corner of Market and Fifteenth Streets, in the heart of the Castro and just a few steps away from the Stop AIDS Project headquarters, someone had stenciled onto the sidewalk "Don't Buy the HIV Lie," an enigmatic rhyme that echoed daily in my mind. What exactly is "the HIV lie," I wondered, as I investigated bareback subculture in San Francisco's Castro and South of Market (SOMA) neighborhoods. Between those who are convinced that antiretroviral cocktails will stave off AIDS forever and those who believe that, conversely, the toxicity of drug regimens (not HIV) is what's killing gay men, the epidemic's early equation HIV=AIDS is steadily being attenuated. To the extent that an HIV diagnosis is no longer regarded as a death sentence, this

28. Rofes, "Barebacking," 17.

29. See Peter Duesberg, *Infectious AIDS: Stretching the Germ Theory beyond Its Limits* (New York: North Atlantic Books, 1996); and Duesberg, *Inventing the AIDS Virus* (Washington, DC: Regnery, 1996). See also http://www.duesberg.com. A University of California, Berkeley, molecular biologist, Duesberg argues that AIDS is caused not by a virus but by AZT toxicity and prolonged use of recreational drugs, both of which take their toll on the immune system. For more on the growing International AIDS Dissidence Movement, including the Group for the Scientific Reappraisal of the HIV-AIDS Hypothesis, see http://www.aidsmythexposed.com, which provides links to 78 different international sites that question the conventional scientific account of HIV pathogenesis. See also the very interesting documentary *The Other Side of AIDS*, dir. Robin Scovill (Hazel Wood Pictures, 2004).

attenuation is to be welcomed. But to the extent that HIV is dismissed as harmless, it is more troubling. The critical interrogation of social norms about sexuality and "health" entails recognizing that science is not value neutral; such interrogation can lead to reassessing—or even rejecting outright—the scientific evidence on which so many contemporary behavioral norms are based. But the fact that we don't know everything about HIV and AIDS does not mean that everything we thought we knew is necessarily mistaken.[30]

Let me be explicit: I am not trying to question whether HIV is the cause of AIDS. Rather, I'm interested in the possibilities opened by skepticism about health imperatives; when sufficiently far-reaching, such skepticism may extend to challenging the construction of aging as a pathological condition and death as an aberrant state. By idealizing optimum health as the human body's normal state, our culture has marginalized death. Too often death is regarded as a sign of either medicine's technological failure or the deceased's moral failure to consistently practice risk avoidance. By making death external to life, we no longer know how to die. Death has been added to the list of health hazards to avoid: it is regarded as dangerous for your health.

Although psychoanalytic theories typically credit the superego with driving tormented individuals to suicide, we should acknowledge that, conversely, superegoistic health imperatives also insist on our living forever. "If you're physiologically old and don't want to be, then for you, aging is a disease," argues nanotechnologist Rob Freitas, anticipating a not-too-distant future when medical technology will enable a privileged few to live for centuries. "A rollback to the physiology of your late teens might be easier than your 10-year-old self, and more fun. We could live about 900 years," he insists.[31] The

---

30. For up-to-date information on "the HIV lie," see http://www.virusmyth.net, which archives a range of alternative explanations for the AIDS epidemic. For a delusional psychoanalytic explanation, see Casper G. Schmidt, "The Group-Fantasy Origins of AIDS," *Journal of Psychohistory* 12, no. 1 (1984): 37–78; Schmidt argues that "the epidemic of AIDS is an awesome demonstration of the power and destructiveness of so much concentrated shame." In other words, rather than a virus, gay men's shame about their sexuality compromised their immune systems. An especially glamorous critic of the viral explanation is gay porn legend Jeff Palmer (http://www.jeffpalmer.net), who comes close to Duesberg's line in arguing that HIV medications are poisonous. See Michael Thorn, "Barebacking with Jeff Palmer," *Instigator Magazine*, April 2003, 18–24.

31. Rob Freitas, "Death Is an Outrage" (lecture, Fifth Extreme Life Extension Conference, Newport Beach, CA, November 16–17, 2002), as reported in David Rakoff, "I'm Dying to Meet You in the Next Life," *GQ*, May 2003, 196–201, 213–14. This fascinating article on the vogue for cryogenic suspension describes a hi-tech industry of postmortem deep freeze and its underlying belief that, at some future point, science will be able to revive those who have paid to have their bodies placed indefinitely in cryosuspension. In his critique of the conviction that technology will overcome the limit even of mortality, Rakoff connects this fringe scientific movement to developments in aesthetic

lunacy of such claims belies their grounding in a cultural logic that has made health a calculus of risk and thus has opened it to the superego. It is now a moral duty to remain youthful and beautiful, to cultivate "health." This duty falls disproportionately to women and gay men but also increasingly to young straight men, who now require the assistance of formerly despised homosexuals in order to fulfill their obligation. (Hence the appeal of *Queer Eye for the Straight Guy*, a television show in which a team of *über*fags administers tips to style-deficient heterosexual men.)

Embracing risk, including the risks associated with unprotected sex, offers one way around superegoistic health imperatives. Barebacking may represent a means to resist "health" as an instrument of power.[32] If the desire to be healthy stems from the desire to be normal, then those who appreciate "the trouble with normal" experience less pressure to conform to health mandates. Additional answers to this chapter's opening question thus would be that bug chasers want to resist normalizing power, to express skepticism regarding mainstream ideals of health and risk-avoidance, and to learn how to live with mortality. To the extent that bug chasers aspire to die in their own way, bug chasing could be considered a philosophical practice, in the traditional sense of philosophy as a discipline in mortality.[33] Barebackers embrace the human finitude that modern life, especially modern medicine, has become expert in disavowing. We might say that, in their quest for unlimited intimacy, barebackers are taking on the fundamental limit of death that defines us all; they are fucking without limits precisely because they don't want to live forever. In its more committed forms, barebacking thus offers a different perspective on the future.

---

surgery, such as the increasingly popular Botox, arguing that "the cryonicists are simply one extreme within a cultural moment that has vilified aging to the point where the injection of a neurotoxin to erase wrinkles and halt facial expression is completely acceptable" (ibid., 214). On this subject, see also Muriel R. Gillick, *The Denial of Aging: Perpetual Youth, Eternal Life, and Other Dangerous Fantasies* (Cambridge, MA: Harvard University Press, 2006).

32. See Michele L. Crossley, "The Perils of Health Promotion and the 'Barebacking' Backlash," *Health* 6, no. 1 (2002): 47–68. Crossley makes a similar argument in more psychological terms, specifically those of "reactant theory": "As certain behaviours become the receptacles for all that is valued and moral, a curious process takes place. Not only do their 'opposing' behaviours—non-exercise, unsafe sex, eating junk food, drinking heavily, smoking, using drugs—become associated with a sense of 'irresponsibility' and 'immorality,' in the process of doing so, they may take on a certain *cachet* and value of their own" (49).

33. In attributing to bug chasers an aspiration to die in their own way, I have in mind both Freud's psychoanalytic discussion of the subject's wish "to die only in its own fashion" and Nietzsche's philosophical discussion of the principle of "dying at the right time." See Freud, *Beyond the Pleasure Principle*, in vol. 18 of *Standard Edition*, 39; and Friedrich Nietzsche, *Thus Spoke Zarathustra*, trans. R. J. Hollingdale (Harmondsworth, UK: Penguin, 1961), 97–99.

THE FUTURE ILL

The paradox of the superego is that compliance with its dictates exacerbates rather than diminishes them. The more you obey superegoistic imperatives, the worse things get. This paradoxical logic helps explain the encroachment of risk into our understanding of health: the healthier we try to become, the more we appear subject to danger. As medical emphasis shifts from specific infectious pathogens to multifactorial chronic diseases, the pressure to imagine future illness intensifies. Advanced medical technologies have created what historian of science Charles Rosenberg calls "protodisease states," ordinary health conditions, such as high blood pressure, that may lead to future sickness. "With our increasing diagnostic capacities, we have provided altered narratives for millions of individuals who might otherwise have lived out their lives in ignorance of a nemesis lurking in their bodies," Rosenberg contends.[34] Not only do supersophisticated diagnostic technologies enlarge the scope of health moralization to virtually medieval proportions (if you don't alter your "lifestyle," you should expect to get sick), they increasingly identify disease with risk itself by making one's current freedom from disease nugatory in comparison with one's sickness potential. No longer an integral part of being alive, risk is redescribed as the cause of future illness. To live riskily is to *be diseased*, even in the absence of pathological symptoms. In other words, this new medical perspective regards risk itself as a symptom.

Of course, a life wholly free from risk would be impossible to achieve, since the most ordinary daily activities—climbing out of bed, stepping into the shower, driving to work, eating a sandwich, boarding a plane—all entail risk. Every bodily movement involves minor risks, as does prolonged corporeal immobility. Adam Phillips reminds us that "wanting is a species of risk"; in other words, there is no desire that does not have risk built into it. "What became known, after Freud, as psychoanalytic theory is nothing but an encyclopedia of modern risks," Phillips observes.[35] From a psychoanalytic perspective, then, the attempt to eliminate all risk (rather than the cultivation of risk) would be deemed pathological. Defining health in terms of risk situates "health" forever out of reach, in a manner akin to the superego's sadistic positioning of virtue beyond one's grasp. Moral judgments about what constitutes acceptable risk are built into contemporary definitions of illness. To take risks that the majority considers unacceptable is to make oneself the target of pathologizing

---

34. Rosenberg, "Banishing Risk," 45.
35. Adam Phillips, *Side Effects* (New York: HarperCollins, 2006), 19.

definitions; hence the notion of "risk groups" as an epidemiological category gives rise to the prejudicial ascription of pathological identities. In this context, I remain skeptical about the wisdom of distinguishing too strictly between barebacking and bug chasing, since such a distinction tends to depathologize barebacking at the expense of bug chasing, which thenceforth bears the entire moral baggage of sexual risk taking.[36]

When illness is conceived in terms not of present physical conditions but of a future that must be forestalled at all costs via scrupulous risk management, then we "create a new class of lifetime pariahs, the future ill," argues Susan Sontag.[37] Even before AIDS, homosexuality tended to be understood as a doomed identity, a "protodisease state" that would lead inevitably to misery and death, despite any particular queer person's seeming perfectly well. AIDS has reinforced this prejudice about homosexuality, since as members of a "risk group" gay men are considered susceptible to HIV infection and therefore tend to be regarded generically as a class of "the future ill." Sontag elaborates this predicament:

> Testing positive for HIV (which usually means having been tested for the presence not of the virus but of antibodies to the virus) is increasingly equated with being ill. Infected *means* ill, from that point forward. "Infected but not ill," that invaluable notion of clinical medicine (the body "harbors" many infections), is being superseded by biomedical concepts which, whatever their scientific justification, amount to reviving the antiscientific logic of defilement, and make infected-but-healthy a contradiction in terms.[38]

By destigmatizing seropositivity, those who identify proudly as "poz" are reclaiming the notion of "infected but not ill." And by thus resisting the "logic of defilement," gay men have attempted to disentangle seropositivity from illness and death—that is, to challenge stereotypical narratives about homosexuality as a doomed identity. Yet in seeking to interrupt the sequence of inevitability whereby homosexuality leads to HIV infection and thence to AIDS and death, these attempts have succeeded in revising only the narrative's dénouement. The predictable development from HIV infection to AIDS

36. See Gregory Tomso, "Bug Chasing, Barebacking, and the Risks of Care," *Literature and Medicine* 23, no. 1 (2004): 88–111. Tomso offers good arguments for distinguishing more carefully between barebacking and bug chasing, but he overlooks the invidious implications of any such distinction.

37. Susan Sontag, *AIDS and Its Metaphors* (New York: Farrar, Straus, and Giroux, 1989), 33–34.

38. Ibid., 32, emphasis in the original.

and death has been contested, but less so the inevitability of gay men's se-
roconversions. Instead, seroconversion has come to be regarded as a rite of
passage into the world of hot queer sex. By embracing risk one eliminates risk,
in the tautological sense that seroconversion alleviates the perpetual worry
about HIV infection (and, given the inconclusive scientific evidence, very few
barebackers are concerned about reinfection). Paradoxically bareback subculture institutionalizes risk as a permanent condition of existence, embracing
and eroticizing it, while promulgating the idea that seroconversion renders
moot one particular risk. In this way, bug chasing provides a way of eluding
superegoistic health imperatives, even as it simultaneously offers a mode of
conforming to the imperative of enjoyment.[39]

HOW TO DO THINGS WITH HIV

Bug chasers replace one story about the queer future with another. In place of
the stock narrative about inevitable sickness and death, they have invented a
story about kinship and life—a different version of the queer future to which
HIV transmission nevertheless remains central. Although it has become com-
monplace to observe that the narratives through which we understand disease profoundly affect the experience of disease, with no modern illness is
this more the case than with HIV/AIDS. Bug chasers have not only different
stories about HIV but also a different experience of the microbe. We might say
that bug chasers are living a different mythology of HIV, one that treats the
virus as a gift rather than as a punishment.

"Considering illness as a punishment is the oldest idea of what causes illness," notes Sontag; "AIDS is understood in a premodern way, as a disease
incurred by people both as individuals and as members of a 'risk group'—that
neutral-sounding, bureaucratic category which also revives the archaic idea
of a tainted community that illness has judged."[40] It is striking that a pathological syndrome whose identification depends on the most advanced medical technologies should be apprehended culturally in such primitive ways.

---

39. A different line of reasoning than the one I'm pursuing here might see the superegoistic
imperative to "Enjoy!" as motivating bareback subculture and perhaps gay culture in general; such
a line of reasoning would contradict my claim that bug chasing represents a way of eluding superegoistic imperatives. The work of Slavoj Žižek tirelessly elaborates the Lacanian logic whereby the
superego commands not moderation but intensification of enjoyment. See Jacques Lacan, "The
Subversion of the Subject and the Dialectic of Desire in the Freudian Unconscious," in *Écrits: A
Selection*, trans. Alan Sheridan (New York: Norton, 1977), 319: Lacan characterizes the superego's
categorical imperative as "*Jouis!*" to which the subject responds "*J'ouis*" ("I hear").

40. Sontag, *AIDS and Its Metaphors*, 45–46.

Since HIV "hides behind other diseases"—nobody dies from AIDS as such but from diseases that prey on compromised immune systems—it required diagnostic techniques that emerged only during the late 1970s in order to make it visible.[41] In this sense, AIDS represents a nosological entity invented by postmodern medical technology. Yet this postmodern invention tends to be understood through archaic narratives, whether of defilement, sin, and punishment, on one hand, or of initiation, gift giving, and fraternity, on the other. Online bug chasing involves an appropriation of twenty-first-century technology in the service of archaic fantasies.

According to subcultural nomenclature, the partner for whom a bug chaser searches is known as a gift giver or "gifter." Based on the model of sperm donors, gift givers are men willing to consensually inseminate other men with HIV. They transmit the virus intentionally rather than inadvertently and understand their actions as creative rather than as unequivocally destructive. Since most states have criminalized deliberate HIV transmission, it is hardly surprising that gift givers remain shadowy figures.[42] Research suggests that, although the proportion of North American men who enjoy barebacking is surprisingly large, the proportion of those in bareback subculture who identify as gift givers is very small. (I think that what I find disturbing about the occasions on which strangers I'm barebacking ask me to ejaculate inside them is the impression that I'm being interpellated as a gift giver—a sense that I'm being misrecognized as an HIV-positive man willing to transmit the virus deliberately yet casually, without discussion of the matter.)

Self-identified bug chasers significantly outnumber gift givers. Indeed, many barebackers subscribe to the principle that, as one man put it, "I don't do conversions"—in other words, they'll have unprotected sex only with those presumed to be already HIV positive. A notable example is the bareback pornographer Dick Wadd, whose work I discuss in chapter 3 and who describes his distinctive approach to performing conversions thus:

> There were three young HIV− men in my past who assumed that, because of my work, I am HIV+ and who wanted to take my charged load. I invited them [separately] to my playroom, lit the candles, put on my best music, set the scene, tossed them in the sling, bored into their eyes with mine right before

41. Mirko D. Grmek, *History of AIDS: Emergence and Origin of a Modern Pandemic*, trans. Russell C. Maulitz and Jacalyn Duffin (Princeton, NJ: Princeton University Press, 1990), 56.

42. See http://bugshare.net for an extensive archive of conversations among gift givers and those who pursue them.

penetration, then grabbed them by their harnesses, shook them, slapped their faces and screamed, "What the fuck are you thinking?"[43]

Here the individual selected as a prestigious gift giver uses his subcultural authority to question rather than fulfill bug chasers' desires for infection. A bareback pornographer who thus paradoxically might be regarded as inventing new techniques of safer-sex education, Dick Wadd makes the refusal to perform conversions a dramatically active principle, even as some subcultural participants claim to specialize in seroconverting others.[44] Yet it is worth observing that the principled refusal to perform conversions—or even to indulge a fantasy about deliberate infection—concerns community and kinship, not just disease prevention, since choosing to have sex only with other seropositive men establishes a sense of camaraderie among those who, in the 1980s, were treated as pariahs.

The example of Dick Wadd makes clear that some in the bareback community, despite their commitment to unprotected sex, remain vehemently opposed to viral transmission. One research study calls this subset of barebackers "anti-bug-chasers" (although they might as aptly be characterized as "anti–gift givers").[45] On bareback Web sites, it has become necessary to specify explicitly one's disinclination to pursue certain fantasies of transmission—an indicator of just how common such fantasies have become. Yet it is also a telling artifact of how our culture thinks about sexuality in terms of *identity* that research studies even attempt to quantify the number of bug chasers, gift givers, and now anti–gift givers. Everyone wants to know how many bug chasers and gift givers are out there, as if these expressions of subcultural nomenclature designated specific categories of persons amenable to classification, enumeration, and ultimately regulation. It seems reassuring to learn that self-identified bug chasers outnumber gift givers—until one grasps that "bug chaser" and "gift giver," like "top" and "bottom," are merely temporary crystallizations of desiring positions that can be occupied, albeit at different moments, by the same individual. Thus it is less the case that bug chasers outnumber gift givers than

---

43. B. J. Cavnor, "Dealing with Dick: An Interview with Dick Wadd," *Instigator Magazine*, March 2005, 35.

44. Paul Morris refers to a man who "is a specialist at doing conversions because he makes the bottom bleed, and so the semen goes directly into the blood system. He has a PA [a Prince Albert, or pierced-penis ring], and he . . . fucks really roughly. . . . He won't stop until there's blood, and he has a 100% success rate, of which he's very proud." See "Visual AIDS," 21.

45. See Christian Grov, "'Make Me Your Death Slave': Men Who Have Sex with Men and Use the Internet to Intentionally Spread HIV," *Deviant Behavior* 25, no. 4 (2003): 339n.

that the identity of bug chaser is more easily inhabitable, especially if one is already HIV positive. Perhaps surprisingly, in this subculture receiving the gift is regarded as less disturbing than giving it.

The general reluctance to assume full responsibility for someone else's seroconversion helps explain the phenomenon of conversion parties—ritualized group initiations into the "bug brotherhood"—during which men are penetrated bareback by multiple partners, thus making the specific source of infection difficult to identify. On a practical level, such arrangements lend participants a measure of legal protection; bareback parties often are advertised with the motto "Don't ask, don't tell." As I suggested earlier, gay men have appropriated the U.S. military's homophobic policy of nondisclosure for their own ends. Yet the convention of nondisclosure during group bareback sex also enables the source of infection to be given over to fantasy: one may entertain whichever narrative he finds most appealing about the paternity of his virus. In this way, the presence of HIV allows bug chasers to exit a bareback encounter or conversion party with considerably more than just memories.

One variant of this practice is the "roulette party," in which sexual risk is choreographed through provisions such as those in the following online solicitation:

> B[irth]day fuck fest at my hotel in SOMA just off Harrison [Street]. I have a few neg bottoms lined up to take some Neg and Poz loads. Here is the party format. Everyone will arrive around 9:00pm at my hotel room. When you arrive you will write down your hiv status on a card. You will be the only one to see this card. It will have a fake name on it but one that you will be known as. Once we are all done fucking and the tops leave[,] the bottoms will reveal the cards and see who took what. The tops can remain for round two if they like or you can bail if this freaks you out. No one will discuss status until every one is done with the breeding. If this sounds hot to you email me with a current chest and cock shot, face if you like, and I will get back in touch with you close to the date of the party. This will be my 37th b[irth]day and I want a gift to keep on giving.[46]

Coded as a unique birthday gift, the virus is regarded with considerable ambivalence, not only because the host's own serostatus remains unclear but

---

46. Posting from http://www.ultimatebareback.com (previously http://www.barebackcity .com), May 27, 2003.

also because he recognizes that potential gift givers might be "freaked out" by the prospect of viral transmission. Although treating HIV as the prize in a party game appears disturbing, even pathological, we should not overlook the significance of this attempt to coordinate birth and death, to make one's birthday the occasion for "breeding" or initiating new life. It is as if one could transform the vagaries of sexual risk into a controlled scientific experiment, with a protocol and measurable outcomes, thereby mastering one's erotic destiny. In this misplaced attempt to reclaim agency vis-à-vis HIV, there lurks the fantasy of gaining control over something that hitherto has dominated gay men's lives.

On the surface, the idea of HIV as a gift seems utterly perverse. To become infected with the virus can feel catastrophic rather than a boon. However, the subculture's loosening of medicine's stranglehold on HIV/AIDS, like Deaf culture's demedicalizing of deafness, endeavors to make it seem less catastrophic. Giving rise to community, it becomes something one can live with, rather than being construed as irremediably tragic. As Scott O'Hara, one of the earliest advocates for bareback sex, put it:

> I've had many worse things happen to me than being infected with HIV; most of them resulted from long-term relationships, which our society regards with benevolence. Being Positive, in the current climate of fear and anger, is the best thing that could have happened to me. I look around me at the Negative world, and I see men who are in the closet about their desires: mustn't admit to wanting to get fucked—mustn't admit to liking rimming—mustn't admit to drinking piss—mustn't admit to frequenting sex clubs or bathhouses.... Having AIDS has, in the long run, given me back my sexuality and my voice.... Because I know, first-hand, the advantages of being Positive, I don't feel the need to warn people away from the virus.[47]

O'Hara was one of the first and therefore most controversial HIV-positive gay men to reinterpret the virus as a gift, even before the community that would provide support for that reinterpretation came into existence. Doubtless O'Hara's articulate advocacy—including his telling comparison between the relative costs of seropositivity and those of long-term relationships—laid a foundation for bareback subculture's emergence. Yet more than individual experience or autobiographical testimony warrants the subcultural transvaluation of HIV as a gift. Significant etymological and cultural histories rationalize

---

47. Scott O'Hara, "Talking with My Mouth Full," in Colter et al., *Policing Public Sex*, 83–84.

the otherwise deeply counterintuitive understanding of what infection means. A cultural logic beyond that of bareback subculture underwrites thinking about the virus in these terms.

THE LOGIC OF GIFT GIVING

Pierre Bourdieu summarizes a principal conclusion of the vast anthropological and philosophical literature on gift giving when he observes that "the major characteristic of the experience of the gift is, without doubt, its ambiguity."[48] This ambiguity lies partly in a gift's power to bind its recipient to the donor, to create a potential state of indebtedness. The greater the act of generosity, the greater its power over the recipient, who thus simultaneously gains and loses as a result. Behind the munificence of the bequest may lurk an aggression that seeks to dominate, even enslave, the recipient. Classically, this underside of generosity comes to light in the potlatch, the festival of competitive giving. The gift that cannot be adequately reciprocated links donor and recipient in a bond that may be resented as well as desired.

The ambiguity of the gift, together with the ambivalence it has the capacity to evoke, is encoded in the history of the word itself. In his *Problems in General Linguistics*, Emile Benveniste notes that, in various Indo-European languages, the verb for *to give* "was marked by a curious semantic ambivalence" that enabled it to be expressed by its opposite, such as the verb for *to take*.[49] Etymologically, "gift" comes from the Latin *dosis*, signifying a dose of poison (this meaning is retained most explicitly in German, in which *das Gift* is the noun for poison). Commenting on this antithetical meaning, Marcel Mauss claims that "the kinship of meaning linking gift-present to gift-poison is ... easy to explain and natural." He unpacks it by reference to the gift systems characteristic of early Germanic cultures, arguing that

> the typical prestation for the ancient Germans and Scandinavians is the gift of drink, of beer; in German, the present par excellence is what one pours. . . .
> [O]ne can see that the uncertainty about the good or bad nature of the presents could have been nowhere greater than in the case of the customs of the kind where the gifts consisted essentially in drinks taken in common, in libations

48. Pierre Bourdieu, "Marginalia—Some Additional Notes on the Gift," trans. Richard Nice, in *The Logic of the Gift: Toward an Ethic of Generosity*, ed. Alan D. Schrift (New York: Routledge, 1997), 231.

49. Emile Benveniste, *Problems in General Linguistics*, trans. Mary Elizabeth Meek (Coral Gables, FL: University of Miami Press, 1971), 272.

offered or to be rendered. The drink-present can be a poison; in principle, with the exception of a dark drama, it isn't; but it can always become one.[50]

When the gift is a liquid to be shared, partaking of it involves—along with nourishment—the risk that it might be poisoned. The risk lies in not knowing whether the vital fluid, offered in the spirit of generosity, has been tainted. This gift ritual of sharing libations illuminates the subcultural rituals of sharing semen, passing it from mouth to mouth, consuming it. These rituals are documented in Treasure Island Media's "D.O.C." ("Drunk on Cum") series, as the men who have fellated dozens of guys and imbibed multiple loads of semen in a session are described. Even though oral sex generally is regarded as "safer sex" (it represents a low-probability transmission route for HIV), there remains in the figure of intoxication an idea about being affected by what one has consumed. To be "drunk on cum" is to be intoxicated with a potentially toxic fluid.

A double etymology connects the gift with HIV. It is not only that a gift (especially in fluid form) may be poisonous, but also that "virus" comes from the Latin word for poison. The Latin *virus* stems from an Indo-European root that also means fluid and gives us the word *viscous*. Far from a counterintuitive leap, then, the subcultural coding of virus as gift may be explained by reference to a linguistic history—a chain of signifiers—that composes part of what should be understood as a properly impersonal unconscious. In the unconscious, it may not be possible to distinguish a virus from a gift, just as it is often impossible, in this register, to distinguish positive from negative. Freud makes this point in his brief essay "The Antithetical Meaning of Primal Words": he does not cite the gift-poison case as an example, but he does observe that the unconscious inability to distinguish positive from negative "is identical with a peculiarity in the oldest languages known to us."[51] Although

---

50. Marcel Mauss, "Gift, Gift," trans. Koen Decoster (1924), repr. in Schrift, *Logic of the Gift*, 30. Subsequently, Mauss commented, "This theme of the fatal gift, the present or item of property that is changed into poison is fundamental in Germanic folklore. The Rhine gold is fatal to the one who conquers it, Hagen's cup is mortal to the hero who drinks from it. A thousand stories and romances of this kind, both Germanic and Celtic, still haunt our sensibilities." From Marcel Mauss, *The Gift: The Form and Reason for Exchange in Archaic Societies*, trans. W. D. Halls (New York: Norton, 1990), 63.

51. Sigmund Freud, "The Antithetical Meaning of Primal Words," in vol. 11 of *Standard Edition*, 156. Freud begins this essay by quoting an observation from *The Interpretation of Dreams*: "The way in which dreams treat the category of contraries and contradictories is highly remarkable. It is simply disregarded. 'No' seems not to exist so far as dreams are concerned. They show a particular preference for combining contraries into a unity or for representing them as one and the same thing. Dreams feel themselves at liberty, moreover, to represent any element by its wishful contrary; so

he appears to be discussing the unconscious of individual persons, in fact Freud is intuiting an impersonal unconscious that depends on linguistic mediation. Hence Lévi-Strauss's observation, in his *Introduction to the Work of Marcel Mauss*, that "it is linguistics, and most particularly structural linguistics, which has since familiarized us with the idea that the fundamental phenomena of mental life, the phenomena that condition it and determine its most general forms, are located on the plane of unconscious thinking. The unconscious would thus be the mediating term between self and others."[52] It is this sense of the unconscious as sociolinguistic mediation that Lévi-Strauss discerns in Mauss's work on gift giving.

For Mauss, gifts are paradigmatically what mediate relations among individuals and between groups. In his classic treatise on the subject, Mauss describes how premodern cultures organized social relations around the reciprocal giving and receiving of gifts of all sorts. Such cultures have gift economies (rather than market economies) in which giving occurs primarily between groups (tribes, clans, families), not between individuals, and in which all cultural members and institutions are engaged. Anticipating structuralist anthropology, Mauss characterized gift giving as a "total social fact," insofar as through it "all kinds of institutions are given expression at one and the same time—religious, juridical, and moral, which relate to both politics and the family; likewise economic [institutions], which suppose special forms of production and consumption."[53] From this perspective, gift giving represents a basis for social organization rather than merely a sign of individual desire.

Embedded in this form of social organization is the assumption that donors acquire prestige through their giving (the more you give, the greater your status), at the same time that they impose on recipients the obligation to reciprocate. To give is thus not to lose but to gain, both symbolically (in terms of social status) and materially (in terms of the goods and services that your gifts are expected to elicit). Mauss was fascinated by certain Native American cultures of the Pacific Northwest, such as the Haïda, which, during the potlatch festival of competitive giving, dispensed with virtually everything that the tribe

there is no way of deciding at a first glance whether any element that admits of a contrary is present in the dream-thoughts as a positive or as a negative." From vol. 4 of *Standard Edition*, 318.

52. Claude Lévi-Strauss, *Introduction to the Work of Marcel Mauss*, trans. Felicity Baker (London: Routledge and Kegan Paul, 1987), 35.

53. Mauss, *Gift*, 3.

possessed. As I have indicated, there is an aggressive component to gift giving that tempers its generosity, making the practice prone to ambivalence.[54]

For the cultures described by Mauss, the purpose of giving is neither altruistic nor wholly self-interested. Rather, the social motive animating these elaborate cycles of giving and reciprocation is that of solidarity: gifts establish social bonds; they unite families in kinship networks; and, in general, they help to build collectivities. "A gift that does nothing to enhance solidarity is a contradiction," explains anthropologist Mary Douglas; "the gift [is] an agent of social cohesion," affirms Lewis Hyde.[55] By establishing relations of reciprocity, a gift economy generates social bonds differently from a market economy: when one purchases a commodity, the transaction completes the relationship, but when one makes a gift, he or she initiates a cycle of reciprocation that continues beyond the initial exchange.[56] Through the principle of reciprocity, a gift creates or consolidates the relationship between donor and recipient. As Hyde puts it, anticipating perfectly bareback subculture's distaste for condoms, "in commodity exchange it's as if the buyer and the seller were both in plastic bags; there's none of the contact of a gift exchange."[57] Gift giving thus may be understood as an elementary mode of relating to others, and it is crucial to my argument about the subculture that gift giving establishes relations specifically of kinship.

Gay men have discovered that one of the things they can do with HIV is use it to create solidarity and form communities. The "bareback community" is not merely a derivation or subset of the "gay community," based solely on imaginary identification and symbolic affiliation, since barebackers repeatedly cement communal relations through acts of viral exchange. HIV transmission has the potential to create social bonds that are both symbolic and material; membership is etched into the body like a tattoo. Some barebackers have appropriated the motto of the American Express company—"Membership has its privileges"—to articulate their sense of belonging to something more

54. In a particularly resonant account of gift giving, Lewis Hyde argues that the aggressiveness and competitiveness of the potlatch are post-European inventions—the results, in other words, of capitalism's contact with North American aboriginal cultures. See Lewis Hyde, *The Gift: Imagination and the Erotic Life of Property* (New York: Random House, 1983), 30.

55. Mary Douglas, "No Free Gifts," foreword in Mauss, *Gift*, vii; and Hyde, *Gift*, 35.

56. See also C. A. Gregory, *Gifts and Commodities* (London: Academic, 1982), 41. Gregory argues that "commodity exchange establishes objective quantitative relationships between the objects transacted, while gift exchange establishes personal qualitative relationships between the subjects transacting."

57. Hyde, *Gift*, 10.

than an imaginary community. Bug chasers believe that being HIV positive makes them part of a gang; those with whom they share the virus are known as their "bug brothers." "I wanted to be positive because I wanted to belong," explains one young man. Countering the image of the person with AIDS as an isolated outcast, voluntary seroconversion has come to be understood as a new basis for community formation. In this way, the stigma associated with HIV has been embraced as a badge of honor.

IS THE RECTUM A WOMB?

The exchange of viruses as gifts transforms community into consanguinity. Not only an ambiguous gift, HIV fulfills several roles in the new narratives that gay men are creating. As a putative object of exchange, it allows men to bond with each other; as a shared substance, it permits those bonds to be conceived in kinship terms, thereby materializing a sense of brotherhood. In view of HIV's role as an object of exchange, we might say that cum swapping represents the form that homosocial bonding takes among gay men. Some men establish social bonds with one another not through the mediation of women's bodies (as in the structuralist model famously critiqued by Gayle Rubin, Eve Kosofsky Sedgwick, and others) and not simply through sex with one another, but specifically through the mediation of HIV.[58] In place of the "traffic in women," we have viral trafficking as the latest incarnation of male bonding. Here homosociality does not represent a defense against homosexuality but an extension of it. From a bug chaser's perspective, then, becoming HIV positive involves fraternity more than disease. In a world of casual sex and transient relationships, seroconversion offers the fantasy of a world of permanence.[59]

However, the fact that seroconversion is nonfungible complicates HIV's role as an object of exchange. When two men engage in cum swapping, semen is

58. See Claude Lévi-Strauss, *The Elementary Structures of Kinship*, trans. James Harle Bell, John Richard von Sturmer, and Rodney Needham (Boston: Beacon, 1969); Gayle Rubin, "The Traffic in Women: Notes on the 'Political Economy' of Sex," in *Toward an Anthropology of Women*, ed. Rayna R. Reiter (New York: Monthly Review, 1975), 157–210; and Eve Kosofsky Sedgwick, *Between Men: English Literature and Male Homosocial Desire* (New York: Columbia University Press, 1985).

59. It is not simply our contemporary world that creates the conditions to which such fantasies are a response. In his fascinating study, *Intimacy in America*, Peter Coviello argues that dreams of bodily affiliation—of forms of intimacy with the capacity to transform strangers into kin—have animated national imaginings since the beginning of the nineteenth century. The visions of relatedness that Coviello discerns in early U.S. writers uncannily anticipate contemporary bareback subculture. See Peter Coviello, *Intimacy in America: Dreams of Affiliation in Antebellum Literature* (Minneapolis: University of Minnesota Press, 2005).

exchanged but HIV is not: it may be transmitted but not *exchanged*. Although the notion of semen as a gift is long-standing and durable, the presence of the virus transforms it into a gift that keeps on giving (to paraphrase the online "roulette party" invitation). In terms of the economies described by Mauss, a gift that keeps on giving imposes an impossible obligation on its recipient. A gift of seroconversion, by definition, cannot be returned to the original donor; instead of reciprocity, such a gift establishes an asymmetrical relation. It constitutes an extraordinarily aggressive gift; yet it also betokens a kind of unusual generosity in the sense that it may be donated without expectation of a return. Herein lies the basis for distinguishing between a gift economy and an exchange economy (whether capitalist or otherwise). In his critique of Mauss, Derrida argues that the central Maussian principle of reciprocity abolishes the gift *as gift* precisely by situating it within a cycle of exchange. The obligation to reciprocate, which consolidates the relation between individuals or groups, nullifies the gift by transforming it into something like a loan. A true gift would be given freely, without expectation of return, according to Derrida.[60]

In this way, the gift becomes a central category of ethics; that which is given without expectation of recompense tends to be regarded as ethically exemplary. Paradoxically, the subcultural gift of seroconversion appears to fulfill this criterion for ethical exemplarity insofar as it cannot be returned to the donor. However, the virus as gift circulates within bareback subculture as in a general economy of exchange: the donor (figure A) already has received it from a previous gift giver (figure Z) before passing it on to the next recipient (figure B).[61] Semen and the virus thus can be seen to circulate through nonidentical economies of exchange; to some extent the subcultural rhetoric of "cum swapping" obscures the breadth of the circuit through which HIV moves. This distinction enables us to grasp how the subculture's gift economy always exceeds the couple: bareback sexuality is not paradigmatically that of the intimate pair but that of the group. Barebacking thus may be considered

---

60. Jacques Derrida, *Given Time: 1. Counterfeit Money*, trans. Peggy Kamuf (Chicago: University of Chicago Press, 1992). Derrida's critique is anticipated by Hyde, who argues along similar lines: "In gift exchange the transaction itself consumes the object. Now, it is true that something often comes back when a gift is given, but if this were made an explicit condition of the exchange, it wouldn't be a gift. . . . This, then, is how I use 'consume' to speak of a gift—a gift is consumed when it moves from one hand to another with no assurance of anything in return." From Hyde, *Gift*, 9.

61. See Hyde, *Gift*, 16: "[W]hen the gift moves in a circle no one ever receives it from the same person he gives it to. . . . When the gift moves in a circle its motion is beyond the control of the personal ego, and so each bearer must be a part of the group and each donation is an act of social faith."

a strategy for taking sexuality beyond dyadic relations into the social. It en-larges the horizon of potential intimacy.

Of course, this extension beyond the couple into the social generates great anxiety as well as pleasure, since the gift being shared is regarded as pathogenic. HIV subsists in fluids that cannot always be contained within individual bodies (or couples); as a consequence, there remains a persistent fear of contamination—of receiving the gift unwittingly. This fear has been expressed primarily in terms of sexual pollution; yet anxieties about con-taminated blood (rather than semen) illuminate further what is at stake in the subculture's creation of a community around shared substance. In *Tissue Economies*, a fascinating study of recent transformations in the global circula-tion of human tissues, Catherine Waldby and Robert Mitchell show how the donation of bodily substances such as blood traditionally has functioned to unite communities according to the logic of generalized gift exchange. How-ever, with the contamination of the blood supply by HIV and hepatitis C virus during the 1980s, the ambivalence of the gift made itself felt to such an extent that today the blood supply is "commonly regarded not as a distributor of health and a benevolent mediator between fellow citizens, but as a distributor of risk and illness and a dangerous mediator between clean and infected sec-tors of the population."[62]

In fact, this transformation is as much a result of the shift from a gift to a market economy, in which human tissue increasingly is treated and processed as a transnational commodity. The contamination of the blood supply made clear that what had been perceived as a gift economy—in which individu-als donate whole blood to their fellow citizens—was actually part of a much wider system, in which blood products are transacted by global corporations that procure them in regions (including the United States) where blood is not only donated but also sold by economically disenfranchised individuals.[63] Waldby and Mitchell point out that, in Western Europe and the industrial-ized Commonwealth countries (Canada, Australia, and New Zealand), a gift ethic still dominates tissue donation, insofar as—with the notable exception

62. Catherine Waldby and Robert Mitchell, *Tissue Economies: Blood, Organs, and Cell Lines in Late Capitalism* (Durham, NC: Duke University Press, 2006), 41. For their discussion of blood dona-tion, Waldby and Mitchell draw on—and mount a strong critique of—the influential argument made in Richard M. Titmuss, *The Gift Relationship: From Human Blood to Social Policy* (New York: Pantheon, 1971).

63. On the difficulty of sustaining the distinction between gift and market economies, see John Frow, "Gift and Commodity," in *Time and Commodity Culture: Essays in Cultural Theory and Postmodernity* (Oxford: Clarendon, 1997), 102–217.

of sperm—donors may not legally sell their tissues.[64] Bareback subculture inverts this situation by making spermatic transactions the basis for a distinctive gift economy and thus for a particular kind of community.

EVERY GIFT IS EROTIC

Meditating on gift giving and responsibility, Derrida aspires to conceive the gift as something that does not and should not entail an obligation; he thus is interested in a category of gift called the *dan*, which functions outside regimes of reciprocity and exchange. In *The Poison in the Gift*, an account of ritual giving in South Asia, anthropologist Gloria Goodwin Raheja uncovers the sacrificial significance of nonreciprocal giving. Gifts categorized as *dan*, though otherwise valuable, are considered nonreciprocal because symbolically they transfer "inauspiciousness" from their donors to recipients. In so doing, such gifts procure for donors and, indeed, for the whole village "freedom from premature death and freedom from disease."[65] It is someone's job to receive ritual gifts that are understood as containing poison and thus to safeguard the health and well-being of the community. Although this idea of "poison in the gift" helps to illuminate the ritual giving and receiving of HIV-infected semen, the communities formed around such practices in San Francisco and elsewhere do not appear to be free from "premature death and...disease" but, on the contrary, subjected to them. What Raheja calls the "transferal of inauspiciousness" is not just symbolic in bareback subculture, because HIV marks semen with an irrevocable ambivalence. Although the subcultural project of destigmatizing HIV involves an effort to transform it from a punishment into a gift, the older connotation nevertheless lingers. As much as a gift and a basis for solidarity, the virus also can be used as a weapon.[66]

The fundamental ambivalence associated with poz-cum—the fact that it is sought after as a badge of lifetime membership, yet dreaded for exactly the same reason—lends the practice of gift giving an insoluble ambiguity or

---

64. Waldby and Mitchell, *Tissue Economies*, 21.

65. Gloria Goodwin Raheja, *The Poison in the Gift: Ritual, Prestation, and the Dominant Caste in a North Indian Village* (Chicago: University of Chicago Press, 1988), 248.

66. See Michael V. Relf et al., "Gay Identity, Interpersonal Violence, and HIV Risk Behaviors: An Empirical Test of Theoretical Relationships among a Probability-Based Sample of Urban Men Who Have Sex with Men," *Journal of the Association of Nurses in AIDS Care* 15, no. 2 (2004): 14–26, which tracks how HIV is marshaled as a weapon by some gay men in domestic abuse of their serodiscordant partners. The fact that its use as a weapon occurs less often in anonymous sexual encounters than in long-term gay relationships suggests that monogamy is hardly the solution to bareback promiscuity, as some critics are wont to insist.

doubleness in bareback subculture. This doubleness is conveyed very powerfully when, in the most intense scene of *The Gift*, Louise Hogarth's controversial documentary about the subculture (Dream Out Loud Productions,
2003), we hear spoken for the first time one San Francisco gift giver's seduc-
tive proposition. The scene presents testimony from Doug Hitzel, a young
man whose barebacking career was cut short after he seroconverted and who
features heavily in journalistic accounts of the subculture. Hitzel has become
famous because he so volubly regrets his involvement in bareback sex; far less
media attention shines on those who show insufficient remorse at their initiation into the brotherhood. A poster child for bug chasing, the youthful Hitzel, barely out of high school, offers a perfect picture of innocence sullied. Like
the San Francisco men who find his innocence erotically attractive, Hogarth's
documentary does not fail to exploit the opportunity that this fresh-faced
young lad represents.

There are lots of tears in *The Gift*, but during the scene in which he describes his conversation with a gift giver that he's met online but hasn't yet
fucked, Hitzel becomes so choked up that he can hardly speak. Facing the
interviewer's question, he finds himself unable to repeat what the man who
infected him said: "I'm sorry, this is just really hard to say," Hitzel comments
between sobs. Suspense mounts as the audience's desire to learn how the gift
giver seduced him is inflamed by Hitzel's difficulty in quoting the fateful conversation. "He said, 'I'll charge you up,'" he finally tells the camera.

In this cinematically compelling scene, we witness the gift giver's proposition quoted in subcultural argot but spoken with a diametrically opposing
affect: seductiveness unmasked as deadly threat. The fundamental ambivalence associated with poz-cum is revealed in a flash as two affective worlds
collide—one in which viral transmission is a highly erotic act and the other
in which it is ethically abhorrent. The subcultural vernacular "I'll charge you
up" evokes the act of charging a battery or readying a mechanism for action;
it works rhetorically as a seduction by implying a lack in the one to whom it is
addressed. "I'll charge you up" means *I'll give you something you need or want*,
thereby constituting HIV as desirable, even necessary. Although behind this
proposition may be heard the threat *I'll fuck you up*, the vernacular coding of
infected semen as "charged" suggests that what a gift giver proffers is not
only membership (from one perspective) or disease (from the opposite perspective) but, above all, *power*. A more experienced San Francisco gay man's
telling a recently transplanted Midwestern newbie such as Doug Hitzel that
"I'll charge you up" is tantamount to offering the younger man initiation into

a select community. And it is worth recalling that, since many HIV-positive men are prescribed testosterone supplements with their antiretroviral drug cocktails, they quickly achieve impressive results at the gym—and in the sack. Unlike HIV-positive men in the 1980s, these guys radiate a sexual allure that appears deeply desirable.

The gift giver's proposition also confirms the erotic power of giving. As the poet Sharon Olds formulates it, "every / gift is erotic. The pleasure of giving / is a sexual pleasure."[67] There remains an irreducibly erotic component to giving—regardless of what is given—because the act of giving connects the parties involved, making one body of two (or more than two). Traditionally eros is understood as the force that binds individuals and groups into ever-greater unities—"the Eros of the poets and philosophers which holds all living things together," as Freud observed.[68] In recognition of this power to associate individuals with one another and to combine many bodies into one, Hyde argues that "it is because gift exchange *is* an erotic form that so many gifts must be refused."[69] Thus it is not by denying but rather by acknowledging the erotic lure of the gift that certain prestations may be declined. The secret (or not so secret) disgust that many people experience when confronted with the prospect of HIV as a gift registers in negative form the possibility of this gift's erotic appeal. Indeed, disgust might be understood in this context as a viscerally immediate defense mechanism against that appeal. If so, then the strength of the negative reaction testifies to the intensity of this putative gift's sexual charge.

What I also find striking about the gift giver's offer to "charge you up" is the impression it conveys that a culture's elders are transmitting to the younger generation a material substance along with their wisdom and experience. The inference that HIV transmission represents a necessary rite of passage into full cultural membership makes initiation synonymous with infection. The feature that distinguishes gay culture from national, ethnic, or religious cultures—namely, that no one is born into gay culture and therefore that each individual must discover or invent it for him- or herself—is dissolved by gay men's breeding the virus among themselves and, in Hitzel's case, between generations. Through bug chasing and gift giving, gay cultural membership becomes irrevocable in a way that neither national nor religious

67. Sharon Olds, "More Blessèd," in Schrift, *Logic of the Gift*, xiii.
68. Freud, *Beyond the Pleasure Principle*, 50.
69. Hyde, *Gift*, 73, emphasis in the original.

cultural membership is. It is not so easy to be an expatriate of this subculture once one has been initiated into it.

The sense of intergenerational connection achieved through deliberate viral transmission is dramatized in Dennis Cooper's recent novel *The Sluts*, a postmodern epistolary fiction composed entirely in the form of online postings to gay-sex Web sites. Toward the end of the narrative, a self-identified gift giver named Zack Young makes this confession:

> My thing was and is bareback sex—breeding, bug chasing, and so on. Yeah, I like the "I might be sentencing someone to death when I cum inside him" thing a lot. I love the gambling aspect of raw sex. I love the idea that having hot sex with a bottom could have a permanent, negative impact on his life. I love how barebacking makes having sex heavy and meaningful. I love how gay guys can be like straight guys who wonder how many illegitimate kids there could be out there with their DNA. I love imagining my ex-fucks out in the world infecting others or dying in hospital beds.[70]

An unsympathetic character in the novel, Zack Young represents the gift giver as assassin. Yet even this emphasis on the poisonous dimension of the gift cannot eradicate its constitutive ambivalence, in which HIV transmission generates life and death almost simultaneously. Here "breeding" is compared to the actions of irresponsible straight men, "who wonder how many illegitimate kids there could be out there with their DNA." Barebackers' "breeding" also may be compared with straight men's concern for the welfare (not merely the existence) of their progeny. By organizing viral transmission as a purposeful activity, barebackers infer that a shared bodily substance—whether conceived in terms of blood, DNA, or HIV—represents the basis for not only community but also, more profoundly, kinship.[71]

FANTASIES OF GENERATION

Bareback subculture's ideas about kinship have emerged at a historical moment when mainstream lesbian and gay politics has been focusing as never before on issues of marriage and family. The AIDS epidemic not only made gay sexuality more visible but also led to the promotion of a

---

70. Dennis Cooper, *The Sluts* (New York: Void Books, 2004), 277.

71. On the multiple and thoroughgoing ambiguities of substance as the basis for kinship, see Janet Carsten, "Substantivism, Antisubstantivism, and Anti-antisubstantivism," in *Relative Values: Reconfiguring Kinship Studies*, ed. Sarah Franklin and Susan McKinnon (Durham, NC: Duke University Press, 2001), 29–53.

more socially conservative gay political agenda that centered on winning marriage and adoption rights for lesbian and gay couples. As homosexuality moved from the social margins into the mainstream, becoming by the mid-1990s what Andrew Sullivan proclaimed as "virtually normal," some queers invented bareback subculture to help keep their sex outside the pale of bourgeois respectability.[72] If part of the appeal of gay sex consists in its transgressiveness—whether real or imagined—then barebacking and bug chasing may represent a strategy for reinscribing same-sex eroticism within the sphere of transgression. In other words, if the prospect of same-sex marriage raises the specter of gay in-laws, then bareback subculture ensures that some gay men will retain the status of outlaws—a status that carries considerable erotic appeal. As Scott O'Hara said in 1997, "I believe in exchanging bodily fluids, not wedding rings."[73]

Bug chasing, cum swapping, and gift giving may be considered alternatives to gay marriage not because the former involve promiscuity instead of monogamy but because HIV makes the exchange of bodily fluids somewhat akin to the exchange of wedding rings. They may be regarded as homologous exchange rituals because both confer forms of solidarity on their participants. As far from casual sex as one can get, bug chasing and gift giving entail lifelong commitments—commitments that may be more permanent than those of marriage—in the sense that what is exchanged at a conversion party comes with a lifetime guarantee. It has not escaped barebackers' notice that a better analogy than marriage for viral exchange is that of conceiving and bearing children. As the quotation from a bareback Web site with which I opened this chapter indicates, much of the rhetoric around bareback sex concerns breeding ("Breed, get seed and get on your knees to feed"). One of the earliest and most notorious bareback-porn movies, as discussed in the next chapter, is titled *Breed Me* (dir. Paul Morris, Treasure Island Media, 1999). Breeding the virus in other men's bodies creates simultaneously lateral and vertical kin relations: the man whom one infects with HIV becomes his sibling in the "bug brotherhood" at the same time that one becomes his parent or "Daddy," having fathered his virus. If this man also happens to be one's partner or lover,

72. See Sullivan, *Virtually Normal*; and Andrew Sullivan, ed., *Same-Sex Marriage: Pro and Con* (New York: Vintage, 1997). The classic rebuttal of Sullivan's argument may be found in Warner, *Trouble with Normal*. On the emergence, during the '90s, of gay conservatism as a response, in part, to AIDS, see Robinson, *Queer Wars*. For a consideration of these issues in terms of broader political shifts in U.S. culture, see Duggan, *Twilight of Equality*.

73. Scott O'Hara, "Viral Communion: There's Life beyond Condoms," *POZ*, November 1997, 69.

then by "breeding" him one has transformed what anthropologists call a relational affine into a consanguine; one's "husband" has become one's "brother"
via a shared bodily substance.

With the virus coded as a gift, seroconversion can be understood as successful insemination. Men who used not to worry about condoms because
there was no danger of pregnancy in gay sex now represent their deliberate
abandonment of condoms as an attempt to conceive. One account of the role
of crystal methamphetamine in bareback subculture reports the following:

> Mike, who had an HIV-positive boyfriend for six years before finding crystal,
> losing his boyfriend and only then getting infected, believes he knows when
> he got the bug. "When I had seroconversion sickness, I just counted back the
> days—and although it could have been any of literally a hundred guys, I roman-
> ticize that it was this one positive guy I met at the Westside Club [a Manhattan
> sex club] and spent six hours with," he says. "He was tall and good-looking and
> really just 'it' for me. Somewhere inside I was determined to have myself his
> baby, and the crystal took me where I could enact that fantasy."[74]

A popular gay drug facilitated the enactment of this quite conventional fantasy
of bearing a desirable man's baby. To those whose accounts of bareback subculture emphasize the role of licit and illicit drugs in its emergence (thereby
explaining the increase in unprotected sex as a result of the convergence of protease inhibitors and crystal methamphetamine), my own account doubtless appears to underestimate the destructive significance of crystal in contemporary
gay culture. I would argue, however, that explaining sexual behavior primarily
in pharmacological terms betrays a rather conservative, one-dimensional approach to what is actually a very complex set of practices. The right-wing obsession with drugs colors far too many ostensibly progressive accounts of social

74. Kevin Koffler, "Life vs. Meth," *POZ*, July/August 2002, 53. In this article, a self-described
"recovering crystal-methamphetamine addict," reports that "over a decade of doing meth, I had
thousands of sex partners—and maybe three even *mentioned* using condoms" (emphasis in the
original). Over the past several years, recognition of the synergy between crystal methamphetamine
use and bareback sex has been growing; I'm persuaded that this illegal drug, known variously as
"tina," "hydro," crank," "sparkle," or "speed," is as significant as protease inhibitors in furnishing
the pharmacological conditions of bareback subculture. Koffler claims that the term *barebacking*
was "coined at the cranked-out sex parties of San Francisco around the same time . . . that protease
combos were supposedly making HIV a chronic, manageable disease." By dramatically diminishing inhibition, intensifying sexual response, and energizing its users, crystal methamphetamine
encourages marathon fuck sessions that can last several days and involve multiple bareback partners. All reports suggest that the vast majority of crystal methamphetamine–fueled sex is bareback.
See also Michael Specter, "Higher Risk: Crystal Meth, the Internet, and Dangerous Choices about
AIDS," *New Yorker*, May 23, 2005, 38–45.

problems in the United States. The example of "Mike," quoted above, suggests that drugs furnish the conditions under which certain fantasies may be enacted, but the availability of pharmacological substances does not account for the power of these fantasies or their existence in the first place.

Viral transmission facilitates fantasies of connection, kinship, and generation that may be as familiar to heterosexual as to lesbian and gay readers. The fantasy of bearing someone's child or, indeed, of becoming someone's child is not gender specific or a function of sexual orientation. To those who might object that the joyful outcome of heterosexual insemination could not differ more from that of HIV transmission, we must reply that the unconscious remains blind to any such difference. Although the social outcome differs, the fantasy motivating both kinds of reproduction is essentially the same. Another way of putting this (although it may be cold comfort) would be to say that the unconscious completely ignores heterosexual privilege. Hence the significance of this psychoanalytic concept for queer theory and politics.

Pursuing the comparison between breeding a baby and breeding a virus, we might observe that, until quite recently, childbirth endangered the mother's life and that, even today, babies make their parents more vulnerable to illness by compromising parents' immune systems. Despite the risks, the inconvenience, and the enormous expense involved, straight people seem unable to stop themselves from breeding. Virtually all parents insist that these inconveniences—together with the lack of sleep and the extra coughs and colds that a baby brings—pale into insignificance beside the pleasure and satisfaction of their new child. Having a baby is life transforming and absolutely worth it, my peers assure me. Then again, barebackers attest that the pleasure and satisfaction achieved through unprotected sex and cum swapping is both life transforming and absolutely worth it. The inconvenience of a few extra illnesses, as well as the expense and hassle of extra medications, pale into insignificance beside the rapture of unencumbered fucking. As one barebacker put it:

> Feeling a man's dick inside me, condomless—that's when the sex becomes spiritual in its intensity. Communion, in the truest sense. Integral to that closeness is the knowledge that he intends to leave a piece of himself inside me; his cum, like the sex itself, has a psychological value far beyond anything physical.[75]

The distinction between breeding a baby and breeding a virus may come down to a question of perspective. It is not that children are like viruses but

75. O'Hara, "Viral Communion," 69.

that seroconversion can feel like becoming pregnant. Discovering that one is carrying a desirable man's virus often is experienced as enormously fulfilling.

It should be acknowledged at this point that viruses do not qualify, under most definitions, as living microorganisms. Whatever their effects on a human host, they are not biologically alive, since they lack any cellular structure of their own and cannot survive outside the host organism.[76] Of course, this definition of life derives from a perspective that seems curiously limited, from a viral point of view. Indeed, it is the fact that viruses are not biologically alive that facilitates their immortality and enables them to be imagined not only as the offspring of a human mating but also as the bearers of an imperishable connection. The virus itself permits unlimited intimacy, in the sense that it traces the persistence of multiple prior bodily contacts in the present moment. Thus the virus may be considered a particular form of memory, one that offers an effective way of maintaining certain relations with the dead. It is not necessary to sleep with the deceased in order to get his virus: one need sleep only with somebody who has slept with him or somebody who has slept with somebody who has slept with him, et cetera. The mechanism of this kind of filiation through breeding differs from heterosexual reproduction, even as it routinely is imagined in terms of conceiving a child.

The possibilities of viral connection are illustrated nicely, if inadvertently, by an anecdote that my former colleague the late poet Robert Creeley told about his friend and fellow poet Allen Ginsberg: "Ginsberg claimed to have fucked a man in San Francisco in the '50s who claimed to have fucked Whitman late in his life, the man a teenager at the time"; Creeley added that "Allen was keeping the torch lit."[77] Describing the maintenance of a native avant-garde tradition through bodily, specifically sexual, connections, Creeley highlights the dominance of kinship as a model for thinking about our relations to the cultural past as well as to the future. Through HIV it is possible to imagine establishing an intimate corporeal relation with somebody one has never met or, indeed, could never meet—somebody historically, geographically, or so-

---

76. However, as Lewis Hyde argues, "inorganic gifts do become the vehicles of *zoë*-life when we choose to invest it in them"; he adds that "a confusion between organic liveliness and cultural or spiritual liveliness is inherent in a discussion of gift exchange." From Hyde, *Gift*, 33. Further, in his discussion of how, in the twenty-first century, a genetic style of thinking is being superseded by what he calls a postgenetic style of thought, Nikolas Rose develops Hyde's suggestion in order to argue that "our very sense of what is or is not life, living, or alive is often exactly what is at stake in the politics of the present." From Rose, *Politics of Life Itself*, 48.

77. Reported by Mark Hammer in "Remembering Bob: Final Goodbyes to Poet Robert Creeley," *Artvoice* (Buffalo), April 28, 2005, 13.

cially distant from oneself. What would it mean for a young gay man today to be able to trace his virus back to, say, Michel Foucault? By thinking in genealogical terms, we start to appreciate how HIV can become a basis of authority and pride rather than of merely stigma and shame.

REINVENTING KINSHIP

HIV has become a resource for queer reinventions of kinship because it offers a vital means of showing relatedness. Anthropologist Roy Wagner argues that kinship should be understood not as a set of invariant rules but as a dynamic process of differentiating relational categories that thereby enables a flow of relatedness among them.[78] Considering kinship less as inert substance than as intentional activity, this perspective allows one to find—and to make—kin in unexpected places. For example, advances in biotechnology and information technology have enabled people who are unrelated but who share a particular gene, such as that for Down syndrome, to think of themselves as related. With Down syndrome or Marfan syndrome, genetic disease support groups become the basis for relatedness and thus for a new sense of kinship.[79] In cases such as these, kinship derives from hereditary diseases or syndromes rather than from nongenetic STDs, to which greater stigma is attached. Of course, hereditary diseases require sexual acts in order to be passed to someone else, but, in these cases, sexual activity is redeemed—destigmatized, as it were—by the fact that such reproduction is heterosexual.

How, then, did gay men come to think of viral exchange as a basis for creating kinship networks? There is a historical answer to this question that takes us back to same-sex experiments in kinship that immediately preceded the AIDS epidemic. The communal enclaves that lesbians and gay men formed in places such as San Francisco after World War II tended to be understood as involving an exile from kinship, but, beginning in the late '70s, in the wake of sexual liberation movements and innovations in reproductive technology, same-sex couples started adopting children or conceiving them through what

78. Roy Wagner, "Analogic Kinship: A Daribi Example," *American Ethnologist* 4 (1977): 623 (cited in Carsten, "Substantivism," 38). The critique of kinship essentialism stems principally from the work of David Schneider, Wagner's teacher; see esp. David M. Schneider, *A Critique of the Study of Kinship* (Ann Arbor: University of Michigan Press, 1984). See also the important work of feminist anthropologists such as Gayle Rubin, Marilyn Strathern, and Sylvia Yanagisako, as well as the contributors to *Relative Values*, ed. Sarah Franklin and Susan McKinnon.

79. See Rayna Rapp, Deborah Heath, and Karen-Sue Taussig, "Genealogical Dis-Ease: Where Hereditary Abnormality, Biomedical Explanation, and Family Responsibility Meet," in Franklin and McKinnon, *Relative Values*, 384–409.

came to be known as alternative insemination. The resultant "gayby boom" was only the most visible—perhaps we should say the most recognizable—of multiple experiments in queer kinship. Rather than accepting that homosexuality precluded kinship, the lesbians and gay men who served as informants for anthropologist Kath Weston's groundbreaking study of queer kinship in San Francisco reinvented kin relations in various ways.[80] My suggestion is that barebackers' creation of consanguineous communities through viral exchange represents a less immediately recognizable kinship experiment that emerged from the same context.

Bareback subculture's kinship networks are not easily recognizable as such because they do not involve children (except at the level of fantasy) and they are not institutionalized. That is to say, barebackers practice kinship outside the law. This does not make them necessarily more radical or progressive than the lesbian and gay nuclear families that represent today's readily identifiable face of nonheterosexual kinship. The lesbians and gay men whose relational experiments Weston documented were part of a broad movement to de-essentialize (or de-biologize) kinship by conceiving it more in terms of voluntary association than in terms of involuntary consanguineous ties. To some degree, the assumption that "blood is thicker than water" became outmoded by the conviction that enduring affection and cohabitation create a stronger foundation for kinship than does blood. In this respect, the lesbian and gay critique of kinship essentialism drew on feminist critiques of gender essentialism, even as most nonheterosexual Americans persist in the essentialist superstition that homosexuality is an inborn, immutable trait.

By basing kinship on viral transmission, barebackers have reasserted what might be considered a retrograde emphasis on blood or "substance." Weston's ethnography of San Francisco lesbians and gay men in the mid-'80s suggests that members of this urban enclave already intuited connections between the "gayby boom" and AIDS. What both the epidemic and the experiments with alternative families made apparent were the various ways that people could become related to each other by blood without involving heterosexuality. Weston observes that "as the practice of alternative insemination spread among lesbians, relations conceived as blood ties surfaced where one might least expect them: in the midst of gay families that had been defined in *opposition* to the bio-

---

80. Kath Weston, *Families We Choose: Lesbians, Gays, Kinship* (New York: Columbia University Press, 1991). See also Ellen Lewin, *Lesbian Mothers* (Ithaca, NY: Cornell University Press, 1993).

logical relations gays and lesbians ascribed to straight family."[81] Consanguinity generally assures the legitimacy of kin relations in Western cultures, making it possible to appeal to state protection of those recognized as kin even in the absence of legally sanctioned marriage rights. Without adequate affinal protections, lesbians and gay men naturally fall back on an appeal to consanguineous entitlements.

During the '80s, against the background described by Weston, San Francisco gay men discovered that they were connected to each other in ways they had not anticipated. The identification of a bloodborne pathogen as the cause of AIDS entailed recognizing, among other things, that gay men sharing an urban space such as San Francisco had been creating viral consanguinity among themselves without knowing it. The dawning realization that tricks one had forgotten might have marked permanently one's insides engendered a sense that one's bodily condition could be related to that of strangers with whom ostensibly he shared nothing but a brief interlude of pleasure. Such connections may have affected one's body as much as his genetic inheritance. It was almost as if gay men were discovering in forgotten strangers long lost kin. One of the most remarkable transformations wrought by the epidemic was this overnight conversion of strangers into relatives, without the usual intermediary stages of friendship or cohabitation.

The revelation of consanguinity helps account for the rapid construction of care networks in urban gay communities, as well as explaining why public health authorities tried to establish contact-tracing mechanisms early in the epidemic. Of course, the prospect of recording the identities of those who tested positive for such a stigmatizing disease and, on that basis, attempting to contact their sex partners prompted vociferous objections from activists, who saw immediately how such data could lead to the abuse of civil liberties. Skepticism about the discriminatory uses to which such intimate information could be put discouraged many from being tested for HIV. Yet the public health notion of contact tracing may have inspired recent attempts to form kinship networks based on viral exchange.

One of the most reactionary proposals that was floated early in the epidemic, in conjunction with contact tracing—that mandatory universal testing be followed by tattooing of the infected—has been revived by barebackers almost two decades later. Committed barebackers now sport tattoos featuring the biohazard symbol or, less ambiguously, tattoos saying "poz" or "HIV+" as marks

81. Weston, *Families We Choose*, 169, emphasis in the original.

of subcultural defiance and signals of serostatus to potential "bug brothers."[82] Although such insignia may evoke tattooing practices employed by the Third Reich, we should bear in mind how the pink triangle that gay concentration-camp internees were forced to wear was reclaimed by gay liberation several decades later as a symbol of pride. The stigma attached to HIV as a consequence of its association with gay-male anal sex is still so extraordinarily powerful that it makes sense to create a community, by whatever means, in which relief from stigmatization may be found. Regrettably, mainstream lesbian and gay culture does not seem to have been able to provide that community.

KINSHIP OR BIOSOCIALITY?

Although failing to provide a world in which seropositivity is without stigma, mainstream lesbian and gay culture has created modes of relatedness that enable some people to imagine that world. Nonheterosexuals living in San Francisco constitute a critical mass from whose social and sexual interactions have emerged innumerable relational experiments over the course of several decades. Unsurprisingly, these relational experiments now include configurations that are understood in kinship terms. The campaign for same-sex marriage, which took such a leap forward, in February 2004, with San Francisco mayor Gavin Newsom's decision to grant marriage licenses to same-sex couples, contrasts starkly with barebackers' attempts to create consanguinity through viral exchange; yet both grow out of the same matrix and the same set of concerns. It is no coincidence, in other words, that bareback subculture originated in San Francisco.

Kinship is only one model, albeit the dominant one, for thinking about relatedness. If the recourse to conceiving of relatedness in terms of shared substance seems to revive a fairly conservative idea of what constitutes affinity and solidarity, we nevertheless should not underestimate how queer experiments with kinship alter what kinship is. The anthropological critique of kinship warns that, as a Western epistemic device, "kinship" tends to constitute, or at least to shape, the realities it describes; my description of this subculture in kinship terms likewise could be charged with helping to create what I'm ostensibly just recounting. Yet as an experiment in relatedness, bareback subculture has the distinction of not conforming to any established kinship

82. Scott O'Hara, the self-styled "king of unsafe sex," started this trend in 1994, when he had "HIV+" tattooed on his left bicep, a decision that generated considerable controversy in the gay community at the time. For his own account of this decision, see Scott O'Hara, *Autopornography: A Memoir of Life in the Lust Lane* (New York: Harrington Park, 1997), 127–30.

model. By transforming relational affines (lovers) into consanguines (siblings) and by confusing relations of consanguinity with relations of descent, bareback "breeding" irrevocably contaminates the elementary categories of kinship, even as it appeals to them for a measure of its provocative power.

Understood in terms of kinship, bareback subculture changes what kinship means. Obviously this form of kinship is not heterosexual; instead, it involves homosexual or monosexual breeding.[83] To the extent that it entails erotic relations between persons understood as brothers, bareback kinship is eminently incestuous. Barebackers transform other men into fraternal relatives in order to keep having sex with them, and they do so by means of a virus. Thus bareback kinship is homosexual and incestuous differently from what those terms usually signify. In Western cultures the incest taboo distinguishes a comparatively small number of persons as sexually prohibited; through HIV barebackers have discovered a means for making sex with any number of strangers tantamount to incest. In this way, the "unlimited intimacy" desired by subcultural participants undermines the basic classifications and typologies through which anthropologists differentiate relations. From a conventional perspective, the viral mixing performed by barebackers hardly qualifies as kinship at all.

Since bareback "breeding" is neither heterosexual nor homosexual or incestuous in the usual sense, a question remains concerning how best to characterize the form of relatedness with which this subculture is experimenting. Barebackers are breeding a culture, a distinct way of life, by voluntarily sharing viruses; they are engaging in relational experiments by way of unregulated biological experiments with pathogenic microbes. Insofar as they do not want to die but to give birth, bug chasers apprehend HIV less as a harbinger of death than as a complex generator of life in its own right. One of the

---

83. As an extension of her work on Antigone, Judith Butler has brought to prominence the question of whether kinship is invariably heterosexual. Her dogged misreadings of structuralism and psychoanalysis lead Butler to make unnecessarily heavy weather of a question whose answer will be obvious to anyone who has been paying attention to relational experiments in queer culture. See Judith Butler, *Antigone's Claim: Kinship between Life and Death* (New York: Columbia University Press, 2000); and Judith Butler, "Is Kinship Always Already Heterosexual?" *Differences* 13, no. 1 (2002): 14–44. For a judicious anthropological critique, see Thomas Strong, "Kinship between Judith Butler and Anthropology: A Review Essay," *Ethnos* 67, no. 3 (2002): 401–18; for a critique that identifies the major problems of Butler's handling of psychoanalysis, see Mikko Tuhkanen's review of *Antigone's Claim* in *Umbr(a)*, 2003, 140–44. The most compelling recent psychoanalytic account of Antigone (which Butler pointedly overlooks) may be found in Joan Copjec, "The Tomb of Perseverance: On *Antigone*," in *Giving Ground: The Politics of Propinquity*, ed. Joan Copjec and Michael Sorkin (New York: Verso, 1999), 233–66.

legacies of AIDS activism is the impressive level of sophistication that many gay men have achieved with respect to virology, biotechnology, transmission probabilities, medication regimes, and so on. Far from barebacking among gay men in the United States signaling inadequate safer-sex education, it may be gay men's unprecedented autodidactic relation to HIV/AIDS that enables subcultural experiments in "breeding." Of course, these experiments are uncontrolled, illicit, and involve human subjects; their results are unpredictable and may sometimes be fatal, at least to the humans involved.

Yet the very fact of these experiments' unpredictability—the fact that they count as experiments at all—means that we cannot be certain about their inevitable fatality. The social death caused by HIV's intense stigma so far antedates organic death that, in the meantime, some of the undead have invented their own form of subcultural life.[84] But barebackers are breeding not only each other and a distinctive cultural life; they also are breeding a virus. It is vital to subcultural practice that bareback sex involves exchanging the virus as a sign of indelible connection. The peculiarity of this kind of sex thus resides in its deliberate involvement of a pathogenic parasite; in a sense, bug chasers and gift givers are having sex with a virus as well as with each other. They have opened their bodies to intimate relations with nonhuman life.[85] Standard categorizations such as homosexuality, bestiality, or incest do not capture with sufficient precision the kind of intercourse involved here.

Anthropologist Paul Rabinow has coined the term *biosociality* to describe how, especially in the wake of the Human Genome Project, biotechnological advances can transform human relatedness by making something such as genetic abnormality a new basis for kinship (the Down syndrome gene, as mentioned above, would be a salient example).[86] Rather than "kinship," *bio-*

84. On the notion of "social death," see Orlando Patterson, *Slavery and Social Death: A Comparative Study* (Cambridge, MA: Harvard University Press, 1982). The central resistant insight of Patterson's book (and of recent scholarship that draws inspiration from it) is that social death can function as a source of cultural reanimation.

85. In a fascinating meditation on what he calls "bestiality," Alphonso Lingis suggests that the human disinclination to appreciate our constant intercourse with animals and other nonhuman life stems from the prejudicial misrecognition of our bodies as bounded and individuated. He reminds us that "human animals live in symbiosis with thousands of species of anaerobic bacteria, six hundred species in our mouths that neutralize the toxins all plants produce to ward off their enemies, four hundred species in our intestines, without which we could not digest and absorb the food we ingest. . . . The number of microbes that colonize our bodies exceeds the number of cells in our bodies by up to a hundredfold. They replicate with their own DNA and RNA and not ours." From Alphonso Lingis, *Dangerous Emotions* (Berkeley: University of California Press, 2000), 27.

86. Paul Rabinow, "Artificiality and Enlightenment: From Sociobiology to Biosociality," in *Incorporations*, ed. Jonathan Crary and Sanford Kwinter (New York: Zone, 1992), 234–52.

sociality may represent a better term for characterizing the kind of relational experiments that barebackers are conducting by means of a virus. The fact of sharing some microscopic entity whose existence remained unknown until medical technology isolated it a quarter century ago has become the source of not only new subjective identities but also intersubjectivity and social life. Subcultural nomenclature tends to describe barebackers' biosociality in terms less of marriage, family, or community than of tribes or gangs. Although some bug chasers are searching for Mr. Right to infect them—or have elected to enhance the intimacy of their primary relationship by sharing their partner's virus—most subcultural participants express commitment to intimacy beyond the couple. They are interested more in group membership than in privatized union with another individual. Sociologically these group formations could be described as "neo-tribal," with the qualification that committed barebackers modify the interiors (not only the exteriors) of their bodies for purposes of affiliation.[87]

Since they conceive of relatedness in terms less of marriage or family than of gangs or tribes, barebackers appear unconcerned by the issue of state recognition of their relationships. This absence of concern evokes a central tenet of the queer critique of marriage, namely, that marriage permits an extension of institutional power into spheres of intimacy that we reasonably might wish to keep as free as possible from state intervention. Institutional recognition of intimate relations is always a double-edged sword, in that it legitimates one kind of relationship at the expense of others. As Michael Warner argues, marriage is a discriminatory institution—and should be resisted on that basis—because it confers selective legitimacy.[88] It becomes more, not less, discriminatory when extended to same-sex couples, insofar as the relational recognition that marriage brings inexorably detracts from all the other forms of

87. See Theresa M. Winge, "Constructing 'Neo-Tribal' Identities through Dress: Modern Primitives and Body Modifications," in Muggleton and Weinzierl, *Post-Subcultures Reader*, 119–32.

88. See Warner, *Trouble with Normal*, chap. 3. See also John Borneman's strong critique of the totemic status that marriage holds in anthropological discourse, in which it tends to be regarded as a universal equivalent. Commenting on the way that marriage is counterposed to AIDS and death in U.S. culture, Borneman suggests how marriage also confers its own form of death: "In the United States marriage tends to be posited as the antithesis of death: an escape or way out of death—out of the abyss of chaos, loneliness, singlehood, incompleteness, and, now, AIDS. At the same time that marriage is desired or experienced as a completion necessary for life, a making fully human or a whole of previous halves or parts, it also signals the security of a death to all possibilities for an unexpected history, an end to all histories outside the marriage, as if history thereafter were containable within the consanguinal and affinal relations of the kinship chart." From John Borneman, "Until Death Do Us Part: Marriage/Death in Anthropological Discourse," *American Ethnologist* 23, no. 2 (1996): 228.

intimacy that heterosexual as well as nonheterosexual people have invented and continue to invent. Universalizing marriage serves the enterprise of social regulation by homogenizing relational recognition. Thus although bareback subculture grows out of the same relational matrix as the campaign for same-sex marriage, it manifests a quite different sense of the vital constituents of relationality. Rather than state recognition, barebackers crave witnesses who may become coconspirators in their enterprise of deregulating intimacy. As the next two chapters elaborate, witnessing in bareback subculture takes the form, first and foremost, of pornography.

TWO: REPRESENTING RAW SEX

Can insemination be captured on film?

On April 13, 2004, news broke that "veteran performer" Darren James, a forty-year-old African American actor in the straight porn industry, had tested positive for HIV.[1] In the weeks that followed, three of the thirteen women with whom he had worked after returning to the United States from Brazil, where he contracted the virus, also tested positive. These three women thus were infected on camera. The disclosure of James's seroconversion—the first such positive test result in straight porn since 1999—brought the multibillion-dollar U.S. industry to a standstill. A sixty-day moratorium on filming was declared, with virtually every one of the approximately 200 porn companies in California's San Fernando Valley conforming to the industry's self-imposed freeze. The incident made national headlines, generating a controversy that illustrated how differently the straight porn industry in this country treats HIV compared with the gay porn industry. Amid intensive discussion of condom

1. My account of this incident draws on the following sources: Scott Ross, "AIM Working to Contain HIV: Search for Second-Generation Continues," *Adult Video News*, April 13, 2004, available at http://www.avn.com/video/articles/15719.html; Nick Madigan, "HIV Cases Shut Down Pornography Film Industry," *New York Times*, April 17, 2004, sec. A:11; Nick Madigan, "Sex Videos on Pause, and Idled Actors Fret," *New York Times*, April 25, 2004, sec. 9:1; Andrew Murr, "A Web of HIV Infections," *Newsweek*, April 26, 2004, 8; Alan Clendenning, "HIV Case Airs Secrets of Porn Industry," *Miami Herald*, April 29, 2004, sec. A:16; Tristan Taormino, "Porn Faces Reality: HIV Outbreak in California Porn Industry Highlights Risky Business," *Village Voice*, April 30, 2004, available at http://www.villagevoice.com/people/0418,taormino,53111,24.html; Nick Madigan, "Voice of Health in a Pornographic World," *New York Times*, May 10, 2004, sec. A:14; and Carol Queen, "Porn HIV Scare May Signal Coming Changes," *Good Vibrations Magazine*, May 12, 2004, available at http://www.goodvibes.com/Content.aspx?id=1252&leftMenu=35&lr=y.

use and the prevention of STDs in the production of hard-core pornography, prominent studios in the gay sector of the industry felt moved to issue statements about their policies on safer sex and HIV transmission. Yet despite the fact that Darren James apparently contracted HIV via unprotected anal sex with a woman and then unwittingly passed it on to three others by fucking them in the ass without a rubber on film, nobody described what he did—or what routinely happens in straight porn—as barebacking.

Unlike the mainstream gay porn industry in the United States and the straight porn industry in Brazil, condom use is still far from the norm in straight porn production in California. Although a few U.S. companies are condom only (including Vivid, the industry leader), straight porn production has relied for the past decade—and with considerable success—on a different method for preventing the spread of STDs. San Fernando Valley porn studios require that models document a clean bill of health before they are allowed to perform, namely, proof of negative results on an HIV and other STD tests taken within the last thirty days at the Adult Industry Medical Health Care Foundation (AIM). Established in January 1998 by porn legend Sharon Mitchell, AIM administers regular tests for HIV, syphilis, gonorrhea, and chlamydia to all industry performers; in the wake of Darren James's positive HIV-test result, the foundation started posting test results on its Web site. Records indicate that James was tested for HIV roughly every three weeks (more frequently than the industry standard) and that, as soon as he tested positive, he ceased performing. Further, the thirteen women (and one man) with whom he worked after returning from Brazil—and everybody with whom they worked after having sex with him—were quickly tested by AIM, which uses the PCR DNA test, the best HIV-detection method available. A voluntary quarantine list, containing more than sixty names, appeared on AIM's Web site.

This system was so effective in curtailing a potential epidemic of HIV transmission in the straight porn industry that Sharon Mitchell was invited to contribute an op-ed column to the *New York Times*, to discuss her foundation and the issues surrounding the incident.[2] As porn icon Nina Hartley also pointed out, in response to panicked cries for government regulation of the industry, "AIM has administered literally thousands of tests to adult performers, who have gone on to engage in tens of thousands of on-camera sex acts without a single instance of HIV transmission as a result. This is one of the rare and great

---

2. See Sharon Mitchell, "How to Put Condoms in the Picture," *New York Times*, May 2, 2004, sec. 4:11.

public health success stories in the tragic history of the HIV epidemic."[3] Given that most straight porn is produced without the use of condoms, that the U.S. industry alone produces approximately 4,000 films each year, and that many performers have unprotected sex with thousands of partners over the course of their careers, it is indeed remarkable that Darren James was the first case in five years of an established performer testing positive.

Yet James's case shows that the porn industry's self-devised testing system isn't foolproof. To begin with, there is the problem of the time lag between infection and the production of antibodies: it is the latter (not the virus itself) that show up on a positive HIV test. Darren James received a negative test result on March 17, 2004, immediately after his trip to Brazil, but the absence of HIV antibodies didn't prevent him from transmitting the virus to some of those with whom he worked after his return. An additional problem is that AIM's testing system relies on what sexologist Carol Queen calls "a sort of huge-scale monogamy among the 1,200 or so performers in the business."[4] The system works perfectly only when it remains completely closed. It cannot take account fully of performers' off-screen partners, who are under no obligation to participate in AIM's comparatively expensive testing program (in 2004 each test cost an actor $110, which adds up, over time, to a considerable business expense).

The ideal of "huge-scale monogamy" is compromised also by pornographers' outsourcing operations to Brazil, where the currency collapse has lowered costs dramatically for U.S. producers. The beauty of the landscape and of the population, combined with a well-developed indigenous porn industry, make Brazil especially attractive when the San Fernando Valley starts to feel stale. The trouble is that Brazil's porn industry depends primarily on condom use to prevent the spread of STDs, since testing is prohibitively expensive. In this global market, when two systems come into contact with each other, their respective prophylactic norms clash. Stateside pornographers who prefer to produce rubberless movies typically pay Brazilian women double their usual fee to have sex on camera without protection, believing that the HIV-negative North American men who perform with them are reasonably safe, as long as their unprotected sex remains strictly heterosexual. In the straight as well as the gay world, it is assumed that those who are getting fucked are at greatest risk. AIDS still is seen as a disease of the sexually penetrated.

3. Quoted in Queen, "Porn HIV Scare."
4. Queen, "Porn HIV Scare."

What makes the Darren James case so fascinating is that it stands as an allegory of the unpredictable results that follow from one local culture's contact with another. The clash between two similar, yet nonidentical, sexual ecologies threatens the integrity of AIM's carefully regulated system. San Fernando Valley's AIM system functions effectively because it maintains an elaborate contact-tracing network that relies on word of mouth, pseudonym recognition, and the digital network of the virtual world, which has been so hospitable to pornography. In a context where everyone who fucks on film is a "star"—where, that is, each erotic act includes a legion of witnesses—it is easier to keep track of who has had sex with whom, no matter how frequent the bed hopping.

Sharon Mitchell is a contact-tracing expert. On her Web site, one finds a "quarantine list" that is remarkable for its complexity and sophistication. Not merely a catalogue of names, the AIM quarantine list includes the date of each performer's last negative HIV-test result, alongside the date each worked with Darren James or one of the women with whom he worked. The thirteen women (and one man) who worked with James after he was infected but before he knew it have been designated "the first generation"; the performers with whom they worked subsequently are "the second generation." As soon as a member of the first generation tested positive, new catalogues of the "first" and "second" generations were compiled, based on sexual contacts and the possibility of exposure to HIV.[5] Perusing this complex list, with its kinship-derived nomenclature of generations, one cannot escape the impression that, in a relatively closed group, viral transmission furnishes the basis for affiliations that are more than merely communal or virtual. Darren James and the three women whom he inadvertently infected will always be "porn stars," irrespective of the fact that they are unlikely to perform again in front of the camera, because the connection with porn is now in their blood. They have become related consanguineously.

The metaphor of family—and the imperative, even here, to *keep it in the family*—proves unexpectedly apposite for describing Southern California's porn industry. With the assistance of biomedical technology, Dr. Mitchell has diagrammed in AIM's quarantine list what amounts to a family tree, thus confirming this otherwise counterintuitive perspective on porn's promiscuous relationships. The presence or threat of HIV transforms those ostensibly alienated relationships into a kinship system. Here "keeping it in the family" means

5. From http://www.aim-med.org/Quarantine.html (accessed June 26, 2004).

minimizing contact with foreign sexual systems, whether conceived in terms of national boundaries, sexual identity categories, or serodiscordance. Endogamy necessitates a system of viral apartheid—one reason that there is little overlap between the straight and gay porn industries around Los Angeles.

If the avoidance of condom use in straight porn is rationalized by appeal to a testing system and contact-tracing network designed to insure seroconcordance among the performers, bareback porn is based on a similar rationale: Why bother with prophylactics when those having sex all share (or are assumed to share) the same serostatus? Despite the fact that the straight porn industry remains fairly segregated from the gay sector of the industry and that, within the gay sector, bareback porn is fairly segregated from mainstream gay porn, bareback porn nevertheless uncannily mirrors straight porn in some of its presuppositions. Is it merely coincidental that *bareback* emerged as an explicit subcategory of gay pornography around the time that Sharon Mitchell established AIM, with its kinship-based understanding of viral transmission and contact tracing? If the roughly 1,200 members of the U.S. straight porn industry can be conceived of as an extended family whose protection depends on maintaining "huge-scale monogamy," how does bareback subculture compare as a sexual grouping? What are we to make of the fact that the most extreme forms of heterosexual pornography produced today resemble bareback porn in their obsessive focus on the archetypal scenario of the anal gang bang, in which multiple (condomless) men penetrate a single individual? And why do barebackers refer to such activity by the ostensibly heterosexual term "breeding"? What is the motive for filming these rituals?

I would like to dispel from the outset a glib assumption that, since porn is big business, the primary motive for filming bareback gang bangs must be financial. Pornography is one line of work in which women consistently get paid more than men to perform—often ten times as much per scene. Straight guys who fuck on film have seen their pay decline so rapidly by comparison with their female counterparts that, as veteran performer Buck Adams commented to Susan Faludi in the course of her research for a very interesting article on the gendered economics of the industry, "pretty soon you're going to have to pay to be in a porno movie."[6] This helps explain why some ostensibly straight male performers go "gay for pay," pursuing a career in mainstream gay porn, where remuneration is better. Given that men make more in gay porn than they do in straight porn and that the Darren James case revealed the practice of paying

6. Quoted in Susan Faludi, "The Money Shot," *New Yorker*, October 30, 1995, 85.

Brazilian women double their usual fee to perform without condoms, it would be reasonable to assume that men in bareback porn would be compensated even more than mainstream gay porn models. But this is not the case. In fact, many of the men in bareback movies perform for free. As if confirming Buck Adams's reductio ad absurdum, some men even offer to pay the filmmaker in order to get fucked without condoms on screen. As we shall see, what motivates bareback porn is something other than financial considerations.

Although not motivated primarily by money, a distinct array of material conditions—pharmacological, technological, and jurisprudential—has enabled bareback porn to appear and flourish in recent years. I have suggested how antiretroviral therapies' transformation of HIV infection from an immediate death sentence into a manageable chronic illness made it possible for gay men to begin thinking differently about their bodily fluids. The late '90s also saw the introduction of Viagra, the first "erectile dysfunction" drug, which quickly joined the pharmaceutical options of gay sexual culture.[7] Both kinds of medication entered the market as a shadow epidemic of illegal drugs—principally, crystal methamphetamine—was percolating through sexual communities on the Pacific Coast. This constellation furnished an ideal pharmacological environment for marathon fuck sessions with or without multiple partners, with or without condoms, and with or without regret.

At the same time, increasing numbers of men were taking advantage of virtual technology and reorganizing their erotic lives online. Not only were Internet chat rooms and bulletin boards replacing outdoor cruising and gay bars, but digital technology also was changing the distribution and consumption of hard core. Pornography became a multibillion-dollar industry in the final decade of the twentieth century because, during that period, porn entered domestic spaces where it previously had been unavailable. Cable television and home Internet access meant that it was no longer necessary to go to a porn theater or a red-light district to view hard core, as it had been in the '70s; it also was no longer necessary even to run to the video store, as it had been in the '80s. During the '90s, a revolution in digital technology brought pornography directly to the consumer. Hence, for example, the several hundred thousand commercial porn sites that now exist on the World Wide Web. Pornographers' joining hands, for distribution purposes, with corporations

7. See Michael Scarce, "Something Borrowed, Something Blue: Viagra Use among Gay Men," in *Smearing the Queer: Medical Bias in the Health Care of Gay Men* (New York: Harrington Park, 1999), 137–53; and David Tuller, "Experts Fear a Risky Recipe: Viagra, Drugs and HIV," *New York Times*, October 16, 2001, sec. F:5(L).

such as AT&T and General Motors—as well as with Marriott, Hilton, and other hotel chains—also led to some improvement in porn's general social reputation by making it more legitimate, more accessible, and even more profitable than before.

In view of these transformations, we might say that digital technology has normalized pornography. Yet perversions, fetishes, and minority sexualities all proliferate online. Such apparently contradictory effects are attributable in part to the dramatic decline in obscenity prosecutions during the '90s. Under Janet Reno, U.S. attorney general from 1993 to 2001, the Department of Justice shifted its priorities from pornography to national security. As a result, hysterical symptoms of the conservative preoccupation with porn—such as the infamous Meese Commission and an aggressive censorship agenda—began receding into the past. But it was not only the change in political administration that reduced federal prosecutions of pornography. Since the 1973 Supreme Court ruling in *Miller v. California*, obscenity law has relied on a "community standards" criterion that did not anticipate the virtual world we now inhabit; as a PBS documentary on the porn industry observed, "the Internet inhibits obscenity prosecutions because it fractures the very idea of what a community is."[8]

A law that appeals to "community standards" invariably enforces the majority's biases at the expense of minority viewpoints: reliance on "community standards" leaves nonnormative sexualities especially vulnerable to the incomprehension and hostility of the sexually normative. Erotic tolerance therefore has benefited from the temporary desuetude of the so-called Miller test, even as obscenity has come to be defined in terms less of sexual explicitness than of deviation from the norm.[9] Although John Ashcroft, Reno's successor as U.S. attorney general, reinstated an aggressive antiporn campaign that merely was stalled by the events of September 11, 2001, the broader consequences of these transformations in access to sexually explicit representations still are poorly understood. Doubtless hard-core porn has become more significant in the contemporary organization of sexuality than it was in earlier periods—although my argument will counter alarmist claims that porn

8. See *American Porn*, dir. Michael Kirk (Frontline, 2002). Legal criteria for determining obscenity were laid out in *Marvin Miller v. State of California*, 413 U.S. 15 (1973), reprinted in David Copp and Susan Wendell, eds., *Pornography and Censorship* (Buffalo: Prometheus Books, 1983), 357–66.

9. For a critical account of this shift in legal definitions of obscenity, see Linda Williams, "Second Thoughts on *Hard Core*: American Obscenity Law and the Scapegoating of Deviance," in *Dirty Looks: Women, Pornography, Power*, ed. Pamela Church Gibson and Roma Gibson (London: BFI, 1993), 46–61.

determines its consumers' behavior. Porn has become vastly more pervasive during the past decade or two, but it has not wreaked the damage prophesied by conservative jeremiads. And although the far-reaching changes that I have described help to illuminate the conditions of bareback porn's emergence, they hardly constitute a causal explanation.

MAXIMIZING VISIBILITY

No longer a closet activity, unprotected gay sex has given rise to a subculture that graphically represents itself and aspires to create a visual archive of its actions. If we imagine that HIV-positive men who fuck without condoms tend to remain circumspect about publicizing their sexual behavior, then we misapprehend what makes barebacking the basis for a subculture. Unlike erotic activities (such as masturbation) that elicit little or no representational trace, bareback sex seems to call for witnesses and thus to generate documentary evidence, as well as communal bonds. I'm suggesting that barebackers have been breeding not only a virus but also a way of life, with its own distinct identities, rituals, and iconography, which are amenable to critical analysis.

It is perhaps inevitable that a sexual subculture's self-representation should draw on conventions that are deemed pornographic: the commitment to overcoming limits means that everything must be shown, nothing regarded as obscene. And, indeed, the subculture has produced a remarkable corpus of pornography. In this chapter, I discuss a number of self-identified bareback-porn tapes produced during the past several years by small independent studios (such as Treasure Island Media, Dick Wadd Media, and Hot Desert Knights) that remain separate from, and mostly frowned upon by, the more established gay porn studios (such as Falcon, Catalina, and All Worlds), which are committed to safer-sex practices in the making of their films. Despite the impulse to "show it all" and leave nothing merely implicit, pornography is a genre governed by conventions that regulate what may—and may not—be shown. When we look at porn as more than a provocation to sexual excitement, we find an array of visual and discursive conventions that, even in this uninhibited genre, constrain the appearance of the unconventional. One of my concerns lies with what happens when the attempt to represent nonnormative sex comes up against the norms of representation. I am intrigued by how bareback porn, in its effort to make certain forms of intimacy visible, poses a challenge not just to pornographic conventions but to representation as such. Aspiring to represent "raw sex," bareback porn paradoxically adapts technologies of visual mediation—the digital camera, the Internet—to its project of overcoming mediation.

I am suggesting that bareback porn is more than merely a dubious form of entertainment for risk-friendly gay men—more even than a subculture's privileged form of self-representation. Bareback porn is a form of thinking. As a genre confronted with problems of representation—such as how to capture insemination on film—bareback porn constitutes a mode of thinking about bodily limits, about intimacy, about power, and of course about sex. Despite what is said by its critics in the gay community, bareback porn also may constitute one valid way of thinking about a virus. Unlike "pre-condom" gay porn produced during the '70s and early '80s, bareback porn is far from oblivious to HIV. Bareback porn, in other words, is no more simply a case of "denial" than bareback sex is simply a case of irresponsibility.

In describing bareback porn as a form of thinking, I do not mean that someone's ideas about sex or about AIDS are reflected in the actions these videos record, but that those actions themselves choreograph a mode of embodied thought. Thinking is among the range of actions performed in these videos—thinking less as ratiocination than as working over a problem through bodily activity.[10] Rather than the cognitive labor of an individual such as the director, thinking would be a collective endeavor that constitutes one unpredictable outcome of friction among bodies, including the director's (which sometimes enters the frame of these movies). Usually unencumbered by scripts and pushing against the generic conventions of mainstream pornography, the bareback videos considered here resemble filmed explorations more than performances. There are no actors in these films, just participants. Even the cameramen are participants, occasionally joining in the action and often visible on screen when only filming it. We find few signs of the effort that mainstream porn undertakes to edit out those moments when a cameraman strays into the shot; bareback porn regularly breaks the frame of cinematic illusion. The appearance of cameramen in these videos is evidence not of technical incompetence but of this pornography's blurring the distinction between participants and witnesses, just as bareback sex tries to blur the boundaries that

---

10. My own thinking about the significance of action in pornography has been informed by Frances Ferguson's account of porn's historical role in "the larger cultural project of trying to identify the increased importance of action in modernity," although my emphases and conclusions differ from hers (not least because she discusses only literary pornography, whereas I'm focusing on moving-image porn). See Frances Ferguson, *Pornography, the Theory: What Utilitarianism Did to Action* (Chicago: University of Chicago Press, 2004), xv.

separate persons from each other. It is considerably more than the absence of rubbers that distinguishes bareback from mainstream gay porn.

The skeptical reader may object that, far from being a distinguishing feature of bareback porn, the tactic of persuading viewers that what they're seeing is not a performance but the real thing, raw and uncensored, in fact constitutes a standard device of video pornography. The effect of rawness is part of porn's realism and must be perpetually recreated in order for the action not to register as overly stylized.[11] Hence the appeal of "amateur" porn, in which the couples do not appear as professional actors whose job is to fuck on film. What we look for in pornography are not people going through the motions of sex to earn a living but those who seem carried away by pleasure and desire—those who are genuinely moved, their bodies consumed by lust to the point of oblivion. In other words, what we like in porn is the spectacle of bodies losing control of themselves, bodies overcome by a will other than their own. "Lust," "desire," "pleasure": these are but names that we give to manifestations of this "will-other-than-our-own." When bodies appear to be overcome by an alien will in straight porn, we tend to assume that this overpowering force is masculine; we name that alien will "patriarchal power," identifying it with the men in the film or the men making the film. In my view, this widespread assumption—as common among pornography's most ardent fans as among its feminist critics—misunderstands the forms of power at work in porn.

Porn's appeal lies in its rendering visible, even palatable, that peculiar loss of control entailed in the experience of orgasm. The climax of a conventional

11. The question of pornographic realism has been analyzed primarily in terms of feature-length films, in which sex scenes are interspersed with tedious and poorly acted clothed encounters meant to advance the plotline. Umberto Eco argues that the boring bits between copulations—the interminable highway drives, the mundane fumblings at hotel registration desks—actually establish porn's reality effects. See Umberto Eco, "How to Recognize a Porn Movie," in *How to Travel with a Salmon, and Other Essays*, trans. William Weaver (London: Minerva, 1995), 206–210. Building on both Eco's and Linda Williams's accounts of porn realism, Murat Aydemir contends that pornographic realism lies in neither the brightly lit verisimilitude of hard-core fucking nor the tedious scenes between fucks but in "the specific manner with which the genre separates, and alternates between story and number, between dreary realism and theatricalized sex." From Murat Aydemir, *Images of Bliss: Ejaculation, Masculinity, Meaning* (Minneapolis: University of Minnesota Press, 2007), 147. Aydemir's point, following Williams's ingenious characterization of hard-core sex scenes as analogous to the song-and-dance scenes in musicals, is that without the contrast of the boring bits, porn would lose much of its reality effect and thus its power. Such analyses of pornographic realism fail to account adequately for the reality effects of the bareback films described in the present chapter, since these are structured neither as feature-length narratives nor as compilation tapes but rather as documentaries. For a useful analysis of the techniques of documentary realism, see Jane M. Gaines and Michael Renov, eds., *Collecting Visible Evidence* (Minneapolis: University of Minnesota Press, 1999).

porn scene occurs when a man submits to a corporeal force that he cannot master. Commentators on hard-core film and video pornography are virtually unanimous in characterizing the spectacle of male ejaculation—the "money shot," "cum shot," or "pop shot"—as the most important element of the genre, in both its gay and straight variants. "If you don't have the come shots, you don't have a porno picture," insists *The Film Maker's Guide to Pornography*.[12] This formula could be rewritten to suggest that if you don't present the spectacle of *a man submitting* to the loss of bodily control, then you don't have a porno picture. The visual evidence of momentarily losing control—the sight of something that can't be faked and therefore can't be performed, only undergone—remains indispensable to hard-core porn. Narrative climax coincides with sexual climax in this genre, because for a few seconds an individual is subordinated to the involuntary action of his own body.

Porn's characteristic overcompensation for this self-subordination consists in making someone else submit to a man's orgasm, by having an actor ejaculate onto his partner's body (usually the face) in a way that confirms the partner's subordination to the spurting penis. This convention predominates in both straight and gay mainstream porn. As fate would have it, the practice of withdrawal before ejaculation was adapted as a safer-sex technique when the cause of AIDS was identified as a bloodborne virus (and therefore external ejaculation came to be understood as safer than cumming inside). "On me, not in me" emerged as a safer-sex catchphrase during the 1980s. This adaptation of one of porn's visual conventions to a lifesaving grassroots campaign generated some comic misrecognitions, as when a young gay man first witnessed heterosexual video porn and, observing the male actor withdraw for the money shot, concluded that straight porn performers practice safe sex too.[13] What interests me here is how the convention of aiming his ejaculate at someone else obscures the degree to which the man having an orgasm is overcome by a bodily action that he ultimately cannot control.

This notion of involuntary action—what I described above as being overpowered momentarily by a will other than one's own—is significant because we are inclined to believe that it reveals a dimension of truth otherwise inaccessible. The body convulses, and truth emerges along with semen; or so we imagine, since bodies are not given to dissimulation in the manner of speech and representation. "A hard cock never lies," wrote Allen Ginsberg in one of

---

12. Stephen Ziplow, *The Film Maker's Guide to Pornography* (New York: Drake, 1977), 34.
13. As reported in Patton, *Fatal Advice*, 3.

his best lines.[14] However, Ginsberg was writing before the invention of Viagra and other pharmaceutical aids for the flagging penis. Better to have said that a cum shot never lies. Certain drugs that are popular in the porn industry enable men to achieve and sustain erections even in the absence of desire, but men cannot fake an orgasm.[15]

Allow me to be precise. Whether gay or straight, men, like women, can fake the *representation* of an orgasm, but we cannot fake orgasm itself—just as one may fake the representation of pain but not pain itself. To put the point somewhat differently, one can fake an orgasm no more than one can fake a Freudian slip, since both consist of *involuntary* actions. The example of the Freudian slip—that lapsus in which the truth of unconscious desire speaks through a mistake—suggests that, in this perspective, it is less a question of bodily veracity superseding the equivocations of speech than of identifying truth with involuntary revelation. Of course, this analogy is limited by the fact that people tend to chase after orgasms in a way that they don't hanker after making slips of the tongue or other kinds of errors. Nevertheless, our culture's commitment to locating the truths of selfhood in sex resembles the way in which psychoanalysis locates subjective truth in unconscious desire, since both "sex" and "desire" are seen as exemplified by involuntary action.

By discussing the money shot in these terms, I mean to emphasize how pornographic sex involves knowledge or "truth," as well as pleasure. Whether gay or straight, kinky or vanilla, porn aspires not just to get its viewers off but also to find out something. In the classic study of the genre, feminist film theorist Linda Williams characterizes hard-core porn as a technology for investigating sexual difference and particularly for eliciting the secrets of women's pleasure. The ambition to make everything visible and thus knowable in hard-core porn encounters problems when attempting to register definitive visual evidence of female orgasms. As Williams puts it, "seeing everything—especially seeing the truth of sex—proves a more difficult project than one might think, especially in the case of women's bodies, whose truths are most at stake."[16] In this account, the spectacle of male ejaculation substitutes for what cannot be

14. See "Love Comes" in Allen Ginsberg, *White Shroud: Poems 1980–1985* (New York: Harper & Row, 1987), 13.

15. In addition to the family of prescription drugs taken orally to enhance blood flow to the penis (most famously, Viagra, but now also Levitra and Cialis), there are also drugs such as Caverject and Edex, which are injected directly into the penis to guarantee an erection. Unfortunately, erection by injection often leads to problems that require surgical solutions.

16. Linda Williams, *Hard Core: Power, Pleasure, and the 'Frenzy of the Visible'* (Berkeley: University of California Press, 1989), 32.

seen: porn's ubiquitous money shots compensate its straight male viewers for the missing visual testimony of women's erotic pleasure.[17]

But what if a cinematic spectacle of the ejaculating penis appears not as a substitute but as the real thing? In other words, what if we were to take the gay, rather than the straight, male viewer as porn's normative audience? Williams discusses only heterosexual hard core, and it isn't clear whether her account can accommodate gay male porn, which manifests virtually no concern for the mysteries of sexual difference or for women's pleasure. Certainly gay porn is obsessed with *gender* in the form of the visual insignia of masculinity, and gender is constituted relationally, such that there can be no spectacle of masculinity without the specter of femininity hovering somewhere in the wings. Yet this does not make gay porn merely a variant or subset of the straight hard core project that Williams delineates so persuasively.

In considering Williams's analysis, we also should take into account the different role that pornography plays in gay culture, particularly its greater degree of acceptability.[18] Porn consumption has long been normative in gay relationships in a way that it is unlikely ever to become in heterosexual relationships, at the very least because imbalances of power between the sexes aren't at stake when everyone involved in the pornography—actors, producers, distributors, consumers—is male. I'm not suggesting that power differentials aren't part of the spectacle of gay porn or that exploitation is never involved in this sector of the industry. Nothing could be further from the case. Rather, I'm suggesting that gay porn's negligible interest in sexual difference might prompt us to wonder whether hard core is pursuing knowledge about something else altogether. I'm suggesting, in other words, that we question the centrality of sexual difference as an explanatory category when making sense of straight porn, as well as gay porn. Williams's account cannot really accommodate gay porn, but perhaps a queer perspective on her powerful argument can generate an account capable of accommodating *both* gay and straight hard-core porn films.

The genius of Williams's book lies in her dissociating the rise of cinematic porn from earlier traditions of sexually explicit representation and connecting

17. See Williams, *Hard Core*, 95. Since the publication of Williams's book, a subgenre of "squirt" videos has emerged, in which female performers ejaculate at the moment of orgasm, often far more dramatically than their male partners. However spectacular this visual evidence of women's pleasure, it does not seem to have become standardized as a convention in straight porn.

18. For a history of the importance of sexually explicit visual imagery in pre-Stonewall same-sex cultures, see Thomas Waugh, *Hard to Imagine: Gay Male Eroticism in Photography and Film from Their Beginnings to Stonewall* (New York: Columbia University Press, 1996).

it instead with modern discourses of sexuality that culminate in "machines of the visible," a phrase she borrows from French film theorist Jean-Louis Comolli.[19] It is not that a preexisting pornographic imagination had to content itself with expression in writing and drawing until the nineteenth-century invention of photography and subsequently cinema but, rather, that these new technologies served the larger cultural project of making sex visible and thus formed part of the massive deployment of sexuality described by Foucault. Williams makes clear how the nineteenth-century "incitement to discourse"—the imperative to speak about sex and produce knowledge about it—generated a correlative "incitement to see" that finds its technological apotheosis in cinema. Speaking not of standard antecedents such as Sade but of photographer Eadweard Muybridge's pioneering studies of animal locomotion, she argues that "with this ability to induce and photograph a bodily confession of involuntary spasm, Muybridge's prototypical cinema arrives at the condition of possibility for cinematic hard core."[20] Williams's history helps explain why philosophers of film as different as Stanley Cavell and Fredric Jameson consider cinema to be intrinsically pornographic.[21]

According to this way of thinking, hard-core porn resembles nonpornographic cinema ontologically more than it resembles erotica, because hard core is driven by what Williams calls the principle of maximum visibility. Hard core shares with erotica the impulse to arouse its audience, but hard core is distinguished from erotica by virtue of its epistemological impulse to make something available to sight. My contention is that the principle of maximum visibility supersedes sexual difference as an explanatory category, since the former principle elucidates mainstream gay porn and bareback porn as readily as it explains heterosexual hard core. What bareback porn has in common with the straight porn movies discussed by Williams is not a concern with sexual difference but an intense curiosity about the body's interior. For example, one visual fetish of recent straight hard core consists in filming what are known as "dilations": after a prolonged bout of butt fucking, the woman's rectal sphincter does not immediately contract when the male performer's penis is withdrawn, and the camera zooms in for a close-up

19. See Jean-Louis Comolli, "Machines of the Visible," in *The Cinematic Apparatus*, ed. Teresa de Lauretis and Stephen Heath (Houndmills, UK: Macmillan, 1980), 121–42.

20. Williams, *Hard Core*, 48.

21. See Stanley Cavell, *The World Viewed: Reflections on the Ontology of Film* (Cambridge, MA: Harvard University Press, 1979), 45; and Fredric Jameson, *Signatures of the Visible* (New York: Routledge, 1992), 1.

of her gaping anus, in a style very similar to the close-ups of freshly fucked or fisted asses in bareback porn.[22]

The fact that heterosexual hard core seems interested primarily in the dilation of women's anuses, not their vaginas, suggests that it is the mysterious privacy of the insides that this pornography wishes to penetrate, irrespective of sexual difference or sexual orientation. I remain unconvinced that the dilation fetish in straight hard core represents a disavowal of sexual difference, any more than a same-sex erotic preference necessarily represents a disavowal of sexual difference. Of course, emphasizing the difference between the inside and the outside of a body by trying to get as far inside as possible could be understood as hard core's latest attempt at representing what remains unrepresentable in sexual difference (what Lacanians call the real of sexual difference).[23] In this line of thinking, sexual difference would be the impossible referent for which the inside/outside difference fetishistically substitutes. Yet only in a heterosexist imagination does sexual difference constitute the primary, structuring difference. My comparison between bareback porn and the most extreme straight hard core suggests that the difference between a body's exterior and its interior may be more powerfully motivating than sexual difference. And it is certainly the case that bodily interiors pose a greater challenge for cinematic representation.

WHAT LIES INSIDE

If the pornographic impulse to see inside the body should not be considered automatically as a disavowal of sexual difference, it nevertheless is hardly innocent. The principle of maximum visibility that Williams extrapolates from Foucault inevitably functions as a mechanism of disciplinary power, since rendering something visible represents the first step toward controlling it. In trying to see the body's interior by dilating its apertures, pornography might be attempting to get a grasp on interiority itself, as though to achieve its desired

22. In his study of the straight porn community during the '90s, photojournalist Ian Gittler describes the following scene on a Los Angeles porn set: "Careena's decimated, stretched-wide-open asshole coated in a drippy window of Jon's semen is the most hard-core thing—maybe the most disgusting thing—I've ever seen. Like a car wreck, it's impossible to ignore." From Ian Gittler, *Pornstar* (New York: Simon and Schuster, 1999), 133.

23. See Joan Copjec, "Sex and the Euthanasia of Reason," *Read My Desire: Lacan against the Historicists* (Cambridge, MA: MIT Press, 1994), 201–36; Cynthia Dyess and Tim Dean, "Gender: The Impossibility of Meaning," *Psychoanalytic Dialogues* 10, no. 5 (2000): 735–56; and Slavoj Žižek, "The Real of Sexual Difference," in *Reading Seminar XX: Lacan's Major Work on Love, Knowledge, and Feminine Sexuality*, ed. Suzanne Barnard and Bruce Fink (Albany: SUNY Press, 2002), 57–75.

effects in an unmediated fashion. The camera's penetration beyond a body's surface into its interior does not provide merely visual compensation to the spectator who is unable to penetrate that body with his own penis, tongue, or finger; rather, it is as if a penis could see—as if, in other words, touch could be translated synesthetically into vision. We might say that porn, beyond its blandishments of erotic arousal and release, promises to fulfill the desire to see inside another person by physically getting inside him or her. Hard-core porn's ultimate fantasy thus works along the lines of that decidedly unerotic movie *Being John Malkovitch*.

The desire for direct scopic access to others' interiority could be diagnosed as but another instance of modern power's relentless incursion into previously unreachable zones of corporeal intimacy. Yet the desire to see inside bears a more historically specific motive, in that AIDS gave gay men new reasons to be curious about what's inside our bodies and how it got there. For the first wave of gay men decimated by the epidemic, HIV entered their bodies, via a sexual means, before they knew it. I'm not sure that the traumatic significance of this historical sequence has been fully appreciated: HIV got inside the bodies of individual men and inside the gay community before we were aware of its existence. Bodily and psychic barriers thus were breached on a massive scale. Once the pathogen had been identified as a bloodborne virus in the early '80s, the gay community's immediate response was to devise techniques for insulating individuals from others' bodily fluids—that is, to keep others' insides separate from one's own. Irrespective of his own serostatus, every gay man was urged to erect and maintain prophylactic boundaries between his body and others, especially those with whom he was intimate. But what kind of intimacy insists on maintaining an impenetrable boundary between the persons involved? And what is at stake in maintaining a barrier against something you cannot see, something that thereby becomes particularly susceptible to fantasmatic investment?

The fact that HIV, like all viruses, remains invisible to the naked eye poses a challenge to which bareback porn may be regarded as a response. Confronted with an invisible agent that nevertheless is known to be transmitted sexually, the pornographic principle of maximum visibility must generate strategies for making appear on screen something that cannot be seen. One might have thought that the regular appearance of condoms in porn scenes of anal sex would have constituted sufficient visual reminder of the real risks involved in contemporary gay sex, but condoms represent a barrier, when it is the overcoming of a barrier that demands to be represented. Put somewhat differently, it is the condition of innocence regarding the real risks of anal sex—an inno-cence once universally possessed by gay men but now irrevocably lost—that clamors for representation.

One of the earliest bareback-porn movies, *What I Can't See* (Treasure Island Media, 1999), engages this representational challenge by having its central figure blindfolded throughout the proceedings. Directed by Paul Morris, *What I Can't See* may be said to initiate bareback porn by graphically representing the genre's prototypical sexual encounter—the bareback gang bang. As Morris describes the scenario, "for an entire evening, one cum-hungry San Francisco bottom was mounted bareback by 25 men, taking over 20 loads."[24] What dis-tinguishes this videotape from its successors in the genre is that the guy who is multiply penetrated remains blindfolded: "he never sees the men who are shooting their loads up his ass." Thus what the audience sees is precisely some-one not seeing; the condition of not being able to see what's getting inside your body via sexual means is transformed into a spectacle that can be witnessed. It is as if *What I Can't See* were allegorizing gay life before the discovery of HIV—a life not of sexual hedonism as much as of an inevitable yet temporary blindness to exactly what may be entering one's rectum. We might say that the fantasy motivating this movie is that of being able to choose that temporary blindness, rather than being subjected to it by historical circumstance.

Dismissing such pornography as irresponsibly nostalgic prevents us from appreciating how its attempt to capture something that has been lost con-stitutes one instance of this genre's persistent effort to picture what remains invisible—whether it be the virus, ejaculation inside the body, or the moment of infection. *What I Can't See* may be trying to record on videotape something as abstract (and therefore difficult to visualize) as "history" or, more specifi-cally, what it means to be sexually subject to history, to be subject in one's own corporeal being to radical contingency. A blindfold bareback gang bang arguably offers quite an accurate picture of what it's like to be at the mercy of forces beyond one's control. Far from recklessly ignoring the consequences of unprotected sex, this pornography may be thinking about sexual risk in a quite deliberate way. The trouble is that its manner of doing so makes people uncomfortable, since the possibility lingers that we may be watching—and getting off on—an attenuated version of a snuff film.[25]

24. From http://www.treasureislandmedia.com/tivideo/whaticantsee.htm (accessed June 16, 2004).

25. For a useful discussion of the anomalous genre of the snuff film, see Williams, *Hard Core*, 189–95. Although in bareback subculture the occasion of deliberate infection sometimes is referred

In bareback porn, the absence of condoms is palpable as a visual presence. Gay viewers cannot help noticing that something isn't there, because over the course of more than a decade's worth of pornography we became habituated to seeing condoms used fairly consistently for scenes of anal sex between men (if you wanted to watch rubberless butt fucking, you had to turn to either vintage gay porn of the '70s or heterosexual hard core). Although the mainstream gay porn industry mandated condom use throughout the '90s for actors' protection, there was also a pedagogical motive at work, since it was assumed that viewers imitate the sexual practices that they witness in pornography. Safer sex among actors on screen would encourage safer sex off screen among porn's consumers. The conviction that audiences respond to pornographic stimuli mimetically, by enacting in real life what they see on film, has reasserted itself as a particular anxiety in the face of bareback porn. We fear that these movies eroticize harmful sexual practices and will encourage gullible viewers, particularly younger men, to try the same thing at home with their partners. It is one thing for two HIV-positive men to make the decision to fuck bareback on camera, but quite another for HIV-negative consumers of porn to conclude that condoms are a turnoff or a waste of time.

In this way, the critique of pornography as intrinsically harmful has been extended to gay male porn, which appeared largely immune to the radical feminist description of pornography as a violation of women's constitutionally protected rights.[26] Throughout the '80s, second-wave feminism took porn as a central target of its political campaigns, arguing that women's social subordination was exacerbated if not directly caused by pornographic depictions of them. Robin Morgan's axiom that "pornography is the theory, and rape the practice" became the rallying cry for a range of influential feminist critiques.[27] It was particularly disturbing during this period to witness

to as "the fuck of death," it is important to bear in mind that all performers in bareback porn are assumed to be HIV positive already. In some bareback gang-bang tapes (such as *Riding Billy Wild*), men entering a hotel room to participate in the gang bang are visible signing release forms in the background. There is full disclosure and consent in the production of these movies in a way that there cannot be in the production of a snuff film.

26. In *Only Words* (Cambridge: Harvard University Press, 1993), Catharine A. MacKinnon argues that pornography should be understood not in terms of speech that is protected by the First Amendment but in terms of discrimination (which is illegal under the "equal protection clause" of the Fourteenth Amendment).

27. Robin Morgan, "Theory and Practice: Pornography and Rape," in *Take Back the Night: Women on Pornography*, ed. Laura Lederer (New York: William Morrow, 1980), 139. See also Andrea Dworkin, *Pornography: Men Possessing Women* (New York: Putnam, 1979); and Susanne Kappeler, *The Pornography of Representation* (London: Polity, 1986).

radical feminism's alignment with the religious right, as evidenced in the notorious Attorney General's Commission on Pornography, whose final report
in 1986 adopted Morgan's slogan—and the Dworkin-MacKinnon antiporn
position more generally—as if it were uncontestable common sense. Although some feminists dissented from this position (and several produced
brilliant critiques of the Meese Commission), the pact with religious conservatism helped feminist antiporn rhetoric achieve maximum political clout
during the Reagan years.[28]

For more than a quarter century, the topic of pornography has not only
divided Anglophone feminism but also troubled its alliance with lesbian and
gay politics. The gay liberation movement took on board feminism's critique of
patriarchy and conventional gender roles, at the same time that it resisted the
policing of male desire and of sexually explicit representations. When pornography was defined as violence against women, it was hard to know whether
this definition let gay porn off the hook or just ignored wholesale the importance of porn to gay culture. Ironically, this feminist critique of porn reached
its zenith at a time when the accessibility of VCR technology, together with
fears about AIDS, was encouraging gay men's consumption of hard core on an
unprecedented scale. During the first decade of the epidemic, as homosexuality became the focus of such misinformation and anxiety, access to affirmative
representations of our sexuality was vital for gay men.[29] Thus while some feminists argued that gay porn (and gay culture in general) glorified masculinity to
the detriment of female equality, arguments about the harmfulness of gay porn
tended to concentrate on the age of consent. Gay porn could be criminalized
most readily if it could be imagined as an extension of child pornography. In

---

28. For dissenting feminist positions on pornography during this period, see Bette Gordon,
"*Variety*: The Pleasure in Looking," in *Pleasure and Danger: Exploring Female Sexuality*, ed. Carole S.
Vance (London: Routledge, 1984), 189–203; Gayle Rubin, "Thinking Sex: Notes for a Radical The-
ory of the Politics of Sexuality," in Vance, *Pleasure and Danger*, 267–319; Ellen Willis, "Feminism,
Moralism, and Pornography," in *Desire: The Politics of Sexuality*, ed. Ann Snitow, Christine Stansell,
and Sharon Thompson (London: Virago, 1984), 82–88; and Feminist Anti-Censorship Taskforce
Book Committee, ed., *Caught Looking: Feminism, Pornography, and Censorship* (New York: Caught Looking Press, 1986). For excellent feminist critiques of the Meese Commission report, see Carole S.
Vance, "The Pleasures of Looking: The Attorney General's Commission on Pornography versus Visual Images," in *The Critical Image: Essays on Contemporary Photography*, ed. Carol Squiers (Seattle: Bay
Press, 1990), 38–58; and Susan Stewart, "The Marquis de Meese," in *Crimes of Writing: Problems in
the Containment of Representation* (New York: Oxford University Press, 1991), 235–72. For more recent
feminist critiques of antiporn feminism, see Gibson and Gibson, *Dirty Looks;* and Jane Juffer, *At
Home with Pornography: Women, Sex, and Everyday Life* (New York: New York University Press, 1998).

29. This argument is elaborated best in Simon Watney, *Policing Desire: Pornography, AIDS, and the
Media* (London: Methuen, 1987).

kiddie porn, as in straight porn, it was easier to feel certain about whom men were exploiting.

Of course, the glorification of masculinity in gay porn tends to discourage direct representation of children's sexuality: what gay men want to see are real men, not kids. It is straight pornography that has popularized video series such as *Barely Legal* and *Extreme Teen*.[30] The point here is that representations of nonnormative sexuality are easiest to regulate when they can be understood as nonconsensual—as, for example, in cases of sex with underage partners, where consent cannot be given legally. More than with simply age-of-consent issues, however, the legal rhetoric of consent tends to be mobilized against representations of SM and queer sex on the grounds that viewers who are relatively unfamiliar with nonnormative erotic practices often find it hard to believe that *any* adult in full possession of his or her faculties would consent to participating in such activities. Conservatives like to claim that porn causes moral decay, contributes to the decline of the family, and leads to the disintegration of the social fabric in general. Needless to say, such fuzzy claims are hard to prove in any compelling way. It is far easier to show a porno flick in which actual violence appears to be occurring on screen and then to obfuscate the validity of consent—as the Meese Commission investigators did.[31]

In this context, bareback porn raises a set of questions that have bedeviled legal and cultural debates over pornography in the United States for several decades. Because bareback porn represents activities in which the participants appear to be exposed to potential harm (understood as infection with the virus believed to cause AIDS), it pulls gay porn into an orbit of debate from which it had seemed mostly exempt. Bareback porn, in other words, revives old fears that those engaging in gay sex will be corrupted and harmed. Further, its viewers are at risk of corruption and harm, too. Spectators may be recruited to not merely "the gay lifestyle" (as if that weren't bad enough) but also the fatal habit of unprotected sex. Fueling this anxiety is an assumption that the harm perpetrated in the movie is so toxic as to contaminate mere witnesses. Since the antiporn lobby regards pornographic harm as liable to spread like disease, it follows perfectly that this harm should consist of propagating an actual virus.

30. The popularity of representations of mature men having sex with teenage girls may be gauged by observing that *Hustler's* video series *Barely Legal* has turned a profit of around ten million dollars, according to the documentary *American Porn*.

31. See Vance, "Pleasures of Looking," 47–52.

Some bareback-porn producers explicitly acknowledge this concern. For example, Dick Wadd Media prefaced its early movies with an elaborate warning that occupies seven screens' worth of text, in block capitals against a cerulean background, and that includes the following announcement:

WARNING!
MANY OF THE SEXUAL PRACTICES DEPICTED IN THIS VIDEO ARE
UNSAFE
AND CAN SPREAD SEXUALLY TRANSMITTED DISEASES, INCLUDING
HIV, THE VIRUS THAT IS BELIEVED TO CAUSE AIDS.
LIFE IN A FREE SOCIETY INVOLVES DECISIONS AND
CONSEQUENCES. WE STRONGLY SUGGEST THAT YOU ACQUAINT
YOURSELF WITH THE RISKS INHERENT IN VARIOUS SEXUAL
PRACTICES, THEN MAKE INFORMED CHOICES ABOUT THE LEVEL
OF RISK YOU ARE WILLING TO UNDERTAKE, IN LIGHT OF THE
PLEASURE YOU DERIVE FROM ANY PARTICULAR SEXUAL ACTIVITY.
WE HOPE YOU WILL PLAY SAFELY, BUT ULTIMATELY THE CHOICE IS
YOURS TO MAKE.
OK, WE HAVE SAID OUR SAY, SO . . .
ON WITH THE SHOW!!!

On its own line and in a larger font, the word "unsafe" stands out unmistakably: as will become abundantly clear in the next chapter's discussion of *Niggas' Revenge*, Dick Wadd doesn't pull any punches in either the framing of its films or their content. Fifteen years ago, a statement that explicitly characterized unsafe sex as a viable option would have been unthinkable; such a statement was not within the range of things that could be said. Now, however, this announcement figures unprotected sex as a deliberate choice for which the individual must take responsibility (thus making plain that barebacking entails a conscious decision, thereby denaturalizing condomless sex), at the same time that it disclaims responsibility for whatever action its viewers might commit after watching the video. Dick Wadd Media thus appears cognizant of the possibility that it could be charged with promoting unprotected anal sex— that is, potentially felonious activity. The warning announcement reveals this studio's eminently reasonable desire to protect both its customers and itself.

Yet the very idea of such a warning depends on the notion that pornography conditions its viewers' behavior and therefore could be held accountable for it. Legal and political evaluations of pornography tend to remain unsatisfied by the claim that porn leads to erotic fantasy and masturbation but no further. When considering the influence of bareback porn on gay men's behavior, we need to remember that this genre appeared in response to subcultural practices that already were fairly well organized. The assumption that pornography conditions the behavior of its viewers, whether for better or for worse, fails to explain the emergence of bareback subculture, since if gay men had been conditioned by gay porn during the '90s, then they never would have invented barebacking. The relationship between pornography and its audience's sexual activities therefore must be considerably more complex than a mimetic or behaviorist model allows.

Defenses of pornography tend to appeal to the category of fantasy when explaining the unpredictable effects on behavior of any sexually explicit representation.[32] Porn provides material for erotic fantasy, not a prescription for sexual behavior—or so the argument goes. In demystifying a literalist approach to pornography, the standard defense maintains that fantasy necessarily mediates between representation and action, such that there can be no unequivocal correspondence between representational content and individual action. Of course, this defense must confront the literalist objection that, unlike written porn, hard-core film and video cannot be produced without the sexual behavior that is represented actually occurring between live persons, but this objection can be answered by reference to the facts of consent and therefore does no substantial damage to the standard anticensorship argument. The psychoanalytic category of fantasy still seems to me a politically vital concept in the cultural struggle over pornography.[33] Attempts to regulate sexually explicit imagery always aspire to control the kinds of erotic thoughts that people may entertain. Such efforts are rooted in chronic anxiety about sexual variation, particularly the uncontrollable variety of sexual scenarios that proliferate at the level of the unconscious.

DOCUMENTING A SUBCULTURE

Given the terms of recent debates about pornography, it is striking that the most articulate defense of bareback porn appeals not to fantasy but to its ostensible opposite, documentary realism. As Linda Williams observed in her

32. See, for example, Laura Kipnis, *Bound and Gagged: Pornography and the Politics of Fantasy in America* (New York: Grove, 1996); and Linda S. Kauffman, *Bad Girls and Sick Boys: Fantasies in Contemporary Art and Culture* (Berkeley: University of California Press, 1998).

33. I find it remarkable that any psychoanalyst—anyone whose profession involves thinking seriously about fantasy—would censure porn. A prime example of such simpleminded moralism may be found in Joseph Glenmullen, *The Pornographer's Grief, and Other Tales of Human Sexuality* (New York: HarperCollins, 1993).

discussion of SM porn, "the very conventions of pornography work to en-
force a realism similar to that of documentary film."[34] Progressive defenses of
porn have struggled hard to dissociate it from the literalist implications of the
documentary genre; independent bareback pornographer Paul Morris thus is
swimming against the tide when he makes the case for porn as documentary.
Arguing in his manifesto that he feels a moral imperative to document sexual
variation, Morris explains:

> I think it's a job of porn to reflect the experience and the character of the
> people who watch it. Since danger and risk are so much a part of the sexual
> experience, it's necessary that dangerous activities be represented, and that
> the danger be at least occasionally real and shocking.... [A]ll acts of queer sex
> should be represented on screen with equal honesty. The entire spectrum of
> behavior from innocent to depraved, from life-affirming to death-enhancing
> should be available for the viewers.[35]

Morris characterizes his work as documentary porn—movies that capture
what adventurous San Franciscans are doing in their everyday lives—and
compares it to visual ethnography. There is thus a sense in which his work
could be regarded as one vernacular equivalent of what I'm trying to accomplish in this book.

For the past decade, Morris has been conducting interviews with men
about their sexual practices and recording the results, sometimes—though
not always—on film. He's an amateur anthropologist as much as a pornographer, except that his commitment to recording the full gamut of erotic styles
and practices is not primarily in the service of any analytical or classificatory
project. It is simply in the service of pleasure. One of the most noticeable
features of the movies produced by his studio, Treasure Island Media, is how
much the men in them seem to be enjoying themselves. These men are performing risky sex on film not because they're paid to do so (many are unpaid)
but because they enjoy it. Indeed, Morris notes instances of men offering
to pay him to appear in his videos. For example, he describes the origins of
Breeding Mike O'Neill (Treasure Island Media, 2002) thus:

> This video had its start when young Mike O'Neill came in for an interview. I
> instantly recognized in him the kind of man I'm always on the prowl for. He
> has the most easygoing and happy attitude I've encountered in a long time—

34. Williams, *Hard Core*, 203.
35. Morris, "No Limits," 2, 8.

and he's also an insatiable, world-class, cum-hungry bottom. The first thing he did was to offer to pay *me* if I'd tape him getting fucked by a bunch of guys.[36]

Such requests provide strong motive—beyond his status as an avant-garde pornographer who merits study as a significant auteur in his own right—for examining further Morris's place in the subculture.

Morris makes bareback porn because, by his own account, that is how the men he associates with have sex: he's documenting their behavior. Since he produces films that feature ordinary guys (rather than porn superstars) having sex, ordinary guys regularly approach Morris asking to appear in his films. Unlike mainstream gay porn—which requires its performers to be either beautiful, superathletic, very well endowed, or preferably all three—conformity to narrow aesthetic criteria is not a prerequisite for appearing in "a Paul Morris porno tape." Although consequently most of the men he films aren't professionals, Morris's realist aesthetic remains distinct from that of "amateur" porn, the appeal of which lies primarily in a voyeuristic thrill of seeing ordinary, nonprofessional couples fucking at home. Unlike amateur porn, his work aspires to represent a sexual community to and for itself, a community organized around specific erotic practices rather than around identity (he makes no claim to be documenting anything as broad or identity based as the "gay community").

Not only is Morris interested in representing "all acts of queer sex... with equal honesty," he's also committed to representing on screen the full spectrum of men who engage in those acts. His bareback gang bangs mix good-looking men with the less prepossessing, muscular men with skinny guys and the out of shape, smooth with hirsute, and younger men with the middle-aged. Filmed primarily in the multicultural city of San Francisco, Treasure Island Media videos also tend to be racially and ethnically mixed, without advertising racial categories as fetish items. By aiming to picture a sexual community, Morris's work forms part of that new wave of gay pornography committed to "the eroticism of inclusion," as the founders of Titan Media, a popular gay porn studio established in 1995, describe their enterprise.

The ideal of inclusion developed in response to mainstream gay porn's promulgation of a highly specific sexual ideal during the plague years: "How many men could really fit the image of the hairless, ripped, disease-free twenty-

36. From http://www.treasureislandmedia.com/tivideo/breedmike.htm, emphasis in the original (accessed July 6, 2004).

something? Men of color, men who were underweight or overweight, men with hair on their bodies, older men, men with HIV . . . simply no longer existed in the images of gay sexuality being presented."[37] Titan Media shares with Treasure Island Media an avowedly realist aesthetic, grounded in the assumption that gay porn should reflect its audience's experience rather than offer escape from that experience through fantasy. Nevertheless, Titan Media remains staunchly committed to the use of condoms in all film production, as its announcement immediately before the Darren James case made clear.[38] It is perhaps disconcerting to realize that porn's realist rationale, which remains so distinct from its justification as pure fantasy, depends on a notion of social responsibility that conduces as readily toward bareback sex as toward condom use.

The "eroticism of inclusion" is this medium's version of multiculturalism. According to this ethic, all one-handed consumers—regardless of race, age, body type, or serostatus—should be able to see themselves represented in contemporary pornography. What Morris adds to this ideal of inclusion is an imperative to represent the full array of sexual acts, not just a broader range of physical types. In addition to bareback videos, he also produces a line of "swallow" tapes that focus exclusively on oral sex and semen ingestion; in these videos, "diversity" takes the form of the range of men on which—and the variegated physical settings in which—expert cocksuckers such as Damon Dogg practice their art. Morris even markets a two-part video that documents one man's obsession with having pies thrown in his face. Of *Pie-Face* he says:

This is not a tape for many people. Only buy it if you love pie, if you love unusual compulsions, or if you're a serious student of human nature. I personally think it's great and in its own way very beautiful (and weirdly funny). But if you're looking for regular porn-sex, you won't find it here at all.[39]

Morris offers this video as testimony to the startling variety of nongenital practices that can be eroticized; he thus provides testimony to the fundamental psychoanalytic distinction between the sexual and the genital. Documenting

37. Robert H. Kirsch, Brian Mills, and Everett W. Charters, "The Eroticism of Inclusion: A Gay Pornographic New Wave" (paper presented at the World Pornography Conference, Los Angeles, August 8, 1998), 8, available at http://www.titanmedia.com/wpcpaper.html (accessed November 20, 2000).

38. See "Titan Media Public Policy Statement—'Bareback' or High Risk Behavior," available at http://www.titanmedia.com/promotions/public/NEWS/pages/barebacking. Although this statement was issued on April 6, 2004, one week before news about Darren James broke, discussion of Titan Media's policy has been fueled by the furor surrounding James's case.

39. From http://www.treasureislandmedia.com/pieface (accessed July 10, 2004).

sexual variation enhances our appreciation of just how far human sexuality exceeds mere genitalia—even in a genre that exposes and emphasizes genitalia.

It is worth noting that the eroticism of inclusion substitutes one ideal for another: in place of the specific physical ideal that dominated gay porn for more than a decade, we have the more abstract ideals of multicultural inclusion and representational verisimilitude. Thus in a cultural form—hard-core, gay, moving-image porn—in which we might least have expected to encounter any concern with moral ideals, we find intense debate about the best and most responsible way to represent men having sex together. On the one hand, it may be reassuring to discover evidence of a well-developed sense of representational responsibility in gay hard-core porn; on the other hand, the ideal of inclusion assumes that every viewer should find himself and his preferred erotic practices reflected in pornography. That is to say, the ideal of inclusion derives from a politics of recognition characterized by an understanding of identification that differs little from the naive mimeticism customarily invoked by porn's opponents. Not only does the ideal of inclusion not guarantee representations of condom use in gay porn (as we have seen), but the entire project of making sexuality a source of self-recognition generates intractable problems. When pornographers focus so intently on producing representations in which viewers can find themselves, they neglect porn's promise of an experience in which viewers may lose themselves.

Another way of putting this would be to say that, although the eroticism of inclusion invokes a familiar U.S. ideal of pluralism, it also serves the principle of maximum visibility. Including everybody in the on-screen action provides one more means of showing everything. In this context, "exclusion" would be tantamount to censorship, porn's antithesis. What better way to show everything and everybody than to record a regularly scheduled gang bang that customarily takes place without the presence of a film crew? This is the conceit behind *Fucking Crazy*, a Treasure Island Media offering that explicitly announces itself as a "documentary of a raw gang bang" and explains in its opening frames that "this video was shot at one of the 'Cute Boy Bareback Gang Bang Parties' held monthly in San Francisco." The film documents a local ritual that formalizes the subculture's activities and beliefs; it is thus an ethnographic as well as a pornographic text.

FROM ETHNOGRAPHY TO SEXOLOGY

San Francisco's "Cute Boy Bareback Gang Bang Parties" are described in some detail online. Two men, credited in the video as "Troy and Tracy," make their apartment available once each month for a sex party that advertises in advance who the bottom will be. On the occasion recorded by *Fucking Crazy*, the bottom was sometime porn performer Max Holden. Other gay porn icons, such as Jeff Palmer, have been featured as the bottom at these events, but so have many men with no professional relation to porn. An element of competition pervades the parties, and close attention is paid to how many "loads" the bottom takes inside him on a single evening. The Web site advertising these parties includes a "Loads of Fame Gallery," which lists record holders in the art of semen ingestion; "King of Loads" is the honorific bestowed on Jeff Palmer, who took an astonishing 56 loads at the gang bang in February 2003. Max Holden appears to hold the bronze medal, for taking 32 loads at the August 2002 party, presumably the occasion memorialized in *Fucking Crazy*.

As with any competition, these gang bangs are regulated by a system of self-devised rules. Only one man may take the role of bottom at each party: "versatility" is forbidden. Each of the tops who shows up at the event is obliged to ejaculate in the bottom's mouth or butt, preferably the latter and preferably more than once. Aspirants apply for entry to the party online by sending details about themselves, along with photos, to the organizers; rules and selection criteria appear to be quite stringent but boil down to someone's measure of sexual attractiveness. Access to the event seems to be determined by whether an individual qualifies as "cute" and how amenable he is to following the rules. What issues from this format is something of a sexual marathon; on screen it exemplifies Linda Williams's characterization of hard core as a "frenzy of the visible."

I will have more to say, in chapter 4, about the formal organization of these San Francisco bareback gang-bang parties. Here I want to consider how the documentary ambition of *Fucking Crazy* clashes with the hard-core staple of screening male ejaculation. If the money shot represents a sine qua non of straight pornography, how much more crucial must it be in gay porn, where the spectacle of male sexual pleasure proceeds uninterrupted by lingering concerns about female desire. Although both the documentary impulse and porn's investment in the money shot conform to the principle of maximum visibility, in *Fucking Crazy* they conflict. The problem is that bareback sex involves not just the absence of condoms but also a commitment to internal ejaculation. This problem defines bareback porn as a genre, since the visible evidence that is most wanted is precisely what cannot be achieved without compromising the subculture's values. A sexual subculture that relies on porn for its self-representation must confront the paradox that pornographic convention works against the faithful depiction of its central erotic practice.

In *Fucking Crazy*, this conundrum translates into an extended yet unstructured sequence of shots in which a series of quite disparate men mount Max Holden, some of them numerous times, without it ever being fully clear when someone dismounts whether he has cum inside or is just letting the next guy take his turn. As with most Treasure Island Media movies, there is no mise-en-scène but simply an immediate cut to the action, with a shot of an unsheathed erection about to enter Holden's ass. One of the distinguishing features of this video is that a mise-en-scène of considerable duration—in which we see Holden preparing for his erotic marathon and being interviewed about his expectations by the director—*is* included on the tape, but it comes after the sexual action rather than before it. Prefaced with the intertitle "Erich Lange interviews Max Holden (before the party)," this fascinating exchange, which takes place in Holden's San Francisco apartment, augments the video's documentary status by treating its hero as a sexological subject. Viewers get to see the star in the privacy of his middle-class urban home, as well as peering into his motives for participating in the gang bang.

The interview begins as Holden steps out of the shower, and the camera follows him into his bedroom, where he dresses—in a chain-mail jockstrap, jeans, and faded cutoff T-shirt—for the evening. As with any sexology, the questions that Lange casually lobs at him—"What's it like to feel a guy explode inside you? Can you actually feel it?" "What do you do with the cum after it's inside you?"—are designed to elicit the secrets of Holden's desire. Although one suspects that Lange (who also acts as cameraman in these scenes) must have prepared the questions in advance, Holden's frequent pauses and thoughtful responses lend the interview an unscripted quality that enhances its effect of intimacy. Rather than the intense focus on explicit visual imagery that pornography gives us, in these scenes we hear two men, both of whom are well-known porn performers, talking frankly in a domestic setting about their erotic practices and preferences. Here the secrets of sex come through words rather than images, by virtue of a kind of aural voyeurism. In response to Lange's inquiry about the imminent gang bang, "What makes this hot for you?" Holden responds that it enables him to live out a fantasy and that "the hottest thing is thinking about it beforehand."

"You don't feel degraded?"

"Personally, no."

"Do you feel empowered?"

"I don't think of it in those terms. I feel like I'm honoring, or I'm living out, something that I've spent a lot of time fantasizing about."

Rather than for money or self-empowerment, Holden consents to be gang-banged in order to honor a cherished fantasy; he takes his fantasy seriously enough to work to realize it. We might note that realizing his fantasy remains quite distinct from Holden's experiencing a genital orgasm: at no point during the scenes captured in *Fucking Crazy* does he exhibit an erection or even a semi-erection. This man's *jouissance* is located somewhere other than in his penis.

Another long and informative interview, titled "Max Holden and His Dildos," appears only on the DVD version of *Fucking Crazy*. Once again we are in Holden's apartment, where we hear Lange remarking pointedly, "I just want to know what's in those greasy shoe boxes." The greasy shoe boxes piled in the hallway are loaded with dildos, which Holden unpacks for the camera, narrating stories about each of his "toys" before demonstrating what he likes to do with them. These toys have not only identifying characteristics (in terms of shape, size, and color) but also identifying mythologies. Many are named for porn stars—"This is the Ken Ryker dildo," "This is the John Holmes dildo"—and even the anonymous ones have stories associated with them. Having encountered firsthand some of the genitals on which these toys are modeled, Holden and Lange agree that the dildos tend not to be exact replicas but exaggerations. Inevitably they are larger than life. Indeed, much of Holden's discourse about his toys focuses on how difficult it was to fit these gargantuan objects inside his butt when he first purchased them. "My Dad used to tell me when I was a kid that my eyes were bigger than my stomach, but now my eyes are bigger than my hole." As with taking multiple loads at the gang bang, Holden wants more inside himself than seems physiologically possible. But as his body increases its capacity, he moves on to larger toys, and his dildo collection expands along with his rectum. He speaks not only of the succession of favorites, in which one beloved toy is replaced by another, but also, with some nostalgia, of "retired dildos," "dildo memories," and an earlier collection that a previous boyfriend "made me throw away because he thought that if I had these huge dildos I wasn't going to want his dick, but that's not true." Through this second interview, we glimpse an astonishing libidinal investment in material objects that illuminates their potential for condensing entire sexual histories. Put somewhat differently, we see how erotic narratives quicken inanimate things.

To the extent that these interviews unearth Max Holden's sexual history and his motives for undertaking the gang bang, they function as sexological testimony about one barebacker's desires, fantasies, and pleasures. These scenes resemble the kind of interviews conducted by Alfred Kinsey in the 1940s and '50s, except that here both interviewer and interviewee are porn actors who feature in a gang bang captured on the same tape. The curious blending of pornography and sexology illustrates how these ostensibly discrete discourses both serve the broader principle of maximum visibility, since both aspire to reveal things that usually remain hidden from view. This ambition also animates the documentary as a genre, which—as Louis Menand has observed—is defined by the paradoxical intention to "show you what was not intended for you to see."[40] *Fucking Crazy* thus combines a popular cultural discourse (porn) with a discourse of expertise (sexology) by adapting conventions of another film genre (documentary) to further a general cultural impulse (maximum visibility) that exceeds all three discourses and genres.

If the lengthy interviews that follow the gang bang contribute to *Fucking Crazy*'s documentary status, then so does the striking diversity of participants. These include Erich Lange himself—a strawberry blonde, still youthful-looking veteran of gay porn who must have been working in the adult industry half his life and is now fortysomething—as well as anonymous men of similar age, race, fitness, and sexual proficiency. There are also an unidentified African American and several Asian American tops, in addition to a couple of younger, skinny white guys, one of whom (a bleached blonde) has a prominent scar running from sternum to belly button. While each of these men takes turns fucking Holden on a bed covered with a black comforter, the others watch, stroking their penises and glancing self-consciously at the camera. Lange, the documentary's would-be director, halfheartedly tries to orchestrate the action between bouts of pounding Holden himself.[41]

Fucking Crazy appears unconcerned about contravening the racial stereotype in U.S. gay porn that assumes Asian men should take the role of bottom

---

40. Louis Menand, "Nanook and Me: *Fahrenheit 9/11* and the Documentary Tradition," *New Yorker*, August 9 and 16, 2004, 90.

41. In order to be clear, I should point out that, although Paul Morris customarily directs the movies produced by his studio (Treasure Island Media), *Fucking Crazy* credits him as producer and Lange as director. The tape is introduced as "Paul Morris presents an Erich Lange video," with the understanding that it has the novelty value of being directed by someone who usually appears in front of the camera.

in sexual relations.[42] And, as with other Treasure Island Media productions, this movie betrays no qualm about showing men whose serostatus is visibly apparent. Late in the game, after many of the tops have mounted Holden more than once, a hitherto unseen figure enters the fray, a guy who looks to be in his fifties and whose body bears the unmistakable traces of HIV medications, as well as perhaps of steroid use. His cheeks deeply scored by lipodystrophy, a characteristic side effect of protease inhibitors, this man fucks Holden several times and cums at least once. At one point, he also French kisses the object of all this sexual attention; he's the only participant shown doing so.

Although we assume that those taking part in bareback gang bangs are all HIV positive, it violates a taboo of pornographic representation to show on screen an unmistakably poz guy fucking a healthy-looking man without protection. The anatomical iconography of such a scene makes the presence of HIV palpable. Yet although the moment of the kiss marks this visibly seropositive guy as special, the movie doesn't attempt to distinguish further his cocktail-ravaged body from the scarred body of the skinny blonde or the various nonwhite bodies of other participants. Bareback porn represents as sexual and, indeed, as sexy those bodies that depart in various ways from corporeal norms. The sexual indiscriminateness of these gang bangs militates against the kind of social discrimination all too evident elsewhere in our culture, including in mainstream gay porn.

The sexual action of *Fucking Crazy*, which is confined to the small bedroom of a typically modest apartment in San Francisco's Fillmore district, mimics while nonetheless differing from that of a standard gang-bang loop. What intensifies its gonzo "reality porn" effect is the regular appearance within the frame of one or another of the two cameramen, one of whom (the infamous Damon Dogg) appears to be getting blown by a participant while filming. There is also a balding, middle-aged guy in a blue tank top who periodically gets caught in the shot as he snaps photographs of the proceedings, presumably for the group's Web site. Thus emerges a concentric circle of witnesses to the scene: first the gang of men themselves, who alternate as witnesses and participants; then the film crew, one of whom gets drawn into

42. For critical analysis of this stereotype, see Richard Fung, "Looking for My Penis: The Eroticized Asian in Gay Video Porn," in *How Do I Look? Queer Film and Video*, ed. Bad Object-Choices (Seattle: Bay Press, 1991), 145–68. For an analysis of alterations in this stereotype—specifically, the recent emergence in mainstream gay porn of an Asian American actor "popular for being a fierce top"—see Nguyen Tan Hoang, "The Resurrection of Brandon Lee: The Making of a Gay Asian American Porn Star," in *Porn Studies*, ed. Linda Williams (Durham, NC: Duke University Press, 2004), 223–70.

the action even as he works his camera; and finally the man taking stills. Further witnesses are created when online visitors inspect these pictures on the group's Web site, perusing the photographic record alongside application instructions on how to participate in the next monthly event. And with the filming of this gang bang as commercial porn, another group of witnesses comes into existence, similarly cognizant of the fact that the scenes they're witnessing are of a kind in which they could, if they wish, participate. We might say that *Fucking Crazy* aspires to obviate the distinction between witnesses and participants by converting the former into the latter, thus breaking the cinematic frame and eliminating the distance between observer and observed.

DESIRING WITNESS

Witnessing is central to bareback subculture. The gang bang may be this subculture's paradigmatic sexual form because it guarantees the presence of witnesses even in the absence of a camera. And it is owing to the fact that the activities recorded in *Fucking Crazy* constitute a subcultural ritual, rather than merely a manifestation of unbridled lust, that witnesses are required. Considering the bareback gang bang as a ritual illuminates this pornography's raison d'être. As Morris details the genesis of this particular film:

> One of our passions here at Treasure Island is showing intense, balls-out sex among men exactly the way it really happens. The thing that gets us most excited is when guys approach us and tell us that they want to use us to fulfill and document a fantasy of theirs. Hot and muscular Max Holden gave us a call and said that he was going to be the cum-hole bottom for a San Fran bareback fuck-party. He wanted to know if we'd like to tape it so he could show off to the Treasure Island men his slutty and talented sperm-hole.[43]

Morris also reports receiving requests from ordinary men who wish to become infected with HIV on camera. Of course, since seroconversion usually occurs several weeks after infection, it is impossible to establish until some time after the event whether unprotected sex caught on film achieved the desired outcome.[44]

---

43. From http://www.treasureislandmedia.com/tivideo/fucd.htm (accessed June 24, 2004).

44. See "Visual AIDS," 12. Discussing the ethical issues raised by these requests, Morris also notes pragmatically that, were he to fulfill them, "I'd be putting myself in a felonious position."

These requests testify to both a pervasive desire to be witnessed in non-normative erotic practices and a widespread subcultural knowledge that this pornographer is committed to documenting such practices. This desire and this knowledge have significant bearing on the question of pornography's influence over gay men's behavior. Rather than assuming that the existence of bareback porn encourages gay men to cultivate sexual risk, we might consider how the desire to be witnessed enables an enterprise such as Morris's to exist. The desire to be witnessed precedes the medium through which, these days, it so often is fulfilled. In keeping with the previous chapter's argument about kinship, I want to suggest that the apparently mind-boggling request for a photographic or video record of one's seroconversion (or infection) could be regarded in light of the wholly conventional desire for wedding photographs or a digital recording of one's nuptials.

The desire to be witnessed when undergoing meaningful sexual rituals should not be pathologized as exhibitionism, since it manifests a wish for cultural rather than individual sanction that is particularly important in the case of nonnormative or stigmatized erotic activities. It is less a psychological than a cultural—or subcultural—desire for recognition. Yet given that bareback sex remains a stigmatized activity even in sectors of the gay community, there are those who wish to partake in it without being recognized. These men participate in the subculture, with its impersonal desire for witnesses, while never quite relinquishing their personal desire for the protection of the closet. They show up in Morris's videos wearing costume masks or with their faces hidden by computer-generated devices that the filmmaker introduces during editing. In *Riding Billy Wild* (Treasure Island Media, 2003), another gang-bang tape, each participant is identified by his "nom-du-porn" flashing on screen the first time that he enters the fray; two of the tops in this movie are identified simply as "Don't Show My Face #1" and "Don't Show My Face #2." And in *Breed Me*, the video that established Morris's notoriety, we see almost no faces: the director acknowledges the taboo status of what he's filming by confining camera shots mostly to close-ups and medium shots of dicks and asses.

Men who don't want to be recognized even as they wish to be recorded barebacking on videotape obviously have no professional relation to porn. Although pornography offers a ready apparatus for witnessing, the desire for witnesses is more primitive than the technology through which, these days, it tends to be satisfied. In a fascinating essay on the history of New York's now-defunct Mineshaft sex club, pornographer John Preston elaborates on the significance of witnesses for nonnormative sexual practices:

> The men who climb into the sling to be fist-fucked are *enduring* the act, and they have an audience to prove that they passed the test. While many participants report great pleasure in accomplishing taking a fist up their ass, it's impressive to note that many men report that they have to have the act witnessed for it really to have meaning for them.
>
> This is even more apparent when dealing with whippings. Obviously, the person being flagellated is *enduring* a punishment. It is not sufficient to analyze that action as the expression of a poor self-image.... The performance of a whipping actually has many models in the same primitive societies that the masculinists admire and cite in their literature. This is the Sioux Indian enduring hooks in his chest; this is the walk across hot coals in Polynesia; this is the way a male can enter manhood.[45]

We need to embrace less a masculinist than an anthropological perspective to grasp how witnesses are necessary for initiation into adulthood—or into a particular position within a symbolic order. Preston's reference to "primitive societies" may be understood as a way of indicating how these rituals are modeled on something other than modern heterosexual forms. Unlike animals, which mature into adulthood as part of a natural process, humans require rites of passage—and gay men have had to invent their own. Especially in our culture of adolescence, with its intense pressure to remain youthful, adulthood is not something that one attains merely by staying alive for a certain allotment of time: it requires symbolic initiation and thus witnessing.

The sexual rites of initiation described by Preston—and dramatized in *Fucking Crazy*—may be about establishing generational distinctions that help make evident what adulthood without heterosexuality means. By creating generational distinctions, these rituals provide a structure that enables transmission of the culture (or subculture) from one generation to the next. In other words, the ritual enacted in a bareback gang bang involves sexual contact among not only all members of the group, via the intermediary of the bottom, but also with what the "primitive societies" invoked by Preston would call their ancestors, via the intermediary of the ritual form. By taking all the other men inside him and storing their semen inside his body, the bottom in

45. John Preston, *My Life as a Pornographer and Other Indecent Acts* (New York: Richard Kasak Books, 1993), 60, emphases in the original.

a bareback gang bang may be establishing communication—via formal iden-tification—with previous generations of the subculture. This kind of connec-tion through ritual is especially important for a subculture that has lost whole generations of its members. It is owing to their role as impersonal intermedi-aries—and not just because they endure so much pounding and take so many "loads"—that gang-bang bottoms such as Dawson, Max Holden, Jeff Palmer, and Billy Wild are regarded as subcultural heroes.

THE REVERSE MONEY SHOT

Having characterized the gang bang as this subculture's defining ritual, I now want to consider the various solutions proposed in response to bare-back porn's defining problem—that is, the difficulty of screening money shots when ejaculation occurs internally. One common solution, found in *Riding Billy Wild* and earlier Treasure Island Media gang-bang tapes such as *Knocked Up* (dir. Paul Morris, 2002), is what might be called a *compromise shot*. In a compromise shot the guy pulls out immediately before cumming, so that the camera can record his climax, but then quickly reinserts his penis to finish ejaculating inside. This technique, which calls for considerable discipline on the part of the man having an orgasm, offers a compromise between porn's demand for maximum visibility and the subculture's demand for internal ejaculation. The closer bareback porn approximates Morris's documentary ideal, the fewer compromise shots are present; in *Fucking Crazy*, we see only one such shot. Information online suggests that Max Holden took 32 loads on the occasion documented in this video, but, apart from the single compro-mise shot and one instance when somebody ejaculates visibly into Holden's open mouth, no conventional money shots are provided.

Following theorists of the genre, such as Linda Williams, I have noted how indispensable the money shot is for hard-core film and video. Traditionally male performers are remunerated according to their proficiency at ejaculat-ing on camera—hence this term for the genre's climactic moment. If it is true that you don't have a porno picture without the money shots (to paraphrase Stephen Ziplow), it also is the case that without a money shot the actor prob-ably won't be paid. "Money shot" describes both the volley of semen onto an adjacent body and the technical term for capturing that action on film. One profits from showing it, and pornographers assume that it is what their audience most wants to see. The question that this desire raises for hetero-sexual hard core—why straight guys insist on seeing another man's penis in the throes of orgasm on film, when the sight of an erection in the locker room would send them scurrying for cover—may be answered by reference to the pornographic principle of maximum visibility. The desire to behold what usually cannot be seen encompasses hidden portions of the anatomy, such as the genitals, as well as physiological processes that occur internally. Since this desire remains irreducible to the psychological preferences of individual viewers, it cannot be grasped in terms of psychologistic notions such as sexual orientation. Instead, the principle of maximum visibility refers to an impersonal desire—an operation of biopower—that saturates modern culture independently of identity categories such as straight or gay.

Bareback porn confounds the hard-core imperative to produce money shots and thus motivates generic innovations of various kinds. Besides resorting to what I have called the compromise shot, some Treasure Island Media productions have recourse to a convention of the medium rarely seen in pornography, the subtitle. In *Plantin' Seed* (Treasure Island Media, 2004), a compilation tape glossed as *What Men Do with Spooge, Part 1*, Morris employs the sort of intertitles that have been used to introduce porn scenes since the dawn of hard-core cinema—for example, "Boning Billy Wild." He also employs frequent subtitles, in a white font toward the bottom of the screen, for two purposes—to make fully intelligible what's occurring on screen and to make fully audible what the participants are saying. Although shot professionally and in good light, the copulations unfolding in various locations apparently offer insufficient visible evidence; the subtitles are meant to provide supplementary proof. One category of subtitle consists in legends such as "Jesse unloading inside Nick" or "Jesse dumps another load," which signal the moment of internal ejaculation. Viewers are told explicitly what's happening in the scene when the conventional visual iconography—the money shot—is absent.

In addition to subtitles describing action, *Plantin' Seed* uses subtitles to confirm what the on-screen participants are saying. Often their words are audible, though indistinct. Most contemporary hard-core porn, especially that without plot or dialogue, betrays zero concern for the unscripted words its protagonists utter as they negotiate their sexual paces, preferring to substitute a generic musical soundtrack that is punctuated only by equally generic grunts and moans. In the pre-video age, these grunts and moans often were dubbed, during the postproduction phase, by actors hired for their voices rather than for their bodies (twenty years ago, I met an unusually handsome and beefy Englishman whose looks had earned him a role in a U.S. gay porn flick but whose dialogue had been dubbed by someone with an American accent and a deeper voice). Plotless porn—that is, the majority of today's medium-to-low budget porn—supplements the space of potential dialogue with background music: porn stars are meant to be seen and not heard. Thus it is highly unusual to find a low-budget porn tape taking the trouble to ensure that its actors' unscripted words are not lost but actually emphasized.

For example, during the scene alluded to above, in which ornately tattooed Jesse pounds Nick, a character identified on screen as Tom Sawyer, who is dressed in grubby overalls and a red baseball cap, encourages the action with audible but indistinct lines that appear as subtitles: "Tom: 'Yeah, knock him up and feed me too.'" Viewers familiar with the subculture will recognize this as a vernacular instruction for Jesse to ejaculate inside Nick and thereby provide Tom with an opportunity to felch semen out of Nick's butt. Immediately before the descriptive subtitle "Jesse unloading inside Nick," we get another telling dialogue subtitle: "Tom: 'Ah fuck man, I can feel it kicking.'" The speaker's hand is clasping Jesse's genitals as the latter ejaculates internally; the subtitle thus offers surrogate evidence for what cannot be seen. Visually Tom Sawyer is in the same position as the video's audience, unable to witness a money shot, but he is in a superior haptic position and can testify to feeling with his fingers the shudder of the other man's orgasm. Subsequently, while felching Jesse's semen out of Nick's butt, Tom pauses to murmur his satisfaction, and we read on screen, "Tom: 'Damn, that's good eating, man.'"

Doubtless these subtitles function in part to preserve the colorful vernacular—"Tom: 'Put those swimmers in there deep man and I'll eat them out'"—that appears to be muttered spontaneously by this individual. Far more literate than most contemporary pornographers, Morris understands the erotic appeal of an idiosyncratic verbal discourse accompanying sexually explicit visual images. Instead of the generic background music that typically furnishes porn soundtracks (often an electronic version of disco in the case of gay videos), Morris heightens his movies' documentary effect by retaining all the contingent noises—traffic roaring by, a radio show playing intermittently, his own enthusiastic remarks to the participants, periodic silence—that occur during filming. The graininess of the soundtrack thus complements the grittiness of the action. As he notes in his online description of *Fucking Crazy*:

> It's been a general rule in Treasure Island Media's videos not to use music in the soundtracks. FUCKING CRAZY has, as one element of its soundtrack,

ongoing "house" music throughout. This was not a decision by Erich Lange or
T.I.M., but was part of the given ambience set up by the party-givers.[46]

So strong is his documentarian commitment that Morris refuses to edit even
the auditory intrusion of generic background music when it constitutes a
noncommercial choice on the part of the men whose ritual he's recording.

In keeping with his challenge to pornographic conventions, Morris likes
to capture not the generic but the idiosyncratic. Preserving Tom Sawyer's col-
loquial diction clearly contributes to that project. But one cannot help noticing the image repertoire from which Tom's lingo is drawn. When he says, "Ah
fuck man, I can feel it kicking," he is referring not to intrauterine life but to
the spasm of internal ejaculation that, in other circumstances, might create
it. And when the action is over, he gazes at Nick's butt and declares, "That's
a knocked-up hole." Groping Jesse's penis, he says admiringly, "Damn, that's
a big cunt wrecker he's got" (all these utterances are subtitled). Pornography
through the ages has invented many synonyms for *penis*, but this is the only
occasion on which I have encountered the term "cunt wrecker." Hearing this
dysphemistic vernacular pronounced unselfconsciously in Tom's low drawl,
we gather that it is the subcultural argot of *breeding* that Morris wishes to
capture for his audience—even if it entails the potentially alienating device
of subtitles in order to do so.

Yet the subtitles are doing more than preserving a subcultural vernacular.
Paradoxically they are using verbal language to translate visual action into
sense, thereby betraying the impotence of vision alone to capture raw sex. The
audience sees subtitles rather than semen; testimony substitutes for visible
evidence. We could say that, instead of the image of whitish fluid suddenly
coming out of a penis, viewers are given, in white lettering at the bottom of
the screen, a representation of something suddenly coming out of someone's
mouth. Subtitles thus constitute another kind of compromise shot. Porn
shows us all manner of part-objects entering the body—a penis, a tongue, a
finger, a hand, a dildo, bodily fluids, a speculum, the eye of a camera—and it
must show us what comes out, even if that amounts to little more than words.
Insofar as it aims to capture what bodies release involuntarily—what they
have to be coaxed into discharging—bareback porn exhibits its most distinctive version of the money shot when all the "loads" that have been ejaculated

46. From http://www.treasureislandmedia.com/TreasureIslandMedia__2007/xcart/product
.php?productid=16156.

inside a single bottom come back out again. I call this spectacle the *reverse money shot*.

Breed Me opens with a reverse money shot, rather than ending with one; it thus inverts porn's traditional narrative sequence as well as the direction in which audiences are accustomed to seeing semen flow. Without warning the screen is filled with a close-up of a pale, hairy ass being worked by a dildo with one hand, while another hand holds a blue measuring cup that collects the remarkable volume of semen emerging from the guy's butt. After three almost intolerably long minutes of this footage, the camera cuts to a close-up of the measuring cup, which contains what appears to be a dozen or more loads of ejaculate. With its harsh lighting, minimal production values, and the untanned, untrimmed, stretched-out butthole, this scene has an amateur-ish, anti-aesthetic quality. But in terms of the history of AIDS, the scene is extraordinary. Gay men watching it realized that they were witnessing the most dramatic visual evidence of "unsafe sex" ever presented on film. Although the image is graphically unmistakable, it comes out of nowhere, with no mise-en-scène or even minimal narrative context; it thus may be regarded as traumatic, since the audience is unprepared for such an image and cannot escape the impression that what it is witnessing is taboo. The reverse money shot thus was established as a principal convention of the subgenre by way of visual trauma. With this opening sequence, Morris restored to gay porn a sense of transgressiveness and a capacity to shock that largely had vanished from the genre. It was for this reason, I imagine, that *Breed Me* became the top-renting gay porn video for April 2000 in the Castro.[47]

The reverse money shot that begins *Breed Me* does not present an aesthetically pleasing or even a conventionally sexy image. It is meant to disturb, and its abrupt appearance contributes to the disturbing effect. In characterizing the function of pornographic imagery, German film theorist Gertrud Koch suggests that "only through the image can the observer confront that which would otherwise frighten him."[48] Her comment helps explain the popularity of *Breed Me* at this historical juncture, since many of the men wishing to view such imagery would not necessarily have wanted to be in the position of the man whose reverse ejaculation they're witnessing. This scene inhibits identification rather than soliciting it. The video, whose opening credits reveal its

47. As reported in "Visual AIDS," 13.

48. Gertrud Koch, "The Body's Shadow Realm," trans. Jan-Christopher Horak and Joyce Rheuban, *October*, Fall 1989, 21.

full title as *Paul Morris Diaries, Vol. 1: Breed Me*, thus serves both documentary and fantasy functions simultaneously. It offers an image calculated to arouse, although with considerable ambiguity about what sensations its audience is meant to experience.

I have noted that contemporary hard-core porn centers increasingly on anal eroticism in both its gay and straight variants. Although representations of ass fucking have become virtually de rigueur in heterosexual as well as gay hard core and although dilations of the anal sphincter appear across the board, viewers are accustomed to seeing their butt sex headed, as it were, in only one direction. As dirty and nasty as it gets in one sense, pornographic images of anal sex are expected to remain meticulously clean in another sense. The market for scat is small indeed. Seeing any bodily product coming out of an anus tends to provoke a visceral reaction of disgust in most adults, irrespective of sexual orientation. I think that this is what gay medical sociologist Michael Scarce was referring to when he characterized the opening scenes of *Breed Me* as having "a high ick factor."[49] The spectacle of a reverse money shot takes some getting used to; various sensations have to be overcome before one can find such an image unequivocally erotic. Fluids that trace the pathway of shit as they leave the body almost inevitably recall our earliest taboos about what's sexually enjoyable.

The opening scenes of *Breed Me* include a close-up of the remarkable volume of seminal fluid collected in the measuring cup but stop there. We are never shown what happens to all that ejaculate or the uses to which it might have been put. Subsequent offerings from this pornographer betray no such reticence. In *Fucking Crazy*, as in *Breed Me*, there are various scenes of guys felching their own cum out of the bottom's ass; this is standard bareback-porn fare. The climax of *Fucking Crazy* comes at the end of the gang bang, when Holden squats on the bed and squeezes the accumulated semen from his ass into a black bowl held carefully beneath him. Following this reverse money shot, he lies on the bed and slowly tips the bowl so that the fluid pours into his open mouth. Having at last emerged from his shapely butt, it all immediately goes back down his gullet.

In the interview "Max Holden and His Dildos," we learn that what looks like a stunt (and perhaps inspired the video's title) in fact constitutes "a normal thing in my life." Having discussed his dildo collection with Lange, Holden prepares to demonstrate how he plays with his toys. At this point,

49. Comments in "Visual AIDS," 16.

it becomes apparent that, to Lange's surprise, Holden has semen inside him from sex the night before. He then relates the details of his usual practice: "If I go out and get fucked and I have cum, loads, inside me, I save it inside me, and then the next day I squat it out into a bowl, and then I'm playing with my toys and I eat it." He proceeds to demonstrate this by squatting over a color-less glass bowl and releasing the contents stored in his rectum. "It's sorta like milking a cow," he comments as he pushes a stream of milky liquid from his butt. An hour or so later, after the seminal fluid has grown cold in the bowl while he works his butt with dildo upon dildo, Holden drinks from the bowl and the movie ends.

The spectacle of someone consuming what has emerged from his own rectum challenges another level of disgust. It is one thing to felch your own freshly laid semen out of the butt that you've just been fucking or to mess around with what has been ejaculated inside you, but it is quite another to feed on an accumulation of substances that you have expelled from your anus. When barebackers take "No Limits!" as their rallying cry, we see that they're emphasizing how sex can function as an arena in which the most basic barriers—including those of disgust and shame—may be negotiated or overcome. Freud claims not only that desire is capable of overcoming disgust but that "the sexual instinct in its strength *enjoys* overriding this disgust."[50] Sexual desire might be described as that which can be satisfied only by ex-ceeding a limit, specifically, a boundary of one's own psychic constitution. It is not just culturally conventional boundaries but one's own real limits that must be defeated in order to achieve complete erotic enjoyment. The motto "No Limits!" thus entails the challenge of locating new limits to repel, as if in an imperialism of desire.[51]

50. Freud, *Three Essays*, 152, emphasis added. On this topic, see also Jonathan Dollimore, "Sex-ual Disgust," in Dean and Lane, *Homosexuality and Psychoanalysis*, 366–86.

51. This is especially apparent in pornography that aims to push the envelope of sexual rep-resentation, such as that produced by Rob Black and Lizzie Borden of Extreme Associates, a con-troversial straight-porn company in North Hollywood that became the central target of Attorney General Ashcroft's antipornography campaign. See Kevin Gray, "What, Censor Us?" *Details*, De-cember 2003, 132–37. See also Michael Kirk's documentary *American Porn*, which focuses on Ex-treme Associates and the production of its indicted video *Forced Entry* (dir. Rob Black, 2002), a rape-fantasy movie. In Extreme Associates' *Cocktails* video series, heterosexual gang bangs conclude with the female star being forced to ingest a mixture of semen, spit, and bile generated during the scene. Likewise, the video *Creampie Milkshakes* (dir. Rob Black, Extreme Associates, 2004) is described thus in a publicity flyer: "Watch as 6 girls get their assholes stretched out by speculums then filled with cum and milk. Then every girl drinks this asshole milkshake to the last drop." As with Morris's *Fucking Crazy* and *Plantin' Seed*, this kind of pornographic action pushes the limits of sexual disgust by focusing on performers who consume substances that have been expelled from

INTIMACY AT A DISTANCE

To say that Morris and his associates lack squeamishness would be to understate the case. In fact, they are connoisseurs of semen. Not content with ingesting seminal fluid the moment it is ejaculated, they specialize in devising uses for "spooge" that has been stored somewhere awhile. We have seen Max Holden's technique for getting the same batch of cum both up his ass and down his throat—consuming it at both ends, as it were. Another variant of bareback porn's money shot consists in collecting semen from various sources, mixing it together, and then funneling it inside somebody at a later date. This is the bareback version of artificial insemination—being bred by guys you've never touched or met. We might call it the paradox of unlimited intimacy at a distance.

This conceit animates *Plantin' Seed*, one of Paul Morris's more recent films. The sequence of gang bangs that composes the movie is punctuated by scenes of an expert cocksucker, named Joey Summers, blowing a series of anonymous men through a glory hole at Folsom Gulch, a notorious adult bookstore in San Francisco's SOMA neighborhood. Released in spring 2004, the season for seed sowing, *Plantin' Seed* plays on the idea that semen can be used to grow things—an idea that was foreign to gay culture before the development of an elaborate discourse surrounding HIV transmission. The film opens with a solo model ejaculating into a funnel apparently held by the cameraman. The funnel's presence suggests that this conventional money shot is to be enlisted in the project of defying pornographic convention by representing not a terminus but a beginning. As an initial deposit, it represents the mise-en-scène of a larger narrative that includes the subsequent, apparently unrelated scene, identified by subtitle as "Joey milks two at Folsom Gulch, San Francisco." The point of a glory hole is anonymity, and this scene of an average-looking guy— pale complexioned, with short beard, pierced tongue, and backward baseball cap—sucking off two random dicks in succession could have been filmed al-

---

the throats, anuses, and penises of various individuals. Although one cannot help registering the similarities between nominally straight and gay forms of extreme porn, a crucial difference lies in the fact that Treasure Island Media men perform these actions voluntarily and often for free, whereas the women in Extreme Associates movies perform them only because they're making money to do so. The difference lies not in the question of consent but in desire: Max Holden wants to perform these elaborate transfers of bodily fluids on and for himself, whereas the guys employed by Extreme Associates want to make a woman perform these actions while themselves remaining spectators. For details of the obscenity prosecution against Extreme Associates—the federal government's first major prosecution for obscenity in more than a decade—see *United States of America v. Extreme Associates, Inc.*, 352 F.Supp. 2d 578 (W.D. Pa. 2005).

most anywhere. However, Morris's documentarian commitment prompts him to supply the identifying details, and it is clear that the action is not occurring on a stage set constructed for the purpose of filming, as is usually the case in porn scenes of glory-hole sex. Subsequent scenes, subtitled "Joey milks three more" and "Joey milks another four," confirm the impression that this probably is how Joey spends a significant portion of his time.

The difference between what might be Joey's habitual practice and what is represented on screen lies in not only the presence of a camera but also the fact that Joey doesn't swallow. Instead, he takes the men's ejaculate in his mouth and spits it into a Tupperware container that slowly accumulates "seed." (These scenes of Joey spitting out the fruits of his labor might be considered weaker versions of bareback porn's reverse money shot.) The rationale behind this accumulation of seminal fluid is not revealed until the concluding scene, in which we are introduced to a handsome young man—identified via subtitle as "Jonas: his first time taking seed"—who has it all funneled into his rectum at the climax of the final gang bang. After several men have fucked Jonas, ejaculated inside him, dressed, and departed, the blue plastic funnel that we saw in the opening scene and the Tupperware container observed earlier reappear, along with what looks like a standard hotel-room wineglass. As Joey transfers the contents of his Tupperware bowl to the wineglass, we hear an off-screen voice commenting, "Joey worked hard for that." The funnel is placed in Jonas's anus and, against a background of street noise (the hotel room's window is open) that includes sirens wailing and a clock striking five, a remarkable volume of viscous fluid is poured into the funnel, from which it seeps slowly into his rectum. The next shot shows Joey using his fingers to milk the seminal fluid back out of Jonas's butt and into another man's mouth waiting below.

Through aggregation and ingenuity, *Plantin' Seed* has transformed the pornographic convention of discrete money shots into numerous transfers of fluid—what might be termed a *multiple displaced money shot*. Alluding to "funneling," a drinking practice common in college fraternity subculture whereby alcohol is siphoned directly into the esophagus via a funnel and tube in order to accelerate intoxication, this film evokes also the dynamics of initiation and competition—how much can you take?—that characterize membership in exclusively male groups such as fraternities. Rituals of excessive ingestion enable homosocial bonding with men whom one might never have met: one acquires membership by undergoing what previous generations of brothers have undergone. In *Plantin' Seed*, Jonas is inseminated with the ejaculate of men whom we have every reason to believe he's never encountered. The subtitle claiming that what we're witnessing is "his first time taking seed" encourages us to view the funneling ritual as Jonas's initiation. And although Jonas looks as though he could be a college student, the conceit of initiating a newbie—of capturing "the first time" on film or of deflowering a virgin—is a well-established porn convention that dates back at least to Sade.

But what if this really were Jonas's "first time taking seed"? What if he were HIV negative prior to these scenes in *Plantin' Seed*? What might this film be documenting? Such concerns are compounded by the fact that we cannot be sure whether the men getting blown through the Folsom Gulch glory hole were aware either that their anonymous sex was being videotaped or that their ejaculate was going to end up anywhere other than inside the guy blowing them. HIV is a weak virus that is killed by exposure to air; nevertheless, there is an ethical problem in appropriating men's semen without their knowledge or consent. Given the low risk associated with oral sex, a seropositive man in San Francisco might consent to an anonymous blow job, whereas he wouldn't necessarily consent to having his ejaculate transferred into a third party's rectum. In the final interview of *Fucking Crazy*, Max Holden observes that guys who fuck him bareback are often "totally disturbed" to learn his elaborate plans for what they've ejaculated inside him. What's disturbing is the notion of a hidden intention or alternative trajectory for one's semen beyond the immediate circumstances of ejaculation. Once expelled from a man's body, semen is outside his control. But he does not expect it to be under someone else's control. The possibility that one's ejaculate might be used for unknown purposes—that something could be done with it about which he remains ignorant—conjures a fantasy of alien abduction in which otherworldly beings extract human genetic material for sinister ends.

Or perhaps this popular fantasy offers a narrative to explain a common masculine anxiety, namely, that we cannot always be certain about the destiny of what we often so casually ejaculate. For gay men this anxiety is intensified by the specter of HIV pervading our sexual communities. Thanks to the virus, our lives are intimately connected with men we've never even seen, not only those we may have slept with and forgotten. The epidemic has shown how something that belongs to a complete stranger can get inside me for good. Thus the point of funneling and the multiple displaced money shot of *Plantin' Seed* may be less to document an actual initiation than to allegorize these complex relays of viral transmission—to picture how a man can get something inside his body from some guy he's never met. Funneling may be bareback porn's way of dramatizing the sex-education dictum that each time you have sex with someone, you're also having sex with all the people he's had sex with. From this perspective, every sexual encounter amounts to a gang bang—as Freud once noted, albeit in somewhat different terms.

In a letter to Fliess on August 1, 1899, Freud commented that "I am accustoming myself to regarding every sexual act as a process in which four individuals are involved."[52] Speaking in the context of a budding theory of bisexuality, Freud was inferring that every heterosexual encounter involves a man's "feminine disposition" interacting with a woman's "masculine disposition," as well as an interaction between the man's masculinity and the woman's femininity. The comment reveals his conception of the unconscious in terms of differently gendered persons—an early instance of Freud's revising the conventional understanding of heterosexuality via a notion of the unconscious. Sexual difference becomes less recognizable once the unconscious is taken into account. As his theory of identification became progressively complex, however, Freud saw more than four people in even the most conventional coupling. No longer a question of constitutional bisexuality but of an individual's identifications with and ambivalence toward his or her parents of both sexes, every sexual encounter involves multiple generations, as well as multiple ghosts. The Freudian bedroom is a densely populated space. We might say that when classical psychoanalysis pictures people having sex, it can't resist conjuring a gang bang. Group sex thus represents not only a paradigmatic form in bareback subculture but also the typical form that sex takes in the psychoanalytic imagination.

Another way of putting this would be to acknowledge how certain activities count as "group sex" even when no more than two persons are physically present. By way of its inventiveness with what I'm calling the "multiple displaced money shot," bareback porn is particularly adept at making apparent how sex involves persons who are not physically present—except as fragmentary, material traces—and therefore how sex regularly explodes the couple form through which it typically tends to be misrecognized. A vivid dramatization of this insight may be found in the subcultural practice of fashioning what is known as "the Devil's Dick." The recipe for this delicacy entails collecting multiple loads of ejaculate in a single condom, freezing the contents, and then using as a dildo the super-sized cum popsicle that results. Paul Morris's

52. See Sigmund Freud, *The Complete Letters of Sigmund Freud to Wilhelm Fliess, 1887–1904*, ed. and trans. Jeffrey Moussaieff Masson (Cambridge, MA: Harvard University Press, 1985), 364.

Breeding Season (Treasure Island Media, 2006) opens with such a scenario. In a montage sequence titled "Making the Devil's Dick," we see floating across the screen in slow motion various shots of different penises individually spurting into a shot glass, each accompanied by a legend indicating its place in the sequence—"#47," "#23," and so on. After about a minute's worth of screen time, during which fourteen money shots are shown, a legend boasting "73 Loads of Cum" translates remarkable footage in which the ejaculate is poured slowly, without spilling a drop, from a large transparent container into a condom that balloons under the weight of the accumulated liquid.

A quick dissolve reveals an opalescent, frozen-sperm dildo being liberated from its rubber casing and put to work in an erotic encounter between two men in a hotel room. Things get messy pretty quickly, as the Devil's Dick begins to melt and thus to make available a distinctively fragrant lubricant. One of Treasure Island Media's regular tops, Steve Parker, drools melting semen over his hairy chest and erect penis while "sperm-dump Dylan" avidly laps it up, even going so far as to lick out the over-used condom. They comment appreciatively on the aroma, and Parker remarks, as he starts wielding the Devil's Dick as a dildo on Dylan's butt, "This boy's gonna be loaded with spawn." An off-camera voice inquires, "Think you can fuck him with it? Think it'll go in?" When, indeed, the Devil's Dick has been inserted fully inside Dylan (to considerable acclaim), Parker informs him, "You've got seventy loads of cum in you right now." The highlight of this scene occurs when, perhaps unable to bear the frozen object inside him any longer, Dylan shoots it back out of his ass in a spectacular variation of the reverse money shot that happens so fast it has to be caught in a slow-motion action replay in the bottom left-hand corner of the screen. "There it goes," someone cries amid general laughter and cheers.

Melting rapidly, the Devil's Dick is absorbed as lubricant into what becomes a typical bareback gang bang. Yet Dylan's taking inside him the entire load of frozen semen clearly represents an impressive feat, perhaps a new record in sperm ingestion, that is registered formally by Morris's adopting the slow-motion instant-replay convention from televised sports. Addressed by Steve Parker throughout these opening scenes as a "cum pig," Dylan attains the status of subcultural hero through this activity; his masculinity is enhanced, rather than impugned, by his ingestion of the oozing seminal object.[53] As seventy-three loads of ejaculate melt into his orifices and over every

53. This subcultural practice gives the lie to critical claims that, as Murat Aydemir puts it, "sperm may be the male substance that brings about the threat of formlessness to masculinity's de-

surface, it becomes impossible to tell whose semen is inside him and whose is outside; he is pervaded by the erotic traces of others.

If the pornographic boudoir tends toward overcrowding (multiple performers plus film crew), then the Devil's Dick scene that begins *Breeding Season* and the funneling scene that ends *Plantin' Seed* help us to see how it is crowded with not only persons but also ghosts, that is, the residual traces of persons. When the funnel is inserted into Jonas's anus or the cum popsicle into Dylan's, these men simultaneously insert themselves into a secret history through acts of identification with men who have preceded them. One consequence of what might be called this ritual summoning of ghosts is that sexual action generates sexual community, irrespective of how crowded or empty the scene of this action might be. Ritualized bodily movement engenders a kind of impersonal identification with strangers past and present that does not depend on knowing, liking, or being like them. In other words, impersonal identification doesn't require one to imagine—or to believe in—a shared psychological identity. The implication is that certain sexual activities evoke history and community even when practiced alone, thereby complicating still further the contentious debates about "public sex." This implication reverberates into the solo jack-off scene that accompanies the credits of *Plantin' Seed*.

As this film's credits roll, we hear the sound of someone urinating, and the image of a handsome man pissing naked in the woods in bright sunlight appears. The man has not featured in the movie's complex action; he is relieving himself solo, his penis semierect. The next shot shows him squeezing semen out of his cock into his hand; he then proceeds to eat it, grinning in the sunshine. These bucolic images point to the fifth solution that bareback porn proposes in response to the genre's central problem of capturing money shots when ejaculation is internal. The first solution that I described was the *compromise shot*, in which a man in the throes of orgasm struggles to ejaculate partly outside and partly inside the guy he's fucking. The second solution

---

termined maintenance of form." From Aydemir, *Images of Bliss*, xxii. In his interesting deconstructive account of semen's potentially corrosive effects on normative masculinity, Aydemir considers hardcore pornography at some length, although he seems unfamiliar with the bareback genre, which has been doing new things with ejaculate for a decade. In *Breeding Season*, as I've tried to indicate, contact with the melting Devil's Dick (which might be regarded as exemplifying the abject and the formless) serves not to undermine but to enhance dramatically this distinct form of masculinity. Put another way: in light of French feminist Luce Irigaray's query regarding "why sperm is never treated as an object a," we can see how, in these scenes in which it is most strikingly treated as such, the results hardly approximate the feminist outcome that Irigaray envisages. See Luce Irigaray, *This Sex Which Is Not One*, trans. Catherine Porter (Ithaca, NY: Cornell University Press, 1985), 113.

adopts the cinematic convention of subtitles to inform viewers verbally that ejaculation has occurred outside the camera's range of vision. A third solution, which I called the *reverse money shot*, consists of filming seminal fluid as it is expelled anally. The fourth solution involves a complicated relay of ejaculations, storage, and transfers that provoked the awkward designation of *multiple displaced money shot*. The fifth solution employs urine as a spectacular substitute for semen. In so doing, it directs our attention to bareback subculture's proliferation of fetishes and the question of what it might mean to construe unprotected sex—and even HIV—as a fetish. Turning from the work of Paul Morris to that of Dick Wadd, the next chapter develops the present discussion of bareback porn by examining the significance of fetishism in the subculture.

THREE: VIRAL FETISHISM, VISUAL FETISHISM

How does something invisible to the naked eye become a fetish?

In the previous chapter, I anatomized the various techniques invented by bareback porn to deal with the problem of screening internal ejaculation. Bareback subculture depends on pornography for its self-representation; yet hard-core porn's principal visual convention (the money shot) undermines the subculture's commitment to fantasies of insemination or "breeding." Suggesting that one of several solutions to this problem consists in the screening of arcs of urine as a spectacular substitute for absent money shots, I want to consider further how bareback porn specializes in creating visual substitutes for something that cannot be seen. The psychoanalytic term for the process of creating a visible substitute for something perceived as missing is fetishism—a notion that Freud borrows from anthropological studies of "primitive" cultures and discovers everywhere around him in the modern world. Fetishistic practices in contemporary sexual cultures are redoubled in pornography, whose structures of representation rely on visual fetishism; indeed, bareback subculture organizes itself around the fetishizing of numerous images, objects, and activities. What I find most remarkable about this subculture is its fetishizing of not a visible entity but a microbe—the "bug"—that cannot be perceived with the naked eye. Bareback subculture complicates what we mean by fetishism not only because it constructs a pathogen as desirable but also because it focuses so intently on the invisible rather than the visible. This chapter approaches the issue of fetishism by examining the subculture's proliferation of fetishes, beginning with the popularity of piss.

FETISHISM AS SUBCULTURAL DISCOURSE

There is very little pissing in Paul Morris's movies but a great deal in those by Dick Wadd. According to his own account, the man who defiantly took as a business name one of his family's epithets for describing his behavior as a child had trained as a certified public accountant with no intention of starting a porn company: "I was just minding my own business when a dear friend, Walter Wallace of New York, former owner of the infamous Mineshaft, called me and said the world needed a good piss video."[1] Aspiring to fulfill his friend's request, Dick Wadd claims that, in making his first film, *NYPD* (Dick Wadd Productions, 1997), he did not set out to produce bareback porn:

> I am a player, not a spectator, so I had seen only two porn videos in my life when I filmed *NYPD*. I had no idea that it's standard industry practice for men to wear condoms in videos. We just filmed the sex the way we had it that day; not one guy in *NYPD* wore a condom, and we thought nothing of it. Unwittingly, *NYPD* became the first barebacking film of the new generation before the term "barebacking" was even coined. I received a significant amount of fan mail and one piece of hate mail from a guy who felt I was a mercenary ruthless killer who was promoting unsafe sex for profit.[2]

Although it beggars belief that an urbane gay man in 1997 could be innocent of the gay porn industry's convention of using condoms for anal sex, various gaffes involved in the production of *NYPD* suggest that Dick Wadd was mostly fumbling in the dark. The term "barebacking" had been coined when he made his first video, but it had not yet become a commercial marketing category for pornography. What most interests me about his account of *NYPD*'s origins is how Dick Wadd imagined himself as producing a water-sports video, when in retrospect he was making bareback porn. Catering to one fetish, he helped to invent another.

More precisely, Dick Wadd helped to make unprotected sex an item on the fetish menu, recasting it as a fetish rather than as a slipup. From passing unnoticed as garden-variety fucking, condomless anal sex became visibly marked—and thus marketable—as a specific preference, even a condition of arousal. Considering the modes by which something becomes marked and thereby amenable to eroticization, I'm interested in how invisible, virtually

---

1. Parker Moore, interview with Dick Wadd, *Unzipped Monthly*, March 2001, 52. The name Dick Wadd carries particular resonance in the history of hard-core film pornography: one of porn superstar John Holmes's recurring screen characters was called Johnny Wadd.

2. Ibid.

abstract entities such as HIV can be fetishized. In this chapter, I explore how fetishes are constituted through processes of visible identification and, in particular, how the subculture's proliferation of fetishes—its multiplication of the number of identifying marks—poses a challenge to the disciplinary project of normalization that strategically exploits the principle of maximum visibility. In other words, I want to make the case for fetishism as a technique of identifying signs and practices that nevertheless refuse to cohere into identities. And by making this case, I want to go some way toward depathologizing fetishism.

As his company's home page testifies, Dick Wadd counts bareback sex as just one among a myriad of fetishes represented in his porn: "Dick Wadd offers the finest in water sports, bareback, fetish and pig video in the world. If you want piss, raw fucking, fisting, dildo work, spit, cum swallowin', felching, armpit and boot work... and much more you've cum to the right place, buddy!" The list's ellipsis implies that this catalogue could be extended, since every aspect of sex carries fetishistic potential; in this pornographic universe, any visible mark or action is capable of being fetishized. For example, water sports (or urolagnia) concern not merely a fetish for piss but the finer points of whether you prefer to give or receive, whether you prefer urine in your mouth or your butt, whether you wish to drink from the source or have it administered via enema, whether you want to be hosed with it from a distance or gulp it directly from a penis lodged in your throat, whether you prefer recycled beer or the funky stuff that hasn't been watered down. Under the rubric of this single practice, fetishistic possibilities proliferate. I mentioned in this book's introduction my conversation with a man in the cooling-off area of Blow Buddies sex club; among the things he told me was that he offers "Crixivan piss," alluding to a particular HIV medication that, like asparagus, lends a distinctive flavor to urine. "That's definitely an acquired taste," he observed.

The conversation confirmed what Dick Wadd's porn vividly illustrates, namely, that *any* sexual taste can be acquired, because objects and activities apparently unrelated to sex are more or less susceptible to eroticization. Sexual fantasy is capable of colonizing virtually every object and space. One example not mentioned explicitly in Dick Wadd's catalogue of fetishes but evident throughout his videos is leather. Even those outside the "leather community" take for granted that there is something potentially erotic about this material, although nothing makes dead-cow skin necessarily sexual, let alone the basis for group identity. A complex set of semiotic and psychic operations must be performed alongside the technical process of skinning and tanning in order to transform animal hide into "leather." My point is that whatever we happen to find erotic condenses a history of metamorphoses and investments that have made it so. According to the classical Freudian definition, an object becomes a fetish when it stands in for the mother's missing penis. This idea betokens an extraordinarily naive, unpsychoanalytic understanding of sex, insofar as genitalia provide a comparatively negligible component of sexuality—even in many gay contexts. What's fascinating about Dick Wadd porn is the determination, despite its name, to multiply sources of pleasure beyond genitalia by pushing the limits of what may be sexualized. Nothing that enters this pornographic frame is exempt from potential eroticization.

Dick Wadd porn thus operates within a distinctly psychoanalytic worldview. By showing how human sexuality has less to do with genitalia than with the unconscious, Freud argued that nothing is sexual until it is made so. Sexuality conforms to the dictates of fantasy, not to those of anatomy. Even genitalia require sexualization before they can be considered erotic, as any child will tell you. At a certain moment in the history of psychoanalytic thought, Lacan turned Freud's theory of fetishism on its head by declaring that, rather than the fetish substituting for the mother's missing penis, the penis itself "takes on the value of a fetish."[3] Lacan's claim is that heterosexual women fetishize the penis—although he might as well have said that gay men do so too. Indeed, plenty of straight men seem to fetishize their own penises; in the classical account, a fetish protects the normative male's penis by protecting his mother's. According to the canonical psychoanalytic description, then, fetishes function to make sex *safe*.

Freud's theory of sexuality tended to fetishize the penis quite unselfconsciously, attributing to it a value unwarranted by either empirical circumstance or his own theoretical discoveries. Likewise Lacan's theory approaches a fetishization of the phallus, even as it employs the latter concept to complicate the Freudian understanding of fetishism. Theoretical blind spots notwithstanding, these psychoanalytic accounts offer a description of human sexuality as ineluctably fetishistic, in the sense not of referring ultimately to the penis (or the phallus) but of drawing attention to the fantasmatic transformation of objects that have no preordained psychic value.[4] The dense weight of

3. Jacques Lacan, "The Signification of the Phallus," in Lacan, *Écrits*, 290.

4. Here I am summarizing the complex argument of Freud's *Three Essays on the Theory of Sexuality* (in vol. 7 of *Standard Edition*, 123–345), an argument that I unpack at greater length in *Beyond Sexuality*, chap. 6. Freud's later account of fetishism appears in his canonical "Fetishism," in vol. 21 of *Standard Edition*, 149–57. Lacan characterizes human sexuality as intrinsically fetishistic by showing how desire is initiated by *l'objet petit a*, the part-object that remains largely invisible, though no less alluring, in the sexual other.

cultural convention persuades us to distinguish some forms of sex as fetish-istic, while others (such as heterosexual genital penetration) are understood as "normal" sex by virtue of their fetishistic histories having been naturalized. From a psychoanalytic perspective, even vanilla sex counts as sex by virtue of its having undergone a mostly invisible process of fetishization—a process that is largely invisible because it coincides with heteronormative culture.

One implication of this psychoanalytic argument is that, since nothing is inherently erotic, virtually anything can become so. A feat of the imagina-tion has been accomplished when persons, objects, and actions that seem conventionally unattractive or even repulsive are made sexy and pleasur-able. Fetishism should be thought of less as a defense against the "trauma" of sexual difference (Freud's argument) than as a creative strategy; rather than as a precautionary measure, it might be understood as an index of psy-chic inventiveness. When an ordinary or devalued object—one thinks, for example, of a used jockstrap or dirty underwear—is transvalued and made precious, we glimpse the extraordinary power of fetishism to destabilize cul-tural hierarchies. Although plenty of fetishes are predictable (big cocks, big breasts), not every case of fetishistic transformation is as trivial as the ex-ample of used underwear. Predictable fetishes are overdetermined by reign-ing cultural values, whereas less-predictable instances point to the cultural underdetermination of certain fantasies—and hence to the possibilities of erotic creativity.

What I'm calling an aptitude for erotic creativity draws on materials, forms, and practices that already exist in the culture. As Gayle Rubin suggests,

> I do not see how one can talk about fetishism, or sadomasochism, without thinking about the production of rubber, the techniques and gear used for controlling and riding horses, the high polished gleam of military footwear, the history of silk stockings, the cold authoritative qualities of medical equip-ment, or the allure of motorcycles and the elusive liberties of leaving the city for the open road. For that matter, how can we think of fetishism without the impact of cities, of certain streets and parks, of red-light districts and "cheap amusements," or the seductions of department store counters, piled high with desirable and glamorous goods ... ? To me, fetishism raises all sorts of issues concerning shifts in the manufacture of objects, the historical and social spec-ificities of control and skin and social etiquette, or ambiguously experienced body invasions and minutely graduated hierarchies. If all of this complex so-cial information is reduced to castration or the Oedipus complex or knowing

or not knowing what one is not supposed to know, I think something important has been lost.[5]

Understanding fetishism entails some appreciation of developments in technology, shifts in patterns of manufacture and consumption, urbanization, and the formation of different sexual or subcultural communities. To Rubin's list, one would want to add the histories of cinema, video, and now computer-mediated spectatorship. None of these sociohistorical developments in themselves fully accounts for the psychic operations that transform something into a fetish, although they do delimit fetishism's material conditions of possibility.

Perhaps because they have so much experience with eroticizing stigmatized activities—and because their communities came into being by way of the historical developments just mentioned—sexual minorities have become extremely well versed in the art of fetishization. Somewhat akin to how the gay community of the 1960s and '70s fought to depathologize the category of homosexuality (they succeeded in getting it declassified as a mental disorder in 1973), the fetish community has fought to depathologize fetishism by wresting its definition from psychiatric experts. The point must be to expunge the stigma that clings to fetishism as a diagnosis, without rendering it as a purely voluntary practice—that is, without eliminating consideration of the unconscious. We need a psychoanalytic understanding of the unconscious to support the argument that sexuality is determined by fantasy rather than by anatomy, and we need a depathologized understanding of fetishism to explore the limits of this understanding of sex.[6]

5. Gayle Rubin, "Sexual Traffic," interview with Judith Butler, *Differences* 6, no. 2-3 (1994): 78–79.

6. The depathologizing of fetishism as an analytic category has come from two main directions, namely, that of lesbian feminism articulated within a psychoanalytic framework, on one hand, and that of poststructuralist cultural anthropology, on the other. The principal coordinates of the debate within lesbian psychoanalytic feminism are Teresa de Lauretis, *The Practice of Love: Lesbian Sexuality and Perverse Desire* (Bloomington: Indiana University Press, 1994); Elizabeth Grosz, "Lesbian Fetishism?" in Grosz, *Space, Time, and Perversion: Essays on the Politics of Bodies* (New York: Routledge, 1995), 141–54; and E. L. McCallum, *Object Lessons: How to Do Things with Fetishism* (Albany: SUNY Press, 1999). For an interesting critique of the status of fetishism within queer theory, see Brad Epps, "The Fetish of Fluidity," in Dean and Lane, *Homosexuality and Psychoanalysis*, 412–31. For more anthropologically oriented critiques, see the following two collections of critical essays: Emily Apter and William Pietz, eds., *Fetishism as Cultural Discourse* (Ithaca, NY: Cornell University Press, 1993); and Patricia Spyer, ed., *Border Fetishisms: Material Objects in Unstable Spaces* (New York: Routledge, 1998). The sexual minority project of depathologizing fetishism would need to overhaul not only the classical psychoanalytic account of fetishism but also that of classical Marxism, since the critique of commodity fetishism

Dick Wadd pornography explores the limits of sex by fetishizing what might seem, at first blush, unattractive, unpleasurable, or downright repugnant. In the magazine interview from which I've been quoting, Parker Moore concludes by asking him, "What haven't you done that you'd like to do?" Given what's represented in Dick Wadd videos (and described in the interview), it is hard to envisage any sexual taboos left to break. However, the pornographer replies, "One thing I've wanted to do in my work is make a statement about hate, and I will realize that dream with the filming of my next video at the end of January."[7] This "statement about hate" turned out to be *Niggas' Revenge* (Dick Wadd Productions, 2001), described as "the most controversial video of the decade," and the bareback movie that provides the principal focus of this chapter. In addition to its spectacular dramatization of multiple visual fetishes, *Niggas' Revenge* illuminates what usually remains invisible even in pornography. By doing so, the film helps us to grasp how something that cannot be seen can become fetishized nonetheless.

WHITE-BOY TROUBLE

Although it makes no direct mention of racism or homophobia, *Niggas' Revenge* is prefaced by an explicit "statement about hate," which immediately follows the warning about unsafe sex, quoted in chapter 2:

> Hate is born of fear, ignorance, superstition and low self-esteem. Hate breeds on itself and has been responsible for more deaths than any other external force on the planet. Hate crimes, such as those committed against the Jews during the Holocaust, are becoming more commonplace in our society, as people cling steadfastly to ideologies and religions and make no allowances for diversity of being or thought. Hate must be eradicated from the consciousness of the human race if it is to survive.

This statement relies on our assent to various clichés (the commitment to "diversity," the notion that hatred is generated by "low self-esteem"), rather than on logical coherence, to make its point. The fantasy of eradicating hatred from the human race is, in the end, not so distant from that of eradicating homosexuality or Jewishness from the human race; indeed, from a psychoanalytic perspective, the determination to externalize negativity—exemplified in the

---

construes fetishism as an error amenable to political demystification. In my view, a political argument needs to be mounted *against* the standard progressive demystification of fetishism.

7. Moore, interview with Dick Wadd, 54.

belief that hatred "must be eradicated from the consciousness of the human race"—motivates continuing cycles of hatred and violence. One cannot help wondering whether the claim that "hate ... has been responsible for more deaths than any other external force on the planet" is meant to compare hatred with disease—for instance, HIV/AIDS—as a source of human mortality and thus to imply that hatred is both distinct from and more reprehensible than, say, unprotected sex. Despite its incoherence, however, this "statement about hate" dramatically alters the meaning of the scenes that follow.

Alluding to "hate crimes" in a gay porn video conjures the specter of gay bashings (a recurrent motif in mainstream gay porn); yet the example specified here is Nazi atrocities against Jews. Describing the Holocaust as a hate crime, although not altogether inaccurate, risks trivializing it—as if the violent manifestations of bigotry in contemporary U.S. society were straightforwardly analogous to Holocaust violence. Yet our inclination to censure this comparison may be mitigated by learning of Dick Wadd's biographical connection to victims of the Holocaust: "My adopted grand-mom, her husband and daughter escaped a concentration camp, but her son did not. The evils of hate and intolerance were consciously impressed upon me at an early age by her and my teachers."[8] How might a boy who was raised by Holocaust survivors and who grew up to become a pornographer represent that history in a movie? Surely it would be pushing the limits of representation and decency beyond any remotely acceptable point to make a porno about the Holocaust?

The question of pornography surfaces repeatedly in cultural debates about the ethical problems of Holocaust representation. Philosopher Berel Lang identifies the subgenre of concentration-camp porn as the baseline from which other deplorable representations of Nazi atrocities must be measured. But when historians and cultural commentators refer to a "pornography of the Holocaust," as they increasingly do in these debates, the term *pornography* is being employed metaphorically, as a kind of shorthand for the commodification of atrocity, the voyeurism unleashed by media spectacles of suffering, and the diminishment of empathy among contemporary audiences.[9] In her

8. Ibid.

9. See Berel Lang, *Holocaust Representation: Art within the Limits of History and Ethics* (Baltimore: Johns Hopkins University Press, 2000), 7, 19, 48. A sample of unreflective invocations of the "pornography of the Holocaust" may be found in Lucy Dawidowicz, *The Jewish Presence: Essays on Identity and History* (New York: Holt, 1977), 224; Philip Gourevitch, "Behold Now Behemoth: The Holocaust Memorial Museum: One More American Theme Park," *Harper's*, July 1993, 60; Alvin H. Rosenfeld, "Another Revisionism: Popular Culture and the Changing Image of the Holocaust," in *Bitburg in Moral and Political Perspective*, ed. Geoffrey H. Hartman (Indianapolis: Indiana University

exhaustive study of the rhetorical uses of the term *pornography* in European and North American culture since World War I, intellectual historian Carolyn Dean demonstrates how persistently the term is used to evade issues that defy explanation. She argues that, "in most invocations of pornography in the context of Holocaust representations[,] pornography is an alibi for a relationship between cause and effect that is nowhere named or explained: it stands in for a framework able to account for the relationship between moral and political perversion, between the loss of moral and the loss of political affect, between the excitement associated with sadism and the numbness associated with fascism, Nazism, and anti-Semitism."[10] Pornography and, through it, homosexuality thus become associated rhetorically with the greatest atrocities of the twentieth century.

Needless to say, this widespread rhetorical usage is detrimental to sexual minorities and to any argument—whether queer, feminist, or otherwise—in favor of pornographic representation, its pedagogical values, and its specific visual pleasures. When the term *pornography* is coined metaphorically, it tends to be unequivocally pejorative, not neutrally descriptive; when used in this manner to characterize nonsexual representation, the term hinders our capacity to think analytically about sexual representations. As Dean suggests, "pornography is an infinitely plastic, dizzying term: a term whose concentration of rhetorical force and explanatory power is such that its meaning is not really held to account. . . . [The term] does not encourage but freezes discussion, and this function is arguably its most significant accomplishment."[11] It is as if, faced with unfathomable horror and the difficulty of representing it responsibly, otherwise-intelligent commentators resort to the label *pornographic* as something that we can agree to censure without further debate. This strategy leaves little room for thinking clearly about actual pornographic representations or the men and women who make them.

Niggas' Revenge is not directly about the Holocaust, although it does feature three neo-Nazis. In this movie, the neo-Nazis attempt to harass their African American neighbors, who quickly turn the tables and take revenge on their persecutors. Anti-Semitism thus is figured in terms of the most

---

Press, 1986), 90; and George Steiner, *In Bluebeard's Castle: Some Notes towards the Redefinition of Culture* (New Haven: Yale University Press, 1971), 55.

　　10. Carolyn J. Dean, "Empathy, Pornography, and Suffering," *Differences* 14, no. 1 (2003): 106. See also Carolyn J. Dean, *The Frail Social Body: Pornography, Homosexuality, and Other Fantasies in Interwar France* (Berkeley: University of California Press, 2000).

　　11. Dean, "Empathy, Pornography, and Suffering," 93.

common expression of racial hatred in the United States—white racism to-ward African Americans. Dick Wadd draws an analogy between U.S. racism and German anti-Semitism, at the same time that he draws on an established porn convention of representing interracial sex as a punishment meted out by blacks to whites. Transposing anti-Semitism into racism against African Americans makes sense for video pornography in that the black/white differ-ence lends itself to starker, more dramatic visualization than do other racial or ethnic differences. In bareback porn, the black-on-white contrast also may be a way of making visible less perceptible differences, such as that between HIV-positive men and their HIV-negative counterparts. A black man fucking a white man without protection adds salience to the idea of revenge.

It is the "niggas," not the Jews, who take revenge on the neo-Nazis in this movie, as described by Dick Wadd thus:

> White neo-[N]azi supremacists fuck with the wrong niggas and get their comeuppance from the huge-muscled, huge-cocked Blake boys: Bobby, Flex-Deon and Chris... and their Puerto Rican buddy, Eric Top Stud. The [N]azis are arbitrarily and brutally used as fuck holes, urinals and cum repositories in the most controversial video of the decade.[12]

This vernacular description conveys the video's contents quite accurately, ex-cept for one detail. Although the neo-Nazis are indeed brutalized and used re-peatedly as urinals by the African American performers, they are not shown as "cum repositories": the movie concludes with a series of conventional money shots, and there is no evidence of internal ejaculation. Dick Wadd remains too invested in the pornographic principle of maximum visibility—at least in this movie—to accommodate those aspects of the subculture that Paul Mor-ris attempts to capture. Far from documentary, *Niggas' Revenge* is pure spec-tacle, and the astonishing volume of urine unleashed during the proceedings enhances its spectacular visuality.

The film's visuality also is intensified by its endeavor to capture forms of verisimilitude associated with involuntary movements of the body, such as spasms or swooning. In this respect, it is identical to documentary. The con-troversy surrounding *Niggas' Revenge* derives primarily from the movie's mise-en-scène, in which we see bodies losing control and exploding into violence. On hearing the insults hurled at them by the neo-Nazis, the three black men

---

12. Jacket copy of *Niggas' Revenge* (Dick Wadd Productions, 2001).

proceed to beat up and humiliate the white men in an extended scene of startling ferocity. Here is the director's account of this mise-en-scène:

> This video, as all Dick Wadd videos, was not scripted. There was a two-minute
> premise where the neo-[N]azis taunted the Blakes with racist epithets; how-
> ever, the taunts touched upon a genuine anger deep inside the Blakes that had
> been buried for decades . . . and no one had any idea of what was to come next.
> These Blake studs wanted to teach the neo-[N]azis a lesson they wouldn't soon
> forget! Bobby thrashed the white boys with his belt so hard that Chane Adams
> went into involuntary convulsions and Bud was knocked out with a 2x4![13]

In what appears to be real fury, the black men rough up the white men, rip-
ping off their clothes, slapping them, pushing them to the ground, spitting
and pissing on them, kicking and stamping on them, thrashing them with
a leather belt and then a plank of wood, and taunting them by rubbing their
faces in the mud, asking repeatedly, "Who the nigga now?" For a long time
during this scene, the white porn performer known as Bud Hole lies motion-
less on the ground; at a certain moment, we glimpse Chane Adams shaking
uncontrollably and moving off screen to recover. It is in these scenes of violence, rather than in the sex scenes, that we witness most vividly porn's characteristic "frenzy of the visible."[14]

After twelve minutes of this violent action, the neo-Nazis are dragged into
the basement apartment of the African Americans' "Puerto Rican buddy,"
where they are treated as prisoners and locked inside a large dog cage. There
they are forced to drink more "nigger piss" from an aluminum dog bowl. The
sex play that follows consists of the African Americans dominating their
white prisoners by sodomizing them orally and anally, repeatedly spitting
and urinating on them, fisting them, whipping them, and verbally abusing
them. Performing a range of actions recognizable to the leather community as
"fetish" activities, the black men play master to the white men. Doubtless the
erotic charge of these scenarios is overdetermined by the spectacle of African
Americans transforming white men into their slaves. The historical specter of
Southern slavery, as well as that of the Holocaust, hovers over the immaculate
California apartment in which these activities occur. Furnished as a modern

13. From http://www.dickwaddfetish.com/niggasrevenge8.htm.

14. I suspect that the violence in these scenes appears acceptable to viewers in a way that it would
not if the roles were reversed (white men beating up black men) or if the scenario were a heterosexual
one (men beating up women). Because the white actors are coded as Nazis, we are able to overlook
how physically puny they are, compared with the fabulously muscled African American men.

dungeon—a space devoted to fetishistic sex play—the apartment features (along with its dog cage) a leather sling, wooden stocks in which the white men are immobilized for fucking, and a bathtub in which they are pissed on freely. This apartment thus functions as a sexual theater whose backdrop evokes historical violence and trauma.

Not only are the activities, context, and paraphernalia recognizably fetishistic, the participants' bodies also are loaded with fetish insignia. Regarding the shaved heads and musculature of the African American performers, we might say that their whole bodies have been phallicized, engorged through weight training and what appears to be steroid use. They also are heavily pierced and tattooed, especially Flex-Deon Blake, who, in addition to pierced ears, eyebrow, nipples, and navel, sports a formidable Prince Albert through the head of his penis.[15] The thick silver hoops that adorn his body are complemented by the chain-link harness that he dons for the sex scenes, along with black leather boots, which all of the dominant men wear throughout the proceedings. On his enormous shoulder in Gothic script is tattooed "FLEX," a detail suggesting that either this performer is deeply committed to his "nom-de-porn" or he hasn't bothered to take one. The tattoo lends a sense of diminished distance between representation and the real that enhances viewing intimacy.

This sense of diminished distance also is fostered by Dick Wadd's Web site informing viewers that Flex-Deon Blake and Bobby Blake are "real life partners," which contributes to the illusion that we're observing a spontaneous, "unscripted" expression of these men's authentic desire. In the fiction of this movie, the three African American men are represented as brothers, not just "bruthas." This is particularly significant with respect to the film's single instance of "versatility," when an African American takes the bottom role and Bobby Blake fucks Chris Blake next to the stocks. Here the fantasy would be that of witnessing not interracial but incestuous gay sex. The cultural prohibition on unprotected anal sex is by no means the only taboo that this movie contravenes. A fantasy about violating the incest taboo explains the momentary appearance on screen of an African American woman, named in the credits as Crystal Blake, who is shown folding laundry in the Blake brothers'

15. Although a typical accessory in contemporary gay fetish and BDSM sexual cultures, the Prince Albert originated in late-nineteenth-century England, where it was known as a "dressing ring" by Victorian haberdashers, who used it "to firmly secure the male genitalia in either the left or right pant leg during that era's craze for extremely tight, crotch-binding trousers, thus minimizing a man's natural endowment." See Doug Malloy, "Body Piercings," in *Modern Primitives*, ed. V. Vale and Andrea Juno (San Francisco: Re/Search Publications, 1989), 25.

apartment and whom I take to represent their mother. Her appearance defies the most elementary convention of gay porn by interrupting the fantasy of an all-male universe. Yet the interruption of this fantasy facilitates the more profound fantasy of sexual congress between siblings. As I suggested in my earlier discussion of the subculture's experiments with kinship, overcoming some version of the incest taboo represents a decisive aspect of barebackers' commitment to unlimited intimacy.[16]

RACIAL FETISHISM

Violating a taboo is not the same as erecting a fetish, although many fetishes—for example, bareback sex or interracial sex—derive their power from an awareness of transgression. Here I am interested in how *Niggas' Revenge* is using a fantasy of interracial male-male rape to imagine other, less visible forms of transgression. It may be necessary to dramatize the violation of multiple cultural prohibitions—against homosexual sex, against interracial sex, against nonconsensual sex, against incestuous sex, against kinky or violent sex, against urinating on another person—in order to conjure the transgressive charge of unprotected anal sex among gay men. Thanks to its construction as a taboo, something that officially remains impermissible under any circumstances, unprotected anal sex among U.S. gay men has come to seem transgressive and thus amenable to fetishization, when it otherwise might be regarded as ordinary or simply ill advised. Gay men have become so practiced in the fetishistic art of transforming phobic objects into sources of erotic pleasure that some of us have started to fetishize HIV too. The homophobic construction of HIV/AIDS as the ultimate horror positions the virus as available for fantasmatic translation into an object of queer desire.[17] Thus even as this chapter's project involves an attempt to depathologize fetishism by showing how it need not entail a disavowal of specifically sexual difference, I want to indicate the problems attendant on fetishizing a virus.

This perilous dynamic plays out in *Niggas' Revenge* through a complex form of racial fetishization. Thus far I have refrained from stating explicitly

16. Sex between siblings is a recurring porn motif. In *Swallow* (Treasure Island Media, 2000), a Paul Morris video focusing primarily on oral sex, much is made of the fact that two of the young men shown fucking bareback are brothers and that Morris is documenting what they regularly do in their everyday lives.

17. That unprotected anal sex and, in some cases, HIV have become fetishes may be deduced from the disavowal that typically structures gay men's relation to them: "I know very well that HIV is the cause of AIDS, but all the same...." See Octave Mannoni, "Je sais bien, mais quand même...," in *Clefs pour l'imaginaire ou l'autre scène* (Paris: Seuil, 1969), 9–33.

what may be the film's most obvious kind of fetishism, because I wanted to anatomize the multiple visual fetishes involved—leather, muscles, tattoos, piercings, chains, whips, boots, spit, piss—and, by arguing for the affirmative potential of fetishistic practices, to suggest the political importance for sexual minorities of depathologizing fetishism. Insofar as the performers in *Niggas' Revenge* and the audience watching it enjoy not just one but a dizzying array of fetishes, they are not treating objects or activities in the manner of Freud's prototypical fetishist, who fixates on a single "fetishistic precondition" for arousal.[18] Fetishism, that is to say, does not seem to be functioning in the movie as what Freud characterizes as a neurotic or perverse defense. This is necessary to bear in mind when we consider how representations of racial fetishism tend to be interpreted as anxious defenses against the threat posed by racial or ethnic difference.

Critiques of racial fetishism, including queer critiques, tacitly repathologize fetishism in ways that strike me as troubling. The classic instance of the pathologizing of racial fetishism appears in Afro-Caribbeanist Frantz Fanon's account of how his interpellation as a "Negro" reduces the psychoanalyst's subjectivity to his skin, in the process dehumanizing him. "I am the slave not of the 'idea' that others have of me but of my own appearance," he explains.[19] Objectified primarily in phenotypic terms, Fanon attributes this racist response to white anxieties about black sexuality, arguing that a fear of blackness is but the obverse of a desire for it that is provoked by stereotypes about "the sexual potency of the Negro" (157). Although discussed almost exclusively in heterosexual terms, Fanon's point that blackness tends to be construed sexually by whites, whether positively or negatively, holds for same-sex interracial relations too. Experiencing racial difference as erotic is, according to Fanon, part and parcel of the same "massive psychoexistential complex" that perpetuates white racism (12); hence his insistence that "the man who adores the Negro is as 'sick' as the man who abominates him" (8). Desiring blackness entails the fetishizing of skin color according to the same stereotypical conceptions about African primitivism, animalistic sexuality, supersized genitals, and so on that fuel racial discrimination. The eroticization of black skin is thus at one with the dehumanization of black people. By extension, the eroticization of white skin is inseparable from the idealiza-

18. See Freud, "Fetishism," 152.

19. Frantz Fanon, *Black Skin, White Masks*, trans. Charles Lam Markmann (1952; repr., New York: Grove, 1967), 116. Subsequent page references are cited in the text.

tion of white people and therefore compounds the problem. From Fanon's perspective, black men who want to have sex with whites "clearly wish to be white" or are motivated by a "lust for revenge" (14)—an argument that helps illuminate the rationale of Dick Wadd's movie. In this account, there can be no interracial eros that is not ultimately racist, no way of blacks and whites being together sexually that does not contribute to racial oppression.

One might have thought that a later historical moment, a different cultural milieu, or the shift from a heterosexual to a gay context would mitigate this sweeping critique of racial fetishism. But in view of recent complaints about interracial sex in contemporary porn by a hip, gay, African American cultural critic, that does not seem to be the case. In his book *Why I Hate Abercrombie & Fitch*, Dwight McBride devotes a long chapter to rehearsing the very same critique of racial fetishism as Fanon, albeit without mentioning him. Identifying "the fetishistic nature of blackness" in gay interracial porn, McBride laments that "black male sexuality seems to be ever in the process of being both reduced and exaggerated to its central signifier—the big black phallus."[20] As with Fanon's objection to having his subjectivity reduced to stereotypes about his skin, McBride objects to the persistent stereotyping of African American sexuality in gay porn. Pornographic representation flattens the complexity of what it means to be black and thus strays too far from realism for McBride's tastes. Although he claims to be propornography and anticensorship, McBride's argument differs little from that of antiporn feminists in the 1970s and '80s: porn is bad because it represents women and blacks fetishistically, reducing them to cunts and big black dicks, when in actuality they are so much more than that. Like antiporn feminists Dworkin and MacKinnon (and like Fanon in another context), McBride finds that pornographic representation "dehumanize[s]" those whom it fetishizes.[21]

The complaint that pornography traffics in stereotypes and that, in so doing, it fetishizes virtually every physical attribute or social marker seems to me entirely accurate but wholly misplaced. The complaint is misplaced because it objects to the defining structures of pornographic representation. The desire to make porn socially responsible by making its representations

20. Dwight A. McBride, "It's a White Man's World: Race in the Gay Marketplace of Desire," in *Why I Hate Abercrombie & Fitch: Essays on Race and Sexuality* (New York: New York University Press, 2005), 109–10.

21. McBride, "White Man's World," 126. Although it seems strange that he omits any mention of Fanon, it is more surprising that, in this lengthy chapter, McBride fails to mention, much less engage, the argument about pornography elaborated by another African American gay intellectual whose book appeared six years earlier in the same series as his. See Delany, *Times Square Red*.

of sexuality and subjectivity more realistic ignores what makes porn exciting. In asking porn to be more responsibly realistic, we forget that it functions primarily as fantasy and that something akin to stereotypes may be indispensable to fantasy's effective operation. Trying to make fantasy conform to political dictates, no matter how progressive the political principles involved, is misguided and dangerous—misguided because the unconscious remains definitively uneducable and dangerous because such an Orwellian project smacks of thought control and censorship. Sexual minorities have faced such a dispiriting history of demands to make their erotic fantasies and desires conform to more socially appropriate, responsible, or realistic criteria that it is particularly troubling when the same demand comes from someone cognizant of that history.

What may seem to be the politically incorrect tendency of erotic desire has to do not so much with an unwillingness to relinquish nasty stereotypes but with an antihumanist inability to respect the inviolable integrity of personhood in the sphere of sexuality. By this I mean that, under the sway of the unconscious, erotic desire fragments and partializes those totalized forms that consciously we recognize as persons. It is not whole persons whom we find sexually arousing but partial objects; we find an individual to be arousing by discerning in him or her the lineaments of a partial object. I like the curve of his eyelashes or his butt; what gets me is the tilt of his head as he laughs. This is what Lacan means when he refers to objects of desire as "in you more than you"—and it is what makes desire ineluctably fetishistic.[22]

McBride takes exception to this notion of "in you more than you," regarding with righteous indignation the way that sexual desire tends to make people see in others something that isn't actually there. He argues that "the function of both whiteness and blackness in the marketplace of desire is to dehumanize (though toward markedly different ends) the person to whom they are ascribed and to endow them with qualities that they often do not possess."[23] "Dehumanize" is a pejorative way to put it; instead, I would say that desire *impersonalizes* its objects and, in so doing, reveals its origins not in sexual difference but in the fragmenting effects of language on the human body. In my view, the psychoanalytic insight that erotic desire is not founded in sexual difference qualifies as good news for queer politics, because it furnishes conceptual

22. See Jacques Lacan, *The Four Fundamental Concepts of Psychoanalysis*, ed. Jacques-Alain Miller, trans. Alan Sheridan (Harmondsworth, UK: Penguin, 1979), chap. 20.

23. McBride, "White Man's World," 126.

ammunition for the ongoing critique of heteronormativity. Once we recognize that sexual desire is never originally the desire for a person of the opposite sex, heterosexuality loses its privileged status as natural and normative; it then requires explaining as a specifically conditioned object-choice with a particular history, just as much as any other sexuality does. The Lacanian critique of object-choice understood in terms of gendered persons and the queer critique of heteronormativity are, I would argue, versions of the same critique.[24]

If erotic desire does not originate in sexual difference, then there is no reason to assume that it originates in racial difference either, even as it is demonstrably the case that sexual identities are racialized and that, likewise, racial identities are constituted along axes of sexuality. Here I am trying to distinguish between two arguments that, to me, seem potentially compatible but necessarily distinct. The first argument concerns the historical construction of sexual and racial *identities*, whereas the second concerns the constitution of interracial erotic *desire*. Scholars such as Siobhan Somerville have shown how, during the post-Reconstruction period in the United States, racial divisions between blacks and whites were defined and became entrenched according to the same logic that was used to differentiate homosexual from heterosexual identities. The late nineteenth-century invention of homosexuality as what Foucault called a "species category" occurred not merely in tandem with scientific racism's invention of racial types; rather, the two processes were historically and conceptually intertwined in ways that lend sexual identities a racialized aspect, while also giving racial identities a sexual cast.[25]

This represents an important account of the construction and mutual imbrication of identities, but it does not necessarily tell us anything about racial or sexual desires. If, as I have suggested, desire is not determined by difference, then that may be because it also is not determined by identity—neither the identity of the subject who desires nor the identity of the one desired. For all its critiques of identity politics, queer theory often forgets that identity and difference are not actually the causes of desire.[26] From a psychoanalytic perspective,

24. See Dean, *Beyond Sexuality*, esp. chap. 6.

25. See Siobhan B. Somerville, *Queering the Color Line: Race and the Invention of Homosexuality in American Culture* (Durham, NC: Duke University Press, 2000). See also Ann Laura Stoler, *Race and the Education of Desire: Foucault's History of Sexuality and the Colonial Order of Things* (Durham, NC: Duke University Press, 1995).

26. This is the principal limitation of David L. Eng's critique of racial fetishism in *Racial Castration: Managing Masculinity in Asian America* (Durham, NC: Duke University Press, 2001), a critique that repathologizes fetishism by treating it solely as a defense against racial difference. Eng extends the identity-difference axes beyond gender and sexuality to include race, but he remains

identity and desire remain antithetical, in the sense that the unconscious displacements characteristic of desire are intolerable to the structure of the ego or to any stable sense of self. Desire is the enemy of the ego, not its expression. I belabor this point only to insist that the distinction between how an identity is formed, on one hand, and how desire is formed, on the other, must be appreciated if we are to conceive of erotic desire across the color line as anything more than an epiphenomenon of racial inequality.

This distinction sheds light on McBride's critique of racial fetishism, by pointing to how modern notions of identity grow out of the late-nineteenth-century obsession with differentiating sexual and racial types. McBride's account of the contemporary "gay marketplace of desire" keeps stumbling over the distressing realization that gay men's erotic desire tends to be organized around types and that the distinguishing feature of any particular type tends to be fetishized. He offers a partial list of such types in his opening paragraph—muscle queen, swimmer's build, leather, preppy, corporate, pseudo alternative, A&F all-American, boy, bear, homo thug—a list that easily could be augmented with skate punk, boy next door, surfer type, student type, jock, cowboy, cop, construction worker, daddy, granddaddy, chubby, military, rubber pig, and so on. Despite his awareness of the proliferation of erotic types, McBride expresses dismay when he is approached in a gay bar because he's African American, that is, because someone finds his blackness erotically attractive. Like Fanon, he wants people to relate to him as a person, a human subject—to desire him for who he really is rather than for his skin color or what his racialized features might convey in some fantasy not of his making. To be desired according to type (as anyone in a gay bar or equivalent setting invariably is, if he is desired at all) means, for McBride, to fall victim to racial stereotyping; hence his difficulty with the conventions of interracial desire.

There is a point of confusion here that the distinction between identity and desire may help to resolve. Stereotypes concern identity, not desire; by contrast, fetishism is a form of desire largely independent of identity. Since stereotyping and fetishism both involve "types," further clarification is necessary. Historians have argued that, during the nineteenth century, as the category of the normal replaced that of the natural as a standard of comparison for human behavior, quantitative methods such as statistics took on increasing importance for measuring what was typical or normal in human populations. By connect-

---

oblivious to the fundamental psychoanalytic insight that the vagaries of desire are determined by neither identity nor difference.

ing the notion of type to that of norm, the classification of racial and sexual types became central to the project of social regulation through normalization. As part of this project, subjective identities (for instance, the homosexual as a "personage") came into being as strategies of social control—hence the political ambiguity that ineradicably marks such identities. This classification of human subjects according to type generates the problem of stereotyping, whereby variation and diversity are immobilized into homogeneous, static forms that are expected to adhere to tightly defined criteria. Racial stereotyping thus may be understood as a procedure of normalization and control—a technique for managing people's behavior by way of their identity. Such techniques are intensified when, thanks to the growing obsession with "the normal," quantitative (statistical) norms get conflated with qualitative (evaluative) norms, making it seem urgently desirable to be and to feel normal. As the norm comes to signify not merely the typical but, more powerfully, the ideal, racial and sexual types are classified hierarchically, to the detriment of all who deviate in whatever fashion from stringently regulated norms.[27]

Although it certainly is the case that, historically, sexual and racial types came into being in relation to each other, sexual types differ from racial types insofar as the former tend to proliferate in ways that challenge normalizing power. The mobility of desire exceeds the taxonomic imagination's capacity for inventing regulatory identities. In the catalogue enumerated by McBride and augmented by me, so many "types" congregate under the rubric of male homosexuality that the binary division of hetero/homo begins to seem perilously schematic. Indeed, such catalogues are but the starting point for a typology that must discriminate according to not only the kind of *person* one might desire but also the kind of *act* (or acts) one might wish to perform with him, as well as what his *position* might be vis-à-vis that act (top, bottom, or versatile), not to mention the kind of preferred *accessories* to the act or its preferred *setting*. Nineteenth-century sexologists discovered that the permutations were practically endless, and sexual types have only multiplied since then.

Gay liberation initiated its own taxonomic system—the so-called "hanky code"—to help men find the specific "type" that they were seeking more

<hr>

27. Here I am summarizing an argument pioneered by Georges Canguilhem, developed by Michel Foucault, and refined for queer theory most notably by Michael Warner. See Canguilhem, *The Normal and the Pathological*, trans. Carolyn R. Fawcett (1966; repr., New York: Zone, 1991); Foucault, *The History of Sexuality*, vol. 1, *An Introduction*, trans. Robert Hurley (New York: Random House, 1978); and Warner, *Trouble with Normal*. For a nuanced account of racial types, see David Marriott, *On Black Men* (New York: Columbia University Press, 2000), chap. 3.

easily. A card I carry in my wallet lists no fewer than 59 different bandanna colors, each of which signifies a different activity or type and each of which is subdivided according to position: if you're looking for a blow job, wear a light blue bandanna on the left; if you're looking to give blow jobs, wear it on the right. This system discriminates among so many typological possibilities that it requires users to distinguish among, for example, five shades of blue in order to be sure that they signal their preferences accurately. Today the hanky code has been superseded by Internet codes that facilitate cruising online, although these conventions also are sufficiently multiple and complex to warrant their own glossaries. I find reassuring how gay culture's proliferation of types works against that same culture's aggressive idealization of certain corporeal norms: the gym-bodied, twentysomething, hairless blonde may pervade visual representation in gay culture, as he dominated gay porn in the 1980s, but this type is only one of an increasingly diverse range of types that gay men find erotically stimulating. Thus although Leo Bersani is right to insist on "the ruthlessly exclusionary nature of sexual desire" in the face of those who idealize gay desire as democratically utopian, gay culture nevertheless offsets the exclusionary commitments of desire by way of its paradoxical diversification of exclusivity.[28]

It is not merely their rapid proliferation that enables sexual types to outwit the taxonomic ambitions of normalizing power. More significantly, it is desire's investment in partial objects, in actions, and in states or conditions that makes sexuality so difficult to confine to identity categories. In psychoanalytic terms, the object of desire (*l'objet petit a*) is not only multiple but also partial, divided within itself. Thus while it is easy to imagine that the kind of *person* you desire gives rise to a form of psychological selfhood (for both him and you), it is not quite so easy to imagine particular sexual *acts* in terms of identity categories, even though a principal purpose of normalizing power consists in the transformation of acts into identities. The hanky code represents the limit of construing diverse acts in typological terms. Although we mostly seem to have convinced ourselves that temporary *positions* (top or bottom) confer putative identities, our preferred erotic *accessories* and *settings* often are too various or contingent to qualify as identity markers. The barebacking motto "No Limits!" implies a willingness to engage in virtually any sexual act and likewise exhibits the virtue of confounding sexual identity categories.

---

28. Leo Bersani, *Homos* (Cambridge, MA: Harvard University Press, 1995), 107. I discuss this aspect of gay culture further in "Sameness without Identity," *Umbr(a)*, 2002, 25–41.

The idea of sexual fetishism provides a way of thinking about how desire becomes invested in objects without necessarily yielding a sexual identity for the desiring subject or for the desired object. To fully grasp the concept of sexual fetishism, one needs to appreciate not only the familiar argument that subjectivity is irreducible to identity (the critique-of-identity-politics thesis) but also the more challenging argument that objects remain irreducible to identity too. It is not just the subject of desire that is split or disunified, not just the fetishist's ego that is split via disavowal (in classical Freudian terms): the object of desire is disunified too. In other words, the object of desire is never whole, only ever partial. Stereotyping works synecdochically by taking the part for the whole (African American male sexuality is reduced to the big black dick), whereas fetishism works with parts that, strictly speaking, do not form part of a larger whole. Another way of putting this would be to observe that partial objects can be fetishized but not stereotyped: it makes sense to speak of stereotyping a person or a class of persons in a way that does not apply to, for example, a foot.

Since stereotyping has to do with identity (in contradistinction to fetishism, which concerns the partial objects of desire), McBride is both right and wrong when he argues for differentiating foot fetishism from racial fetishism—right because fetishism works differently from stereotyping but wrong because, in the end, he treats racial fetishism as if it were the same thing as stereotyping. To whites who find blackness erotically alluring, McBride responds grimly:

> We don't want to be with any white man whose desire for black dick is fetishistic. In such cases, his desire is not about or for the particular black man but for his idea of whatever the blackness of the black man signifies in his imagination. Some have said that such a position is splitting hairs, that all desire is fetishistic. The degree to which such statements are true render[s] meaningless any number of distinctions, salient and otherwise, making one man's fetishistic desire for black men equal to another's foot fetish. Such sweeping statements do not provide much in the way of distinction and serve only to mask the operation of power in some not-so-very-subtle ways.[29]

I have argued that, indeed, all desire is fetishistic, and I have elaborated a set of analytical distinctions meant to help explain "such sweeping statements" (although they might not be the kind of distinctions that McBride had in mind).

29. McBride, "White Man's World," 124.

If interracial desire is fetishistic, it nevertheless is a mistake—politically and intellectually—to automatically condemn it for being so.[30] The question remains of why *Niggas' Revenge* takes advantage of what makes racial difference so amenable to fetishization in the first place.

"WHO THE NIGGA NOW?"

As in the most interesting pornography, *Niggas' Revenge* unapologetically exploits an erotic dynamic that we usually prefer to ignore, by dramatizing how sexual excitement is generated and intensified by exchanges of power. I stress the word *exchanges* in this formulation, since it is the mobility of power, not its coagulation, that generates excitement. Politically we tend to remain suspicious of disequilibriums of power because we misapprehend them as incompatible with freedom—as if power were bad in itself and therefore something we should try to minimize or outwit. When, in *The History of Sexuality*, Foucault characterized power as productive rather than as merely repressive, he was trying to articulate how power possesses a mobility that makes every subject the agent as well as the object of power: power is understood as a set of force relations (rather than as just a set of institutions) that we constantly make and remake as we move through the world. Sex was important to Foucault as an occasion not for liberation from the grip of power (as, for example, Marcuse and Reich imagined) but for the intensification of power's mobility—with the obvious incentive that in sex the exchange of power generates pleasure.

It is primarily through scenarios of enslavement that *Niggas' Revenge* dramatizes the pleasurable dynamics of power exchange. The black men dominate their captives in the manner of slave masters: wielding whips, issuing commands, and taking their pleasure without regard for the white men's dignity or comfort. Inverting the racial positions of Southern slavery, the film adds salience to its use of leather-SM conventions by conjuring as a backdrop the historical institution of involuntary servitude. In this way, consensual erotic dynamics are intensified via allusion to a definitively nonconsensual power arrangement that itself was covertly sexualized. Although officially sexual relations did not form a part of the institution of U.S. slavery, in prac-

---

30. Here I am in agreement with Kobena Mercer, who, in a revision of his earlier critique of racial fetishism in Robert Mapplethorpe's photographs of black nudes, warns against mobilizing "the unavoidably moralistic connotation of the term [fetishism]" when speaking of interracial erotic visual representations. See Mercer, "Skin Head Sex Thing: Racial Difference and the Homoerotic Imaginary," in Bad Object-Choices, *How Do I Look?* 169–222.

tice white slave masters routinely abused their power by taking advantage of sexual access to their African American slaves. Since evidence of this practice consisted primarily in the birth of mixed-race offspring, historians have tended to think of antebellum interracial relations in exclusively heterosexual terms: same-sex interracial relations were even more covert. The widespread practice of owners raping their black slaves was expressed symptomatically as an anxious fantasy about black men raping white women.

Niggas' Revenge invokes this history of race relations most strikingly at a moment when, from the dog cage, one of the white supremacists yells, "If my daddy finds out, he's gonna come in here and lynch you: you'll be swinging from the trees." This extraordinary "unscripted" utterance condenses an entire history of interracial fantasies and racist violence. Linda Williams suggests that viewers' awareness of this history gives interracial straight porn an erotic charge that often is lacking in other forms of pornography and, further, that historical changes in power relations between blacks and whites permit interracial sex to retain some of its pleasurable sense of transgression without simply duplicating racist acts and assumptions. "Racial fetishization is today not the same as the fixing to which Fanon objected," she argues. "If we are willing to acknowledge that interracial lust evolves out of the taboos initially imposed by the white master, but which now serve to eroticize a field of sexuality that is no longer his sole province, then we begin to recognize the validity of varieties of commodification in contemporary visual culture."[31] I would extend Williams' argument by suggesting that a same-sex context for interracial lust modifies its political valence further, even as the homosexual action of *Niggas' Revenge* draws on the same history of racial and sexual inequality for its erotic pungency.

When, by way of explaining the movie's opening scenes, Dick Wadd informs visitors to his company's Web site that "the taunts touched upon a genuine anger deep inside the Blakes that had been buried for decades," he is not only alluding to a history of racial injustice that continues to the present day but also attempting to represent that history from the perspective of its victims. We might conclude that, far from reducing African American male sexuality to the stereotypical big black dick, *Niggas' Revenge* shows viewers a dimension of black male subjectivity—"a genuine anger deep inside"—that often remains unacknowledged. Along similar lines, we also might note that

31. Linda Williams, "Skin Flicks on the Racial Border: Pornography, Exploitation, and Interracial Lust," in *Porn Studies*, 281.

the inflammatory term in the movie's title is spelled how African Americans would spell it (for example, in hip-hop culture), rather than how white supremacists or ordinary racists would spell it. In this sense, *Niggas' Revenge* might qualify as antiracist—though far from politically correct—porn.

Any reading of the movie in these terms must be complicated by the fact that there is no evidence to suggest that *Niggas' Revenge* was produced by or for African Americans. Although some black viewers may be as turned on by the video as some white viewers, the spectacle of African Americans sexually dominating their Caucasian partners is framed and controlled largely, if not exclusively, by whites. Throughout the proceedings, we catch glimpses of white cameramen and of middle-aged white spectators observing the action from a floor or balcony above the basement apartment where it is set: viewers are reminded periodically that this space contains more bodies—specifically, white bodies—than are featured in the film's diegesis. Yet the notion that *Niggas' Revenge* is framed and thus controlled by racial whiteness is complicated in turn by the director's Jewish heritage and his explicit connection of racism to anti-Semitism. To be Jewish is to count as white in some contexts and as nonwhite in others. Further, the black men's "Puerto Rican buddy," in whose dungeon their revenge is exacted, appears as paler skinned than at least one of the neo-Nazis. Puerto Ricans' combined European and African heritage makes whiteness more relative in the Caribbean than it tends to be conceived of in the United States. When Puerto Rican Eric Top Stud fucks white boy Chane Adams, we witness the dissonant spectacle of a phenotypically lighter-skinned man dominating someone whose complexion and tan makes him appear as darker than the Puerto Rican.

One effect of this dissonance is to remind us that, unlike sexual difference, racial difference is not constituted in a binary fashion: the presence of a Puerto Rican figure and the allusions to Jewishness undermine the standard construction of black/white as an opposition. Once undermined as an opposition, racial difference no longer functions so readily as a visible marker for the imperceptible binary opposition between seropositive and seronegative men. Thus complicated by Puerto Ricanness and Jewishness, the black/white difference becomes instead a means for dramatically visualizing erotic exchanges of power. Racial markers become signs not of identity but of temporary positions in a configuration of power whose very instability—its impotence to confer secure identities—yields pleasure. This, I think, is the meaning of the question that African American performer Bobby Blake repeats as he dominates the neo-Nazis: "Who the nigga now?" No longer an exclusively racial epithet, "nigga" has become a term for the subordinate position in a power relation; it thus is employed synonymously with terms such as "boy," "bitch," and "pussy" to convey expressions, reversals, or transformations of power. In this way, *Niggas' Revenge* uses the visible contrasts of skin pigmentation to represent erotic transfers of power that otherwise might be difficult to visualize. Harnessing racial difference to the pornographic principle of maximum visibility permits relations that usually remain imperceptible to become part of a pleasurable spectacle. For me, the fascination of bareback porn lies in its persistent, inventive attempts to show us things that—irrespective of the kind of sexual activity in which we participate—we mostly fail to see.

CONCLUSION: STRAIGHT PORN MIMICS GAY PORN

I have argued that the history of hard-core pornography has become intertwined inextricably with the history of AIDS. What initially was seen as a "gay disease" now dictates how even straight porn performers organize their sex lives and thus affects what consumers of mainstream porn get to view. In the previous chapter, I described formal measures undertaken by the straight porn industry to prevent HIV transmission. Many people outside the industry cannot understand why most straight porn makers go to such lengths to avoid showing condoms in their films. Yet it remains a tenacious conviction among adult-film producers that condom use damages profits, because consumers prefer to see unprotected sex. In light of this rationale against condoms, we might conclude that porn makers value monetary gain over people's lives.

The emergence of bareback porn complicates this glib conclusion. Porn consumers prefer to see unprotected sex because most men—gay or straight, top or bottom—prefer to *have* sex without condoms. For gay men, witnessing unprotected sex on film may be a way of experiencing in fantasy something that they might be reluctant to do in their everyday lives. Bareback-porn performers thus are engaging in risky sex on behalf of those who are unprepared to do so. Among the many fantasies that porn performers enact is a deep fantasy about bodily contact without limits—a fantasy of intimacy that involves complete exposure to the other and hence requires that all barriers be overcome. In entertaining this fantasy, porn's audience is protected by the barrier of the screen; further barriers are deemed unnecessary and, indeed, undesirable.

As with bareback porn, straight hard core focuses increasingly on anal eroticism, as if, thanks to AIDS, straight porn viewers were fully aware that condomless butt fucking provides maximum exposure to the other. It is the most risky and therefore the most intimate sexual activity: by heightening vulnerability, unprotected anal sex intensifies a sense of closeness. Given my description of the various techniques that bareback porn has devised to negotiate the subculture's investment in internal ejaculation (with the reverse money shot offering the best method for transforming an otherwise invisible moment into spectacle), the reader would be forgiven for assuming that a recent release titled *Anal Cum Drippers* was probably the latest contribution from Treasure Island Media or one of the newer bareback-porn studios. But *Anal Cum Drippers* (dir. Mysterio, Maximum Xposure, 2004) is a heterosexual porn movie, in which internal ejaculation is followed by vivid scenes that furnish the film with its charming title.

Far from an anomaly, *Anal Cum Drippers* is part of a popular subgenre in straight porn known as "cream pie." Often advertised as movies in which "the guys don't pull out," this subgenre focuses on heterosexual intercourse in the way that it usually happens in everyday life, eschewing hard core's conventional money shot in favor of other forms of verisimilitude. The Darren James case that I discussed at the beginning of the previous chapter (in which a straight, male porn performer inadvertently infected three women with HIV) involved a "cream pie" scene. In fact, the occasion on which James transmitted HIV to 19-year-old Lara Roxx entailed what one commentator described as "a bare double anal with an internal pop."[32] That is to say, Lara Roxx was fucked in the ass by two guys simultaneously, and both of them came inside her rectum. Despite the prevalence in straight porn of anal sex, the absence of condoms, and the growing popularity of internal ejaculation, this "bare double anal with an internal pop" qualifies as extreme even by hard core's mutating standards. It represents a mindboggling feat on the part of its teenage female performer and must be regarded as a stunt, something designed to test the limits of what is physiologically possible. I have not been able to ascertain whether this scene is commercially available or, if so, how it is marketed. Since the transmission of HIV was nonconsensual (albeit unintentional), there would be legal as well as serious ethical problems if it were distributed as pornography—if, that is, it were marketed as a scene of viral transmission.

The configuration of the scene in question explains why, after Darren James's positive HIV-test result, the initial quarantine list included one man alongside the thirteen women with whom James had worked since returning from Brazil. Apparently the heterosexuality of these men remains uncompromised by their unsheathed erections rubbing together to the point of orgasm inside an anus, because the anus belonged to a woman. The structure of homosociality—in which putatively straight guys bond with each other through the mediation of a female figure—can tolerate overt physical intimacy between men, provided there is a woman somewhere in the picture who functions as a guarantor of the sex-gender system. Even as the most extreme forms of straight porn come to approximate bareback gay porn, a barrier divides them at the level of discourse: straight pornographers speak of "cream pie" and the "internal pop," whereas their gay counterparts speak of "barebacking" and describe internal ejaculation as "breeding." Yet a consciousness of the risks associated with unprotected anal sex seems to have made the practice visually irresistible in straight porn. Today the presence of a female figure who certifies the heterosexuality of men having sex together—whether in gang bangs or just three-ways—is shadowed by the symbolic figure of HIV, the presence of which overdetermines the transgressive significance of condomless butt fucking.

Has straight porn started imitating gay porn? Although it remains unclear whether the new conventions surrounding internal ejaculation originated in gay or straight genres, the latter increasingly seems to resemble the former. I would argue, however, that these porn conventions find their inspiration more broadly in a culture that, for better and for worse, has constructed unprotected anal sex as a forbidden practice. Creating a taboo around any sexual act invites its enthusiastic transgression in hard-core pornography. Yet the new porn genres involve not only transgression but also a quest for knowledge—specifically, knowledge about the inner workings of the sexual body. For the epistemological project of tracking how something from one body may get inside another permanently, categories of sexual identity are mostly incidental. Gender and sexual identities signify primarily on the body's surface, not in its interior. Thus the question of whether these new conventions originated in gay or straight porn is somewhat misplaced.

The new pornographic epistemology that I've been describing seems to be interested in the body's reproductive capacities only insofar as they involve anal eroticism. In this fantasy of the rectum as not a grave but a womb, we can discern the irrelevance of sexual difference even to straight porn. Another way of putting this would be to say that increasingly the fantasies enacted in pornography are governed by the unconscious, which knows nothing of sexual difference. The difference between the body's exterior and its interior now appears as a more compelling subject for pornographic investigation than do sexual difference, racial difference, or the difference between gay and straight.

Thus even as biopower strengthens its hold on human bodies and populations via the proliferation of sexual identity categories, we also observe its
strategies for opening up live bodies in order to regulate internal affairs. In an
age of AIDS and with the assistance of increasingly sophisticated technology,
the pornographic gaze takes over functions of what we customarily think of
as the medical gaze.[33]

Bareback porn's emphasis on "breeding" makes it less a matter of how
much semen trickles out of an anus than of what remains inside despite the
most spectacular reverse ejaculation. Since the body's interior is not socially
marked in the manner of its exterior, surveillance of and knowledge about the
interior poses a far greater challenge. Tracking viral transmission, whether
epidemiologically or pornographically, represents a potential solution to this
problem. When the body's interior can be inscribed similarly to its exterior,
it can be more readily tracked and more intensively eroticized. In this way,
deliberate HIV transmission might be understood as a practice of internal
tattooing, a technique of marking the inside of the body both literally and
symbolically. "Breeding" thus may represent an updated version of having a
lover's name tattooed on one's bicep.[34]

Having a lover's name tattooed on one's bicep is, of course, a cliché, a joke. The
photographer Charles Gatewood describes a man who has the words "YOUR
NAME" tattooed on his dick: "It's a classic pick-up line at bars and parties: 'Uh,
you'll never believe this, babe, but I have *your name* tattooed on my penis!'"[35] The
genre of a beloved's name as tattoo furnishes an opportunity for humor because
such inscriptions readily outlive the relationships that they are designed to preserve. Then again, they are supposed to outlive those relationships in the sense
that, as with any tattoo, an ostensibly indelible mark constitutes a stay against
mutability. Arguably a tattoo that represents the beloved—whether through his

33. This is especially evident in the controversial straight porn produced by cult figure Max
Hardcore, whose signature techniques include inserting a speculum into one orifice of a woman
while penetrating her remaining orifices with his penis, hands, or other implements. See, for example, *Max Hardcore Extreme*, vol. 7 (Max World Entertainment, 2005).

34. The prospect of an internal tattoo is surprisingly disturbing. Charles Gatewood, a San
Francisco–based photographer of the sexual demimonde, uses a black-and-white close-up of a tattooed fetus as the cover image for his book *Forbidden Photographs* (San Francisco: Flash Publications,
1995). Against a dark background, we see the visage of a bearded, biker-style tattooist wearing sun-
glasses, as if to guard his anonymity; his tightly focused right hand, encased in a filthy rubber glove,
holds up to the camera a preserved fetus, mouth ajar, with the outline of a heart inked approximately
where its tiny heart would be. The horror of this brilliant picture lies in its radical equivocation of
the boundaries between inside and outside, as well as between infant and adult.

35. Gatewood, *Forbidden Photographs*, 25.

name, an image, or some combination thereof—is the popular cultural version of a sonnet or other love lyric, that is, something intended to preserve a love relation from the depredations of time.[36]

Culture offers a storehouse of techniques for conserving love relations in spite of mortality and change. We pen lyrics, carve names into the surface of our skin (or a tree or a rock), and now, through the practice of "breeding," gay men have devised a technique for tattooing the body's interior. The presence of HIV enables the act of internal ejaculation to serve as the inscription of a love relation in the face of mutability. We should recognize that "breeding" concerns the maintenance of a love relation, not merely the intensification of eros by uniting it with the threat of death. This sense of maintaining an otherwise transient connection through inscription has become more, rather than less, important for gay men in the wake of the AIDS epidemic. It also may help explain the impulse to film these breeding rituals, since pornographic representation preserves a record of erotic encounters that otherwise might be forgotten.

The connections among breeding, tattooing, and carving legends into trees are dramatized in the opening scenes of *Meat Rack* (Treasure Island Media, 2005), a bareback movie directed by Max Sohl, who is the New York representative of Paul Morris's West Coast company. Set in the longtime gay oasis of Fire Island Pines, the movie refers in its title to the infamous wooded area of the Pines where for generations men have cruised for sex. Cleverly evoking the permanence-transience dialectic in its credits, the video opens with a shot of its handsome star, Dawson, using a stick to trace on the beach the words "Treasure Island Media presents"; the following shot shows a wave gently washing away his careful inscription. Next, in the wooded area of the "meat rack," Dawson cruises leather daddy Joe Sarge and heavily tattooed Chris Neal, who sports inked designs even on the shaft and head of his penis. After a scene in which Joe Sarge and Chris Neal both fuck and "breed" Dawson at his request, the camera silently pans to a weathered carving on one of the nearby trees, which reads "SAFE SEX 2002." As he walks away, with the camera focused on his cum-filled butt, Dawson passes another slender tree, which bears the legend "SAFE SEX PINES→." Far from ignoring the safe-sex imperative, this film registers it only to consciously reject condom use and

---

36. This is a wholly conventional definition of lyric intention. See, for example, the closing couplet of Shakespeare's sonnet 18: "So long as men can breathe or eyes can see, / So long lives this, and this gives life to thee."

unabashedly celebrate semen ingestion. Behind the deliberate irony of these cuts, there may be an acknowledgement of the strange kinship between words carved into a tree trunk and semen ejaculated into a rectum: both aspire to leave permanent traces; yet both must acknowledge the ultimate futility of their efforts to outpace mortality.

By juxtaposing shots of Dawson's anal breeding with shots of traces left in the "meat rack" some years prior, this scene evokes not only the presence of men who cruised the pines and might return next summer but also the ghosts of those lost to AIDS who will never return in person. Evoking spectral presences in this way creates a sense of history, suggesting that the wooded area in which the sex occurs constitutes not simply a bucolic natural setting but also an intensely historical landscape, a place where memories of previous generations linger. Connecting with a leather daddy and a tattooed punk in the woods, our youthful protagonist may be accessing through sex a connection with gay history and community, even as he differentiates his actions from those of "safe-sex" cruising. The framing of these scenes intimates the continuity of an erotic tradition that necessarily exceeds any individual who might participate in it. Although the sex that transpires from cruising in such settings is usually impersonal (albeit not anonymous in this case), the scene has been shot in a way that illuminates what this impersonality consists of: the casual sexual encounter provides an opportunity for connecting with a mostly invisible erotic tradition peopled by generations of what might be thought of as tribal ancestors.

Performing certain acts in particular settings deindividualizes the participants by making them part of a pattern or ritual that preceded their birth and that will outlive them, whether or not their lives are cut short by AIDS. It is a way of connecting with something larger than oneself and, indeed, larger than any self. The virus offers a figure for that connection via its capacity for leaving an indelible trace; it thus facilitates the fantasy of achieving permanent connection through transient encounters. HIV's propensity for sexual transmission means that the microscopic entity passed along at a breeding ritual might have been transmitted on this exact same spot in a similar fashion years before. I think that this is what Paul Morris is referring to when he says that the subculture and the virus require the same processes for transmission.

This account suggests that cruising involves much more than simply getting off. Far from a defense against interpersonal intimacy, casual anonymous sex may represent a means of accessing impersonal intimacy; it may involve a profound exposure to the other and thus an experience of vulnerability and trust with complete strangers. In fact, cruising alters the status of the stranger in a manner akin to how bareback "breeding" alters the status of kinship. Far from a sign of the failure to commit to a single partner, cruising entails a commitment to something more than just individuals. Rather than rationalizing gay men's cruising habits as the inevitable yet dysfunctional outcome of heteronormative social arrangements and discriminatory laws, then, the final chapter considers what it might mean to adopt an ethic of cruising as a way of life.

FOUR: CRUISING AS A WAY OF LIFE

Why should strangers not be lovers?

This question, taken from gay leatherman Scott Tucker's critique of antipornography rhetoric, defines an attitude characteristic of cruising.[1] Often understood simply as the pursuit of new sex partners, cruising entails a remarkably hospitable disposition toward strangers. Insofar as that is the case, the subculture of bareback promiscuity, far from being ethically irresponsible, may be ethically exemplary. In this chapter, I argue that, in fact, cruising exemplifies a distinctive ethic of openness to alterity and that—irrespective of our view of the morality of barebacking—we all, gay and nongay, have something to learn from this relational ethic. Thus I aim to generalize from the subculture and its multipartner practices in order to develop my introductory remark about thinking promiscuously about promiscuity itself. In other words, I want to begin to assess what's at stake in conceiving of promiscuous relationality beyond the strictly sexual realm.

Having endeavored to suspend moral judgment about the subculture until this point, I now wish to advocate a positive ethics of cruising, while at the same time launching an ethical critique of the degraded form that cruising for bareback sex often takes, namely, hooking-up online. In this final chapter, I'm thus more explicit about what I find to praise and to blame in bareback subculture (what I find to blame is not the absence of condoms). Elaborating an ethics of cruising as a way of life requires my differentiating one form of cruis-

---

1. Scott Tucker, "Gender, Fucking, and Utopia: An Essay in Response to John Stoltenberg's *Refusing to Be a Man*," *Social Text* 27 (1990): 18.

ing, or one distinctive relational outlook, from another: the ethics of cruising is a matter not of how many people one has sex with or what kind of sex one has with them (bareback or otherwise) but of how one treats the other and, more specifically, how one treats his or her own otherness. Ultimately the ethics of cruising is an ethics of the stranger in modernity. This chapter uses the figure of the stranger to focus on the politics of public sex and of urban redevelopment, as well as on the troubling privatization of intimacy through various institutional means. The figure of the stranger evokes concerns about safety and risk that remain irreducible to the question of "safe sex," even as debates over barebacking tend to rationalize anxieties about otherness in terms of disease and contamination. In its critique of safety and its embrace of risk, the subculture exemplifies a relation to alterity that I describe by using the vocabulary of psychoanalyst Jean Laplanche; Laplanche is useful for my purposes here not only because he explains relationality through the trope of seduction but also because he makes fully apparent how every relation to other persons is mediated by a prior relation to one's own internal otherness. Focused on the primacy of the other, his is an explicitly ethical psychoanalysis that illuminates the ethics of that eminently public form of seduction known as cruising.

STRANGER LOVING

Cruising represents an indispensable component of urban gay life, in that metropolitan existence constantly propels city dwellers into contact with strangers. "Isn't wide choice and rich opportunity the point of cities?" asks Jane Jacobs in her classic work of urban sociology. "This is indeed the point of cities," she patiently explains.[2] Although Jacobs is not speaking in terms of specifically sexual choice, cities nevertheless furnish the conditions of possibility for cruising because they offer a wide choice of sex partners and rich opportunities for erotic contacts. Young people, especially young gay men, migrate to big cities for just this reason. Without the potential for regular contact with strangers, cruising of the sort that interests me in this chapter cannot really exist. Cruising is a function of urban modernity, as poets such as Charles Baudelaire and Walt Whitman intuitively understood. The constant contact with strangers that city living entails has the capacity to transform human relationality in ways that I wish to elaborate here.

2. Jane Jacobs, *The Death and Life of Great American Cities* (New York: Random House, 1961), 116. Subsequent page references are cited in the text.

In *The Death and Life of Great American Cities*, Jacobs argues that cities are defined by the salient fact that the vast majority of their inhabitants stand in relation to one another as strangers:

> Great cities are not like towns, only larger. They are not like suburbs, only denser. They differ from towns and suburbs in basic ways, and one of these is that cities are, by definition, full of strangers. To any one person, strangers are far more common in big cities than acquaintances. More common not just in places of public assembly, but more common at a man's own doorstep. Even residents who live near each other are strangers, and must be, because of the sheer number of people in small geographical compass. (30)

The quantitative difference between cities and towns (or suburbs) yields a crucial qualitative distinction, namely, that the definitive experience of urban life is an experience of strangers. No matter one's familiarity with a city, the majority of its denizens must remain comparatively unfamiliar. Since everyone is a stranger to someone, not only the urban other but I myself represent a stranger to most of those whose paths I cross in a city. Being a stranger is a function of context, and in an urban milieu most of us are effectively strangers much of the time. Encountering strangers is the norm, not the exception, of urban life.

Under the rubric of the stranger, we find not only completely unfamiliar persons ("perfect strangers") but also those whose faces may be familiar from the neighborhood yet who have not become acquaintances, much less friends. As Jacobs points out, one's urban neighbor may qualify as a stranger quite as much as would a foreign visitor to the neighborhood, since both are unknown. In premodern societies, the stranger was indistinguishable from the enemy—and may remain so in part of the psyche. The unknown, unfamiliar figure tends to be regarded with suspicion and sometimes outright hostility. Yet one basic tenet of modernity consists in differentiating the stranger from the adversary; as Kant observed, "hospitality means the right of a stranger not to be treated as an enemy when he arrives in the land of another."[3] There is a considerable margin, however, between not treating the stranger as an enemy and treating him as a friend—that is, between letting the stranger alone and inviting him into your home. Comprehending the otherness of the foreigner, the dangerousness of the enemy, the ambiguity of the neighbor, and the erotic

3. Immanuel Kant, "Perpetual Peace: A Philosophical Sketch," in *Kant: Selections*, ed. Lewis White Beck (New York: Macmillan, 1988), 439.

potential of the lover, the figure of the stranger holds an equivocal status that I would not want to resolve prematurely.

Combined with the stranger's omnipresence in urban modernity, this equivocal status helps explain the lengths to which people will go in order to avoid contact with strangers. Parents routinely train their children not to speak to strangers, and most adults navigate urban space equipped with various defenses—whether cell phones, iPods, or spouses—designed to minimize contact with those who appear unfamiliar to them. As unwitting incarnations of otherness, strangers tend to arouse both fear and desire; refusing intercourse with strangers betrays our basic fear of them. Cruising responds to this scenario by discerning the erotic possibilities latent in an encounter with otherness. Yet as we consider the experience of cruising, it will be important to bear in mind that it too sometimes constitutes a defensive response to anxieties elicited by the figure of the stranger. Seducing or attempting to seduce the stranger occasionally may function as an apotropaic mechanism for domesticating his or her provocative otherness.

Possible answers to this chapter's opening question, *Why should strangers not be lovers?* thus branch in opposite directions. On one hand, the sexually cautious are likely to insist that you should not take a stranger as your lover, owing to the manifold risks involved: doing so would be inherently unsafe, because one does not know the person; one might be raped, assaulted, robbed, or otherwise taken advantage of; and, even if no crime occurs, one is liable to contract a disease. When strangers are considered as unsafe in and of themselves, erotic contact with them is regarded as all the more so; one notion of safety tautologically redoubles another. Anyone who has a mother, but especially young women, will be familiar with this line of reasoning.

On the other hand, I have claimed that strangers should not be lovers when the principal purpose for making them so involves overcoming their strangeness. This line of argument concerns the otherness of the other, rather than the safety of the self; here hesitation before the figure of the stranger functions to protect him from my intentions, instead of shielding me from his. In this way of thinking, it is not the stranger's alienness but my own narcissism that may be dangerous. To put the matter more precisely, it is neither the stranger nor I who ultimately requires protection in the encounter between us; what needs protecting most diligently is his otherness. My "getting to know him"—my genial effort to make the stranger more familiar—is partly what his otherness needs protection from. Of course, I'm not suggesting that one shouldn't be friendly to strangers; indeed, it is the general reticence about contact with strangers that I'm trying to critique. But what seems salutary about cruising is how it can involve intimate contact with strangers without necessarily domesticating the other's otherness. Thus I would like to rephrase the opening question more pointedly: *Why should strangers not be lovers and yet remain strangers?*

In some respects, gay men's practice of tricking—casual anonymous sex or one-night stands—turns strangers into lovers so briefly and perfunctorily that it rarely compromises their status as strangers. For example, glory-hole sex, in which one man blows another through an aperture in the wall of a toilet stall or porn-arcade booth, effectively keeps its participants unknown to each other (indeed, this may be its purpose). Another example would be a man I once noticed in Mack-Folsom Prison, a sex club that has been characterized as "bareback central in San Francisco," who stood spread-eagled facing the wall, gyrating gently to the music, as various men (including me) fucked him bareback from behind. This very handsome guy never turned his head to see who was penetrating him; clearly anyone was welcome to do so. He was so good-looking and in such magnificent physical shape that he could have been extremely choosy about his sex partners; I thus found it to be striking that this man seemed to care not one whit what those fucking him looked like, how sexually proficient they were, or whether they wore condoms. In cases such as these, sex occurs between individuals whose status as strangers remains constant. Nevertheless, sex of this kind, though it be between strangers, may function as a means of avoiding any encounter with otherness. By contrast, it is the intimate encounter with the other that does not attempt to eliminate otherness that I wish to advocate as ethically exemplary.

It would contravene the principle of benign sexual variation that has guided this study to advocate any particular form of erotic activity as exemplary. From the very beginning of *Unlimited Intimacy*, I have tried not to praise or condemn any type of sex (with the exception only of nonconsensual sex). In this chapter, I am not attempting to construct an ethical hierarchy of consensual erotic practices. Instead, I'm interested in how sex raises ethical questions insofar as it is understood as a privileged domain in which we encounter otherness. It is because erotic relations condense our ambivalence about alterity, not because one way of fucking is better than any other, that sex becomes a matter of ethical concern. (Although he did not speak of it in terms of an encounter specifically with otherness, Michel Foucault recognized toward the end of his life that the history of sexuality needed to be conceptualized as part of the history of ethics, not only as part of the history of power.[4])

Much critical discourse on sexual ethics misconstrues the encounter with otherness in terms of sexual difference, as if one could establish authentic contact with otherness only by engaging the opposite sex or "the feminine." The conflation of otherness with difference betrays a heterosexist error, a ruse of heteronormativity that I have addressed elsewhere.[5] I wish to develop that point here by arguing not only that an ethical encounter with otherness need not depend on sexual difference but also that it need not depend on sex. Whether straight or gay, vanilla or queer, sex may function as a means of avoiding the encounter with otherness altogether or, alternately, of domesticating its threat to the ego's integrity. But, as we often rightly intuit, erotic intimacy also can serve as a means for encountering something wonderfully strange to the self—something that neither the self nor the other properly possesses but that emerges in the contact between them. The ethics of erotic contact involves far more than hygienic practices of "safe sex" or disease prevention.

The kind of contact that I'm trying to delineate, though often we seek it through sex, remains irreducible to genital contact. That is to say, erotic encounters represent not just an instance of but also, perhaps more significantly, a metaphor for contact with otherness. When I define cruising as *contact with strangers*, both the notion of contact and the category of the stranger require further elaboration. Jacobs's pioneering urban sociology helps us to grasp what is at stake in the notion of contact. But *The Death and Life of Great American Cities* does not discuss specifically sexual contact, except in a dismissively homophobic way. To appreciate how gay cruising in urban space may exemplify contact of the sort that Jacobs advocates, we must turn to the twentieth-century literature of cruising. Since cruising is a practice of the ephemeral and the contingent, it is all the more remarkable that it has given rise to such a voluminous archive. In this archive, I have found Samuel

4. See Foucault, *The History of Sexuality*, vols. 2 and 3, esp. pp. 3–13 of vol. 2, in which Foucault explains the disjunction between these two works and his more widely read introductory volume. See also the alternative, separately published "Preface to *The History of Sexuality*, Volume Two," trans. William Smock, in *Essential Works of Foucault, 1954–1984*, vol. 1, *Ethics: Subjectivity and Truth*, ed. Paul Rabinow, trans. Robert Hurley et al. (New York: New Press, 1997), 199–205.

5. See Dean, "Homosexuality and the Problem of Otherness," in Dean and Lane, *Homosexuality and Psychoanalysis*, 120–43.

Delany's writing, particularly *Times Square Red, Times Square Blue*, to be the most consistently illuminating meditation on cruising as a way of life.[6]

YOU DO NOT WANT THEM IN YOUR HAIR

Although separated by nearly four decades, Jacobs's and Delany's critiques of urban planning in New York City both take aim at the persistent assumption that metropolitan existence should be modeled after small-town life. This notion assumes that small towns are safer and thus more appealing to their inhabitants, because, by contrast with cities, small towns afford fewer encounters with strangers. But when considered in terms of murder rates per capita, for example, cities generally are much safer places to live than small towns. What *The Death and Life of Great American Cities* makes plain is how, far from compromising safety, public contact with strangers in urban space helps ensure safety. It is noteworthy that Jane Jacobs, a wife and mother, advances this argument, since one of the main objections to Delany's account of cruising in the former Times Square sex institutions has been that it is viable only for men. Repeatedly my straight female students assure me that the kind of contact with strangers advocated by both Jacobs and Delany is too dangerous for women. Yet here is Jacobs, in 1961, arguing the contrary:

> Strangers become an enormous asset on the street on which I live, and the spurs off it, particularly at night when safety assets are most needed. We are fortunate enough, on the street, to be gifted not only with a locally supported bar and another around the corner, but also with a famous bar that draws continuous troops of strangers from adjoining neighborhoods and even from out of town. It is famous because the poet Dylan Thomas used to go there, and mentioned it in his writing. This bar, indeed, works two distinct shifts. In the

6. Subsequent page references to Delany's *Times Square Red, Times Square Blue* are cited in the text. The vast literary archive of cruising may be divided roughly into pre- and postliberation texts. I have mentioned already Whitman and Baudelaire, to whose names must be added at least those of Hart Crane, T. S. Eliot, and Gertrude Stein; the modernist and protomodernist literature of cruising overlaps with that of the *flâneur*. Later in the twentieth century, anticipating and following U.S. gay-liberation movements, there was an explosion of literary depictions of cruising in the novels of James Baldwin, John Rechy, Edmund White, Andrew Holleran, Gary Indiana, Reinaldo Arenas, Samuel R. Delany, and Alan Hollinghurst (to mention only the most interesting). There is also a fascinating archive of cruising in French literature, notably in the work of Jean Genet, André Gide, Renaud Camus, Roland Barthes, Hervé Guibert, and Guillaume Dustan. Recent critical accounts of this literature include Dianne Chisholm, *Queer Constellations: Subcultural Space in the Wake of the City* (Minneapolis: University of Minnesota Press, 2005); Michael Trask, *Cruising Modernism: Class and Sexuality in American Literature and Social Thought* (Ithaca, NY: Cornell University Press, 2003); and Ivanchikova, "Sidewalks of Desire."

morning and early afternoon it is a social gathering place for the old community of Irish longshoremen and other craftsmen in the area, as it always was. But beginning in midafternoon it takes on a different life, more like a college bull session with beer, combined with a literary cocktail party, and this continues until the early hours of the morning. On a cold winter's night, as you pass the White Horse, and the doors open, a solid wave of conversation and animation surges out and hits you; very warming. The comings and goings from this bar do much to keep our street reasonably populated until three in the morning, and it is a street always safe to come home to. (40–41)

Rather than lamenting the presence on the street where she lives of bars that attract strangers, Jacobs recognizes that strangers traversing the street make it safe, especially at night when foot traffic otherwise would diminish. Neatly illustrating her overarching thesis about the necessity of a "diversity of uses" for successful urban life, the White Horse tavern accommodates in a single institution disparate social classes, since its customers include local laborers, craftsmen, collegiate types, and aspiring literati. Like the most interesting gay bars, this one furnishes a heterogeneous space in which different social classes come into contact with each other in a casual, unpremeditated fashion. On the basis of Jacobs's brief account, the White Horse exemplifies the kind of institution necessary for a vital public sphere (in the classic Habermasian sense) and thus for democracy.[7]

The Death and Life of Great American Cities mounts a strong case for the importance of contact, even ostensibly trivial contact, among strangers in urban public space. This is what sidewalks can be especially good at fostering when they are part of "mixed-use" neighborhoods, Jacobs argues. Cities require plentiful and populous public space that enables contact among strangers, since "if interesting, useful and significant contacts among the people of cities are confined to acquaintanceships suitable for private life, the city becomes stultified" (56). As she quite unsentimentally explains, "cities are full of people with whom, from your viewpoint, or mine, or any other individual's, a certain degree of contact is useful or enjoyable; but you do not want them in your hair. And they do not want you in theirs either" (56). Here Jacobs is describing how manifold minor instances of contact in public space generate

---

7. See Jürgen Habermas, *The Structural Transformation of the Public Sphere: An Inquiry into a Category of Bourgeois Society*, trans. Thomas Burger (Cambridge, MA: MIT Press, 1989). The most productive negotiation between Habermasian public sphere theory and Foucaultian queer theory may be found in Michael Warner, *Publics and Counterpublics* (New York: Zone, 2002).

an atmosphere of friendliness among people who are not, and do not wish to become, friends. In other words, regular casual contact breeds a general disposition of goodwill among those who, by virtue of sheer numerical concentration, inevitably remain strangers to each other. When cities work this way, living among the multitude becomes a source of inimitable pleasure.

Delany takes the logic of Jacobs's critique a step further by extending it to erotic contact. In *Times Square Red, Times Square Blue*, he argues for the vital importance to urban democratic life of not only outdoor public space devoted to "mixed use" but also public sex institutions that likewise foster diversity through interclass mingling. Just as restricting social contact "to acquaintanceships suitable for private life" stultifies urban experience (in Jacobs's words), "similarly, if *every* sexual encounter involves bringing someone back to your house, the general sexual activity in a city becomes anxiety-filled, class-bound, and choosy," contends Delany. "This is precisely *why* public rest rooms, peep shows, sex movies, bars with grope rooms, and parks with enough greenery are necessary for a relaxed and friendly sexual atmosphere in a democratic metropolis" (127; emphases in the original). Delany's point merely restates in terms of sex Jacobs's frank observation that "cities are full of people with whom . . . a certain degree of contact is useful or enjoyable; but you do not want them in your hair." Arguably the greatest single discovery of urban gay culture is the possibility of sharing erotic pleasure with another person without having to have him or her "in your hair"—and without resorting to a commercial transaction in order to guarantee that you won't have him or her in your hair.

This proposition returns us to the question of whether strangers should be lovers, although now we see that their potentially becoming so depends on the existence of public spaces in which strangers can interact freely and attain a modicum of privacy if they so desire. One cannot cruise at home, only in places where one is a stranger. Yet the elementary insight that cities are more enjoyable *and safer* when they afford plentiful public spaces for intercourse among strangers tends to be forgotten—even by Jacobs herself—when the debate turns to sex. The very idea of public sex seems to arouse a terror of indiscriminate fucking in the streets and a consequent disintegration of civilized society; it conjures the specter of untrammeled bodily violations. Although cruising often occurs on city streets, public sex typically does not—at least not in broad daylight. "Public sex" refers to erotic contact outside the home; its occurrence outside the domestic sphere accounts for no small measure of its appeal. Paradoxically public sex can be private in the sense that it excludes access by non-participants and requires the consent of all who are involved. In other words, public sex violates not personal privacy or bodily integrity but only a privatized, deeply misleading conception of the sexual.

Public sex is not Dionysian, indiscriminate activity but carefully self-regulated and fully socialized behavior, with its own etiquette and conventions. Except for cruising in parks and on beaches, most public sex occurs in institutions that, by definition, are part of civilized society rather than an intrinsic threat to it. Yet because these institutions tend to remain concealed behind a scrim of ignorance and stigma, the notion of public sex appears as uniquely disturbing, not to mention radically incompatible with conventional ideas about sexual privacy. Delany explains the problem thus:

> Many gay institutions—clubs, bars of several persuasions, baths, tea-room sex, gay porn movie houses (both types), brunches, entertainment, cruising areas, truck stop sex, circuit parties, and many more—have grown up outside the knowledge of much of the straight world. But these institutions have nevertheless grown up very much *within* our society, not outside it. They have been restrained on every side. That is how they have attained their current form. They do not propagate insanely in some extrasocial and unconstrained "outside/beyond," apart from any concept of social responsibility—and that includes what goes on in the orgy rooms at the baths. The freedom to "be" "gay" without the freedom to choose to partake of these institutions is just as meaningless as the freedom to "be" "Jewish" when, say, any given Jewish ritual, text, or cultural practice is outlawed. (193–94, emphasis in the original)

Real sexual freedom thus entails access to sexual institutions—or to what queer theorists Berlant and Warner call "sex publics."[8]

Times Square Red, Times Square Blue vividly describes these institutions and bears witness to their callous destruction, clarifying along the way that what the redevelopment of Times Square has annihilated is a sexual culture and, indeed, a whole way of life. With narrative dexterity and a novelist's eye for detail, Delany charts the rise and fall of the Times Square porn theaters over four decades, offering an unvarnished impression of the characters who populated

---

8. Berlant and Warner, "Sex in Public," 322–28. In the critical literature on public sex, I have found the following volumes to be particularly helpful: Richard D. Mohr, *Gay Ideas: Outing and Other Controversies* (Boston: Beacon, 1992); Pat Califia, *Public Sex: The Culture of Radical Sex* (San Francisco: Cleis, 1994); Chauncey, *Gay New York*; Colter et al., *Policing Public Sex*; William L. Leap, ed., *Public Sex/Gay Space* (New York: Columbia University Press, 1999); D. Travers Scott, ed., *Strategic Sex: Why They Won't Keep It in the Bedroom* (New York: Harrington Park, 1999); Michael Warner, *Trouble with Normal*; and Ricco, *Logic of the Lure*.

the theaters, the sexual activity that occurred in them, and the wide range of relationships that such activity made possible.[9] As anybody who ever visited one of the dozens of small theaters that used to exist around Times Square can confirm, most (though not all) of the porn screened in these venues was heterosexual, even as the sexual activity in them occurred almost exclusively between men. By taking us inside institutions that no longer exist in New York City, *Times Square Red, Times Square Blue* educates readers who never may have had the opportunity or inclination to visit them. And by thus revealing the erotic activity that transpired in their shadowy precincts (mostly blow jobs and hand jobs), Delany's study performs a service akin to that of the porn movies themselves, which, as he suggests, "represented a tremendous sexual education for their working-class audience" (78). At the same time (and in case there were any doubt on the matter), he makes plain that such institutions hardly developed outside the knowledge or experience of the straight world. No small part of the fascination of these empires of visual pleasure— and, indeed, of Delany's account of them—lies in their casual blindness to the customary segregation of straight and gay sexualities. The existence of public sex institutions clearly is not "just" a gay issue.

As I indicated in chapter 2, the invention of video, DVD, and Internet technologies helped privatize porn consumption by bringing it directly into the home, thus rendering a trip to the local porn theater or video arcade ostensibly superfluous. Delany neglects to mention how such technological developments contributed to the demise of the Times Square theaters. Yet the technological explanation obscures the point that sex at such places is public and social, by contrast with sex in front of a computer monitor or television, which tends to be solitary. The porn may be the same, but the experience is completely different. Neither Delany nor I am suggesting that there is anything wrong with solitary sex or domestic porn consumption—far from it. But there is something wrong when a metropolis such as New York eliminates access to the institutions of sexual culture on which many of its citizens, especially working-class and minority citizens, depend for their enjoyment of the city. As Jacobs's account demonstrates, a city acts against its own interests when it reduces the number of public spaces in which strangers intermingle in a spirit of goodwill.

9. In so doing, Delany answers queer film theorist John Champagne's impassioned plea for more ethnographic studies of the contexts in which porn circulates and of "the everyday uses to which subjects put such texts," in place of the endless close readings of films that the discipline of cinema studies tends to generate. See John Champagne, "'Stop Reading Films!': Film Studies, Close Analysis, and Gay Pornography," *Cinema Journal* 36, no. 4 (1997): 76–97.

Yet this is exactly what the redevelopment of Times Square has done to New York City. It is sobering to realize that the urban development about which Jacobs was so critical at the beginning of the 1960s represented, in fact, the early stage of plans that, four decades later, led to the destruction catalogued by Delany; *The Death and Life of Great American Cities* (1961) and *Times Square Red, Times Square Blue* (1999) resonate not simply because they focus on the same city but because they anatomize two moments of the same process.

The process of urban depredation that these works describe took so long to accomplish because it encountered resistance from New Yorkers along the way. Starting in the mid-1980s, however, those favoring "redevelopment" were able to marshal a burgeoning fear of AIDS in support of their plans to eliminate the sex institutions and, indeed, all small businesses in and around Times Square. A legitimate desire to make the city safer was harnessed to the rhetoric of safer sex that had been invented by gay men committed to public sex, and then cynically deployed against the institutions of public sex at the expense of all those (but especially sexual minorities) who used those institutions. It is terribly ironic that what made such institutions so vital to peaceable urban life—namely, that they facilitated the easy mixing of disparate races, ethnicities, sexualities, and classes—was exactly what made their destruction so readily marketable as a security measure. Since contact with those different from oneself, especially when they are strangers, tends to be regarded as risky (because unpredictable), institutions that sponsor such contact are easily perceived as hazardous, even when the opposite may be true. As Delany notes, behind the rhetoric of "safety" and "family values" there lurks "a wholly provincial and absolutely small-town terror of cross-class contact" (153).

THE PLEASURES OF CONTACT

Not only does he extend to sex the logic of Jacobs's critique, Delany also develops her idea of contact by comparing it with a contrastive mode of sociality, namely, networking. The difference between the two lies in how *contact* crosses class boundaries in public space, whereas *networking* occurs within a single social stratification and thus is more private (in the sense of not accessible to everyone). Because it tends to destabilize class hierarchies, contact is politically desirable in a democratic society. Yet it is not something in which one engages for reasons of political correctness, as if in conformity with the dictates of the left-wing superego. Rather, one participates in forms of sociality that are classifiable as contact for reasons of pleasure—the pleasures of casual social intercourse as well as, if one wishes, those of casual sex. *Times*

Square Red, Times Square Blue is a hymn of praise to the pleasures and benefits of contact; indeed, the entire first half of Delany's book comprises a series of vignettes of memorable contact scenes in New York's porn theaters.

As I have tried to suggest, sexual connection represents an instance of contact but also a metaphor for contact. In *Times Square Red, Times Square Blue*, erotic interclass encounters constitute the privileged figure for a mode of sociality that generates pleasures irreducible to genital satisfaction. Delany describes contact like this in the second half of his book:

> Contact is the conversation that starts in the line at the grocery counter with the person behind you while the clerk is changing the paper roll in the cash register. It is the pleasantries exchanged with a neighbor who has brought her chair out to take some air on the stoop. It is the discussion that begins with the person next to you at a bar. It can be the conversation that starts with any number of semiofficials or service persons—mailman, policeman, librarian, store clerk or counter person. As well, it can be two men watching each other masturbating together in adjacent urinals of a public john—an encounter that, later, may or may not become a conversation. Very importantly, contact is also the intercourse—physical and conversational—that blooms in and as "casual sex" in public rest rooms, sex movies, public parks, singles bars, and sex clubs. (123)

There is a profoundly democratic, Whitmanesque attitude evident in this catalogue of examples that includes *on the same discursive level* an unplanned conversation with someone behind you in line at the grocery store and a contingent sexual encounter with the guy standing next to you in a public toilet. For Delany, these are the same kind of encounter; neither is obligatory, premeditated, or particularly dramatic, yet both are pleasant and potentially beneficial, in the sense that they may yield something unexpected—the discovery of a shared interest that leads to the exchange of useful information, say, or the discovery of a person with whom you want to spend significantly more time. Delany's point—like Jacobs's—is that contact represents an everyday, minor mode of sociality the overall effects of which are major in terms of the web of trust (and thus safety) that it generates in urban space, as well as in terms of its surprising (because contingent) benefits to particular individuals.

Many of Delany's examples of contact describe interactions with homeless people, in which the crossing of class boundaries is especially palpable.[10]

---

10. "My current lover of eight years and I first met when he was homeless and selling books from a blanket spread out on Seventy-second Street. Our two best friends for many years now are

Since contact occurs outside the domestic sphere and in a public space, it makes sense that intercourse with those who have no home epitomizes this mode of sociality. My own example of the pleasures and benefits of contact involves a homeless person whom I encountered in San Francisco on one of the research trips for this book. I had been roaming around the city and was on my way to the gym (Gold's on Market Street), where I had an appointment that I was anxious not to miss. Realizing that my perambulations had left me somewhat behind schedule in a part of the city with which I was less familiar, I was hurrying along when a sharp gust of wind blew my baseball cap thirty yards ahead of me, into the path of traffic. It was not the first time during that windy trip that my hat had blown off, but on this occasion I was ready to abandon it as lost. A homeless man about forty yards ahead (whom I had noticed because he had been yelling at traffic) ran into the road and, much to my surprise, retrieved my cap.

My first thought was that I would have to fork over cash in exchange for the cap, but he returned it to me without so much as a hint of payment. My next thought, instinctive, was don't talk to strangers, especially if they appear to be crazy. Then I remembered Delany and the line that encapsulates the genius of *Times Square Red, Times Square Blue*: "For decades the governing cry of our cities has been 'Never speak to strangers.' I propose that in a democratic city it is imperative that we speak to strangers, live next to them, and learn how to relate to them on many levels, including the sexual" (193). With Delany's axiom in mind, I made willing conversation with the homeless stranger, who just a moment ago had been hurling invective at passing cars and who now graciously had retrieved my hat.

When I divulged where I was headed, the man showed me a shortcut to the gym that saved me from walking two extra miles and that miraculously got me to my appointment on time. (I have a terrible sense of direction: this man accompanied me on what turned out to be the most direct route to my destination.) Not only did he save me considerable time and energy, the homeless stranger also saved my baseball cap and, as we strolled down Castro Street, provided interesting conversation to boot. In so doing, he opened up a whole new perspective on San Francisco's substantial homeless population and on Delany's account of urban, interclass contact. At the end of our half hour or

---

a male couple, one of whom I first met in an encounter, perhaps a decade ago, at the back of the now closed-down Variety Photoplays Movie Theater on Third Avenue just below Fourteenth Street. Outside my family, these are among the two most rewarding relationships I have: both began as cross-class contacts in a public space" (Delany, 125–26).

so together, as we finished the conversation outside Gold's, the man inquired very casually whether I could help him out with spare change, although he was clear that I should not feel under any obligation. Had he asked for money when we first met, I probably would have refused, but after such a pleasant encounter and such generous assistance on his part, I was happy to help. To my surprise, the homeless stranger then showered me with kisses and offered to fuck me right outside the gym (earlier, as he rhapsodized about his "girlfriend's pussy," I had taken him for straight). An experience that, for me, began in trepidation ended in delight.

Although we parted ways at the entrance to Gold's, I suspect that both the homeless stranger and I benefited from the encounter more than either of us could have anticipated. Apparently minor in themselves and wholly contingent, such experiences have a major effect on quality of life in a city. Yet as Delany notes of the pleasures of contact, "specific benefits and losses cannot be systematized, operationalized, standardized, or predicted" (169). There is no guarantee that a stranger will help you rather than, say, grabbing your purse or making off with your hat. A major distinction between contact and networking is that the former entails more risk than does the latter—so much more, in fact, that interclass contact can seem inherently "unsafe." But as the examples provided suggest, interclass contact, though it involves the risk of unpredictability, is not inherently dangerous or unsafe; indeed, one of the great virtues of Delany's and Jacobs's analyses of city life lies in their demonstration that contact with strangers increases the overall level of urban safety.

We thus confront the paradox that a mode of sociality entailing risk actually makes urban existence safer. This paradox is only apparent: it dissolves as soon as one recognizes how safety and risk are not diametrically opposed—how, in other words, not every risk automatically qualifies as "unsafe." The rhetoric of safety engulfing U.S. society and culture leaves us disproportionately terrified of risk in all forms, including the risks of contact with those of different classes, races, sexualities, or nationalities. This rhetoric of safety exploits our terror of the unfamiliar in the service of consolidating class hierarchies, maintaining racial segregation, and intensifying xenophobia. I might go so far as to say that the rhetoric of safety, by inducing such paralyzing fear, approaches a form of terrorism in its own right. We have reached a point at which it is hard to see how appeals to safety and security can be anything other than politically reactionary. Thus even as Jacobs and Delany demonstrate that interclass contact in public space makes urban life safer, *safety* no longer may be the best rationale for contact. In this respect, the significance of bareback subculture lies in its explicit critique of the value of safety as a governing principle. Without going so far as to advocate unprotected sex, I want to suggest that the subculture's embrace of risk may help illuminate the pleasures and ethics of encountering the unfamiliar. The family-values rhetoric that has achieved such prominence in contemporary U.S. political discourse endorses above all the importance of the familiar, whereas I wish to stress the value for democratic life of contact with the unfamiliar, even the strange.

THE SECURITY OF NETWORKING

Forms of sociability that rely on contact with the familiar beyond the borders of kinship are what Delany categorizes as networking. In contradistinction to contact, networking tends to be class bound and membership oriented. My encounter with the homeless man in San Francisco ended when I stepped inside an institution that requires formal membership and a certain level of disposable income for entry. As Delany observes, "networking is heavily dependent on institutions to promote the necessary propinquity (gyms, parties, twelve-step programs, conferences, reading groups, singing groups, social gatherings, workshops, tourist groups, and classes), where those with the requisite social skills can maneuver" (129).[11] It is not a question of denigrating these perfectly valid institutions and forms of sociability as much as of acknowledging how, although situated mostly outside the home, they encourage privatized forms of sociability. They are not fully public, in the sense of open to all, and their membership criteria function to exclude the "wrong type" of person. My homeless acquaintance knew that he could not set foot in Gold's for a quick shower and some time in the sauna without paying an exorbitant fee. Given the history of gay politics in a city as ostensibly progressive as San Francisco, it is worth considering why such a large, welcoming gay gym seems unable to accommodate such a simple physical desire.

That gyms like this one in the Castro are well known as havens of cruising and public sex permits us to differentiate cruising as an instance of contact from cruising as an instance of networking. The risk entailed in cruising for sex at Gold's is less that one might encounter the radically unfamiliar than that public sex explicitly contravenes club rules. Rather than transgressing a class boundary, one violates a prohibition whose enforcement depends on

11. Despite what the term *networking* might connote for some readers, I should emphasize that, in Delany's conceptual usage, it betokens a homogenizing, restricted mode of sociality, in comparison with *contact*. Networking is not rhizomatic.

the mood of local management. Thus although erotic activity in the saunas, steam rooms, and showers of some gyms is barely distinguishable from that of a bathhouse or sex club, the horizon of interclass contact at a gym tends to be narrower than what one is likely to encounter in the less privatized space of a sex club or porn theater. The fact that it costs roughly as much to use a fashionable gym for one day as it does to join a sex club for an entire year means that sex at the gym involves only those who are reasonably close to oneself in terms of socioeconomic status and thus comparatively familiar. From the democratic perspective of interclass contact, sex at the gym risks privatizing public sex.[12]

In terms of Delany's distinction between networking and contact, cruising at the gym occupies an intermediary point between cruising on the street or in a bar—that is, in a public space accessible to all—and cruising online. What troubles me about online cruising is that it contributes to the accelerating privatization of public life that began in earnest during the first decade of the AIDS epidemic, under the Reagan administration. After considerable political resistance to redevelopment plans in earlier decades, New York City witnessed insufficient organized protest of its destruction of the Times Square theaters in the 1990s, because by then most middle-class consumers enjoyed full access to VCRs, DVDs, and online pornography. It was not just that the theaters were shrouded in stigma; porn's enhanced domestic availability allowed most middle-class men to imagine that the theaters' demise would incur only negligible losses. Yet compliance with the privatization of public space disregards the circumstances of those who do not enjoy complete access to the latest technology. Such acquiescence betrays an antidemocratic assumption that the disenfranchised and homeless bear little or no entitlement to visual pleasure. It is a way of saying, in effect, that those who are less privileged than me have less right to erotic enjoyment than I do. Since this is always how the state has regarded nonheterosexuals, it is dispiriting, to say the least, when middle-class gay men start thinking that way.

It also is dispiriting that middle-class gay men should appear oblivious to the qualitatively distinct pleasures and benefits of erotic contact in public space.

12. In the interest of ethnographic accuracy and to forestall potential disappointment, I should note that Gold's in the Castro bears far less resemblance to a sex club than does the much cruisier 24 Hour Fitness gym located further east on Market Street. For a very illuminating ethnographic analysis of cruising conventions at an upscale gym in Washington, D.C., see William L. Leap, "Sex in 'Private' Places: Gender, Erotics, and Detachment in Two Urban Locales," in Leap, Public Sex/Gay Space, 115–39.

When the public space of contact is narrowed to more-privatized spaces suitable for networking, everyone's pleasure diminishes. To be precise, I should say that the privatization of public space *homogenizes* pleasure, even as it may seem to increase its available quantity. The distinction between different qualities of pleasure—a distinction, that is, between the pleasures accessible through online cruising versus those of bar cruising or street cruising (and therefore between virtual space and truly public urban space)—becomes clear in a recent *New Yorker* article about the problem of crystal methamphetamine in the gay community and its role in HIV transmission.[13] The article suggests that the increase in unprotected sex among gay men can be explained by the ready availability of crystal methamphetamine, protease inhibitors, and online hookups—an explanation that this book has argued is inadequate. Nevertheless, the article throws into relief the insidious appeal of online cruising by making clear how Internet hookups create an impression of unprecedented control over one's erotic engagement with others.

When interviewing a middle-aged gay man at one of San Francisco's STD clinics, Dr. Jeffrey Klausner, director of Sexually Transmitted Diseases Prevention and Control Services in the city's Department of Public Health, asks how many sex partners the man has had during the preceding two months. The answer to that question turns out to be the same as the man's response to the question of how many sex partners he's had during the past *year*. The man explains this increase by telling the doctor "I got online" and elaborating thus:

"I am a fifty-year-old, overweight, HIV-positive man. I am balding; I'm not that attractive. But I can go online any time of the day and I can get a sexual hookup. I can go to this site on AOL and I can say I want to meet somebody now for sex. And that's all there is to it.

"I go online and put out my stats—if I am a top or a bottom, what I like to do. I am a top. I am HIV positive. So I will say, 'Does anyone want to be topped by an HIV-positive guy?'

"I'll get five responses in half an hour. And then I will speak to them on the phone. If I like their voice, I will invite them over and look through my window. If I like what I see, then I will be home, and if not I can pretend I am gone. It's been great. I don't have to talk to anybody to do it. I don't have to go out of the house. I can get it like this," he said, and snapped his fingers.[14]

13. Specter, "Higher Risk," 38–45.
14. Ibid., 40–41.

Cruising online makes finding a sex partner indistinguishable from Internet shopping—except that the sex partner arrives at your home address sooner and returns appear easier. When other persons are thus commodified, the possibility of genuine contact appears remote.

What I find disturbing about this man's testimony to the convenience of cruising online is not the increased number of sexual contacts or the prospect of an HIV-positive guy getting so many responses when he advertises as a top. What's troubling is his evident satisfaction at the discovery that "I don't have to talk to anybody to do it. I don't have to go out of the house." In direct contrast with Delany's ethic of sex with strangers as a means of making contact, cruising online enables one to have sex with strangers *without contact*. It is tantamount to treating a stranger as a blow-up doll or a mail-order sex toy—an approach that betokens a purely instrumental approach to the other, rather than the openness to others that cruising at its best represents. Hooking-up online in a city such as San Francisco or New York transforms public space into private space, thereby reducing the contact sport of cruising to a practice of networking. Instead of an opportunity for conversation with strangers, cruising becomes a way to avoid it.

This privatizing of public space, this narrowing of the risky but exhilarating sphere of contact to the reassuringly homogenous zone of networking, has been under way in the United States for at least a quarter of a century. Conservative politicians, such as Rudolph Giuliani, are not the only ones responsible for facilitating the destruction of public sexual culture in the name of a safer New York. Everyone who traverses city streets while talking on his or her cell phone, or with an iPod attached to his or her head, abets the degeneration of contact space into network space. Confronted with a sea of strangers (as one is wont to be in a metropolis), it is perfectly normal to wish for conversation with someone more familiar. The problem arises when all occasions for contact with otherness are treated as signal opportunities to seek more of the same—when, that is, the possibility of momentarily stepping outside one's comfort zone provokes stringent clampdowns on otherness, contingency, and the incalculable.

Bareback subculture's critique of the insidious rhetoric of safety exemplifies the best aspects of cruising, when the latter is understood as a disposition of hospitality toward strangers. But, as I have indicated, much of the cruising for bareback sex occurs online, where this attitude of openness threatens to deteriorate into a controlled instrumentalization of the other as an object of use. The destruction not only of public cruising spaces but also of the ethic of cruising is especially apparent in the online publicity for those "Cute Boy Bareback Gang Bang Parties" described in chapter 2 (and documented in the video *Fucking Crazy*). Although supposedly open to anyone, these monthly events are regulated by an elaborate set of criteria for determining eligibility and an extensive list of rules governing participation. According to the group's Web site, participants must be (or at least must appear to be) under the age of forty; they must conform to certain physical requirements ("You do not need to be Mr. Super Stud, but you do need to have a nice, fit body"); they must submit photographs of themselves, including a cock shot, and complete an online application form; they must live up to their advance publicity ("If you have misrepresented yourself you will not be allowed into the party"); they must arrive between 7:30 and 7:45 p.m. ("Everyone is free to leave at anytime, but no one will be admitted after 7:45pm"); latecomers or absentees should expect appropriate discipline ("We have a very strict no-show policy—anyone who no-shows will be removed from any future parties!!").[15]

Not only do these bareback-party organizers expect *gay men* to show up on time, they expect them to adhere to a long list of prohibitions once assembled: no smoking, no alcohol, no drugs, no bottoming (except by the "prescreened" bottom selected for the evening), and absolutely no condoms. There is a mandatory clothes check, and participants are expected to ejaculate inside the designated bottom's butt or mouth. By all accounts, nobody present at this carefully controlled scene has the option to change his mind. The organizers provide their catalogue of prohibitions in advance, but nobody gets to say no once there. In many respects, this is a grim prospect. Far from a night of hedonism, one should expect a disciplined evening of following the rules. Along with the various elements of successful parties that the organizers have outlawed, we should note that they go to remarkable lengths to permit no contingency, no negotiation, no imagination, no serendipity, no adventure, no inventiveness, and no versatility—thus, in a sense, no promiscuity or contact. Avowedly unafraid of HIV or semen ingestion, the organizers seem exceptionally squeamish at the prospect of other kinds of risk that usually accompany intimacy with strangers.

I find it telling that this strictly controlled environment is not deemed incompatible with a certain multiculturalism: "We try to include a good mix of all ethnic backgrounds as well as body types." This gesture toward diversity cannot conceal the multiple exclusions considered necessary to "create a hot

15. From http://www.cuteboybbparty.com/GroupInfo.html (accessed June 2003).

atmosphere for all those attending the gangbang." Just as Giuliani's redevelopment of New York in the name of safety has made the city less safe and less appealing for many of its inhabitants (as well as for many visitors), so this gay organization's obsessive controlling for "hotness" renders its parties lamentably dull. Since these events occur in a private residence, the organizers have every right to "prescreen" all who enter their home. But their eagerness to privatize public sex—and the manifold exclusions accompanying this move—remains out of keeping with the cruisy adventurousness that historically has been associated with urban gay life. In cases such as this, when self-identified risk takers hedge their erotic activity with multiple rules and constraints, an erstwhile generosity embodied in the bareback ethic of unlimited intimacy dissipates into something more depressingly familiar and routine. Why impose so many limits on a practice of intimacy that is meant to overcome limits?

SOMA RED

By holding a bareback party in a private residence, one avoids not only those who might wish to participate while wearing condoms but also any discussion of the matter. Private space permits its owners to control what happens in it by providing access to only the like-minded; there is no risk of the momentary awkwardness of negotiation when all variables have been controlled in advance. My criticism of this arrangement is not meant to imply an objection to either sexual privacy or privacy in general. On the contrary, privacy is vital, especially in a city. Rather, it is a question of understanding the relation between public and private, of striking the proper balance between them, and of grasping how sex and sexuality are far from exclusively private matters. Ever since modernity detached enfranchisement from property ownership, democratic societies have aspired to provide access to public spaces, public services, and public benefits for all their citizens, irrespective of wealth, status, class, race, creed, and so on. Cities historically have been very good at furnishing public resources. The privatization of public services and benefits contravenes this basic democratic principle at the expense of those with the least resources. Privatizing public sex, as in the "Cute Boy Bareback Gang Bang Parties," compounds this problem.

As an institution that privatizes intimacy, marriage compounds the problem too. There is inequality not just in same-sex couples' relative lack of access to the institution of marriage but, more fundamentally, in the way that marriage privileges one kind of relationship at the expense of others. Michael

Warner points out that "even though people think that marriage gives them validation, legitimacy, and recognition, they somehow think that it does so without invalidating, delegitimating, or stigmatizing other relations, needs, and desires."[16] The social validation of one relational form over others is strengthened, not diminished, by the extension of marriage rights to same-sex couples. Winning gay marriage rights inevitably would stigmatize even further all those forms of intimacy that don't fit into the connubial couple mold, and it would discourage everyone—whether gay, straight, or other-wise—from undertaking relational experiments. Foucault's point on this matter bears repeating: "We live in a relational world that institutions have considerably impoverished. Society and the institutions which frame it have limited the possibility of relationships because a rich relational world would be very complex to manage."[17] Given that marriage provides the principal mechanism whereby nation-states regulate their citizens' intimate lives, non-heterosexual people might have been expected to express more skepticism about the wisdom of entangling themselves in this institution.

Warner argues that the campaign for same-sex marriage is connected to the redevelopment of Times Square, insofar as both confer on erotic relations a measure of respectability by privatizing intimacy. Queers confront a kind of Faustian bargain, whereby we tacitly agree to renounce public sex—or to sell downriver those who find value in it—in return for the legitimacy afforded by the right to marry. Needless to say, this kind of ideological transaction negates completely the relational forms and intimate practices, including those associated with cruising, that public sex spaces have permitted us to create. For some time I labored under the illusion that this problem was "a New York thing," that the urban depredation anticipated by Jacobs and anatomized by Delany, Warner, and others in Manhattan wouldn't occur in cities with flourishing public sex institutions and staunchly democratic mayors. As Giuliani system-atically devastated New York City's public sexual culture, making the city in-creasingly inhospitable to queers, the working class, and the disenfranchised, I felt confirmed in my long-term preference for San Francisco. It came as a shock to discover that, despite manifold differences between the two cities, a similar

16. Warner, *Trouble with Normal*, 99. What I find especially valuable about Warner's critique is how effective it seems to have been, at least anecdotally, in changing lesbian and gay readers' minds regarding the desirability of marriage. The official debate on this issue has made it appear that same-sex marriage is a question simply of equal rights and full citizenship, whereas it may be more a question of how far anyone is prepared to endure the intensified normalization of their erotic and affective lives.

17. Michel Foucault, "The Social Triumph of the Sexual Will," in vol. 1 of *Essential Works*, 158.

destruction of cruising spaces has been unfolding in what many regarded as an urban erotic haven.

In March 2004, I flew to San Francisco for spring break, just a few weeks after the city's charismatic young mayor, Gavin Newsom, garnered international attention by issuing thousands of marriage licenses to same-sex couples, deliberately violating California state law. Newsom's courage in acting on his convictions about sexual equality and his fearless defiance of state governor Arnold Schwarzenegger seemed remarkable in a politician with presidential ambitions—and hence cause for celebration. The evening that I arrived in San Francisco, I ventured out to my favorite cruise bar, My Place, located South of Market at 1225 Folsom Street, just west of Eighth Street, in the heart of the city's warehouse district, which has been home to a well-developed leather culture of bars, clubs, stores, and sex institutions since the 1960s. My Place is not technically a leather bar, although its down-at-heel, working-class atmosphere and reputation for casual sex on the premises attract a number of leathermen. A narrow room stretching back directly from the street (with its bar immediately on the left as you enter), My Place has a heavy leather curtain shrouding its entrance, principally to conceal the bar and its activity from passersby. The leather curtain lends an air of mystery and, for some, menace to the place. Seated in front of the curtain on a tall stool is a Charon-like figure, whose role seems to be to ensure that those entering My Place know what they're getting into. There is no entry fee, no ID check, and no dress code. When I arrived, near midnight on Friday, March 12, 2004, the bar was closed—not temporarily but for good.

Exactly four months earlier, on Friday, November 14, 2003, near midnight, undercover police from the Department of Alcohol and Beverage Control, who had been investigating My Place for six months and surreptitiously photographing men engaged in public sex there, raided the bar and arrested six patrons. As a statement by the San Francisco–based activist group Gay Shame noted, "it is frightening that, in San Francisco, in 2003, gay men are being handcuffed and interrogated by undercover cops for 'lewd conduct' inside a gay bar."[18] One might have imagined that city police would have more pressing matters to occupy their attention; indeed, one cannot help but wonder about the libidinal investment of officers who get involved so closely in other men's erotic pleasure, who devote their time to spying on guys having sex together, and who plan trip after trip to a gay cruise bar under the cover of

18. See http://www.gayshamesf.org/archives.html.

official business. Given the history of this fabled bar, it would be reasonable to suppose that the spot constituted an entirely appropriate venue for "lewd conduct" among consenting adults. The point of the leather curtain and the man seated at My Place's entrance was to ensure that nobody innocent of the bar's reputation stumbled into its bacchanalia by mistake. Consensual erotic activity at My Place, though technically not legal, had been going on there for decades, and everyone knew it. Sex at My Place was consensual in the sense that the men who participated in it were eager and willing, but also that the bar and its employees tacitly consented to its occurring on the premises, while the SFPD turned a blind eye. Doubtless My Place's reputation as San Francisco's friendliest cruise bar had been good for business and good, moreover, for the city's gay tourism.

What changed? Before it became My Place in 1987, the bar at 1225 Folsom Street had been a popular leather saloon named Ramrod for twenty years. Thus for almost four decades this narrow SOMA space functioned as a haven for leathermen and others drawn to the masculine, blue-collar ethos and raunchy sex associated with leather subculture.[19] It is no exaggeration to say that, from before gay liberation until the end of 2003, the place was a beloved institution of what is viewed around the world as a gay Mecca. That after all this time it should be raided by police for sex on the premises suggests a sea change in public attitudes toward homosexuality. The Gay Shame Web site points out that "handcuffing, detaining, and citing gay men for 'lewd conduct' inside a gay bar—allegedly to halt the spread of syphilis, a treatable disease—does nothing but set us back to the pre-Stonewall 1960s, when gay bars were routinely raided by the cops for virtually any reason at all."[20] Of course, it was the frequency and arbitrary brutality of police raids on gay bars

19. My principal resource for historical information on SOMA leather bars is anthropologist Gayle Rubin's indispensable work. See Rubin, "Elegy for the Valley of Kings: AIDS and the Leather Community in San Francisco, 1981–1996," in *In Changing Times: Gay Men and Lesbians Encounter HIV/AIDS*, ed. Martin P. Levine, Peter M. Nardi, and John H. Gagnon (Chicago: University of Chicago Press, 1997), 101–44; Rubin, "The Miracle Mile: South of Market and Gay Male Leather 1962–1997," in *Reclaiming San Francisco: History, Politics, Culture*, ed. James Brook, Chris Carlsson, and Nancy J. Peters (San Francisco: City Lights Books, 1998), 247–72; and Rubin, "The South of Market Leather History," *San Francisco Frontiers*, September 20, 2001, 20–22. (In "Elegy for the Valley of Kings," Rubin dates the Ramrod's opening as 1966; in the *San Francisco Frontiers* article, which reprises "Elegy" in abbreviated form, she dates the opening as 1968.) Scholars in queer studies eagerly await the appearance in book form of Rubin's legendary doctoral thesis, "The Valley of the Kings: Leathermen in San Francisco, 1960–1990" (PhD diss., University of Michigan, 1994), which doubtless will provide the definitive ethnographic account of this subculture and its rich history in San Francisco.

20. See http://www.gayshamesf.org/archives.html.

that prompted a riot at New York's Stonewall Inn in June 1969, the event that conventionally marks the birth of gay liberation. That a San Francisco gay bar should be raided after so much political progress on the issue of gay rights raises questions about the cost to queer cultures and communities of the "progress" that same-sex marriage is considered to represent.

Police apparently began investigating My Place and other SOMA cruise bars after someone alleged that his friends were contracting syphilis there. It is certainly the case that San Francisco, like other major U.S. cities, has seen syphilis rates skyrocket in recent years and that the increase has been viewed as a measure of an increasing incidence of risky sex (since the symptoms of syphilis become detectable far more quickly than those of HIV infection, syphilis rates generally are considered to be a good prognosticator of HIV-transmission rates). Unlike HIV, however, syphilis is not merely "treatable" but easily *curable*. To my knowledge, health officials never have considered shutting down airlines that provide transatlantic flights on the grounds that anyone's chances of contracting influenza increase dramatically through their wanton participation in long-haul air travel. It is the stigma attached to curable bacterial diseases contracted through sex that makes them such a terrific alibi for state crackdowns on gay culture. Put somewhat differently—and this may be what distinguishes public sex from airline travel—the image of others' contracting disease through their disproportionate access to pleasure provokes a virtually irresistible desire to discipline and punish cruisers.

The spot at 1225 Folsom Street subsequently reopened as a gay bar, though of an altogether different sort. Now it is an upscale cocktail joint called CIP Lounge, specializing in expensive mixed drinks (particularly, high-end champagnes) and boasting a four-page drinks menu. Gay bars regularly change ownership and name while catering to a fairly consistent clientele—for example, the Powerhouse, a leather cruise bar located on Folsom Street one block west of My Place, was known in the early 1970s as the In Between bar, then the No Name, then The Bolt, and then The Brig, until it became Powerhouse in 1985 and subsequently reopened, in 1997, under different management as the new Powerhouse. Yet throughout these various incarnations, the bar consistently served San Francisco's leather community.[21] The same could be said

---

21. Details on Powerhouse's previous incarnations are given in Rubin, "South of Market." The phenomenon of a "gay-bar system," in which specific locales serve a continuous function even as individual bars change hands and names, is discussed in Nancy Achilles, "The Development of the Homosexual Bar as an Institution," in *Sexual Deviance*, ed. John Gagnon and William Simon (New York: Harper & Row, 1967), 228–244, cited in Rubin, "Elegy for the Valley of Kings," 136.

of 1225 Folsom Street when it changed from the Ramrod to My Place, but not of the changeover from My Place to CIP Lounge. Cip was the name of the manager of My Place when it was raided; clearly the bar's new name alludes to his, as well as playing on the image of sipping champagne in a refined atmosphere. Equally clearly, the profit margin on drinks at the new establishment has risen exponentially, leading one to wonder whether the police investigation was motivated by health concerns or managerial greed. Although I have been unable to ascertain whether My Place was closed by city officials or by its owner with plans for a yuppie makeover, I'm confident that there is little overlap between the customers of My Place and those of CIP Lounge.

A working-class gay bar populated mainly by men in their thirties, forties, and fifties, My Place was not filled with pretty boys, perfect gym bodies, or "attitude." Much of the institution's seedy charm lay in its resolute unpretentiousness and its patrons' friendliness toward strangers; it was a space of interclass contact where men of all races and body types (including the disabled) exchanged conversation and pleasure with minimum interference. After evenings at My Place, I regularly would jot character sketches of the guys whom I had met and their fascinating stories, inspired by a sense that this bar constituted an ideal site for informally gathering oral histories. My most extensive interactions with nonwhite men, with disabled men, and with men who have been HIV positive for decades occurred in that bar. Although widely regarded as a pleasure dome of easy oral sex, My Place functioned also as a sort of subcultural school, an institution in which San Francisco's sexual history and culture were transmitted orally to relative newcomers such as me.[22] What I found so appealing about My Place was that merely entering the bar and standing around, looking expectant, was sufficient to encourage people who were totally different from oneself to strike up conversations that, while always courteous, were rarely as superficial as verbal exchanges often can be in gay bars.

Doubtless such conversations were facilitated by the ready availability of erotic pleasure and the minimal barriers separating social space from sexual space: if conversation progressed in the right direction, it wasn't necessary to move elsewhere before translating verbal into oral intercourse. Rather than offering to buy you a drink, the friendly stranger engaging you in pleasant

---

22. In ancient Greece, the institution of pederasty was simultaneously an institution of pedagogy: older men initiated younger not just sexually but also in terms of their civic responsibility as future citizens. Sex between men, even when institutionalized as legitimate, has tended to function historically as a means of transmitting knowledge; in my experience, My Place fulfilled this pedagogical function admirably.

conversation was just as likely to offer to blow you on the spot. Although occasionally the bar opened its large storeroom as a back room, sexual activity at My Place tended to spill out of designated areas until the entire bar resembled a good-natured back room. The site of greatest erotic commotion was usually the tearoom, a dimly lit space perhaps nine feet long by three feet wide, containing a trough-style urinal that was concealed from general view by dark leather curtains at either end. (Those who wished to use the bathroom for conventional purposes availed themselves of a tiny separate room with a single toilet and a door that locked.) Often as many as a dozen men crammed into the narrow tearoom for polymorphous public sex, although the border between purely sexual and nonsexual spaces tended to remain permeable at My Place. The bar displayed striking erotic murals on its walls, and, in the years after the ban on smoking in public accommodations, it exhibited inventive, Keith Haring–inspired fluorescent graffiti on the walls of an external hallway constructed for smokers. My Place's two decrepit video monitors played mostly gay porn, typically of the leather genre.

With the metamorphosis (one might say *redevelopment*) of My Place into CIP Lounge, prime contact space has been reduced to an arena for yuppie networking. One wonders where the older, working-class men who utilized My Place but who cannot afford the hundred-dollar "bottle service" at CIP Lounge will spend their leisure time. The loss of this gay institution—along with the opportunities for interclass contact and erotic sociability that it sponsored—marks a moment in gay history characterized by a bid for respectability at the expense of non–middle-class persons and values. Unlike the Times Square porn theaters, My Place was not closed as part of a systematic rezoning plan; however, the police raid that led to its closure has had a chilling effect on other SOMA cruise bars. As I discovered in March 2004, shortly after finding My Place padlocked, the back room at Powerhouse is now more brightly lit, more regularly patrolled, and as a consequence less cruisy. The Loading Dock, a leather and uniform bar at 1525 Mission Street with a strict dress code on weekends, closed in March 2005, after nearly nine years of operation. And the Strand, the city's largest porn theater, on the south side of Market Street at Civic Center, was boarded up in March 2004 (thus precluding a Delany-style encounter). It remained boarded up two-and-a-half years later, in November 2006, when I last visited.[23]

23. While this book was in production, I learned that, in April 2008, 1225 Folsom Street opened as a new leather bar named Chaps II. The bar, which revives the spirit of Ramrod and My

The closing of My Place is a symptom of transformations in the SOMA landscape that have been under way for decades. As long ago as the 1950s, before it became established as the home of leather culture, SOMA was identified as the principal target for redevelopment in San Francisco, because it "offered hundreds of acres of flat land with low-density use, low land prices, and, to the corporate eye, expendable people and businesses."[24] The disappearance of My Place—and the displacement of the blue-collar men, leatherfolk, and other minorities that it served—is part of a process of gentrification that has reduced the SOMA leather-oriented institutions from several dozen at their acme, in the late 1970s and early '80s, to a meager handful today. That this process of gentrification accelerated during the first decade of the AIDS epidemic encouraged a misperception that the disease, rather than redevelopment, was primarily responsible for the decimation of SOMA as a gay neighborhood. As with the invocation of syphilis transmission as a rationale for closing My Place, stigmatized erotic practices readily are viewed as precipitating the demise of public gay culture, even by some gays themselves. In the face of such fantasmatic spectacles of queer sex, the mundane yet nonetheless effective agents of this demise—namely, class warfare and the corporate greed fueling redevelopment—are easily overlooked.[25]

Gavin Newsom, who served on the city's Board of Supervisors for several years before taking office as mayor in 2004, also represents a symptom rather than a direct cause of these changes. As urban historian Chester Hartman observed several years before millionaire Newsom's ascension to power, San Francisco

---

Place, is described online thus: "Chaps Bar San Francisco is a leather and gear bar. It's not just leather, but leather is a very big part of our bar. Here at Chaps, you will always find all the team in gear—from the owner to the manager to the bartenders to barbacks to music people to door-security. It's all about the gear. It's not dress up. It's not a costume. It's a lifestyle. It's a frame of mind. . . . Some patrons gear up. Some patrons don't. Either way, it's a frame of mind. And we encourage you to gear up with whatever shit you are into. At Chaps, nobody will look at you funny, or think you are strange because of your gear. We get it. We honor it and support you in your kink and fetish. Some patrons might not gear up—but are fucking kinky as hell. In that case, wear some flip flops, Abercrombie shorts and a tank top—who the fuck cares? If you are kinky and twisted—you'll fit right in." From http://www.chapsbarsanfrancisco.com/mission.html (accessed June 2008).

24. Chester Hartman, *City for Sale: The Transformation of San Francisco*, rev. ed. (Berkeley: University of California Press, 2002), 8. On the catastrophe of redevelopment for all but corporate profiteers, see also Rebecca Solnit and Susan Schwartzenberg, *Hollow City: The Siege of San Francisco and the Crisis of American Urbanism* (New York: Verso, 2000).

25. In "Elegy for the Valley of Kings," Rubin argues persuasively that "the patterns of urban succession in the South of Market area resulted from geographic competition for the area that had long preceded AIDS, and from public policy decisions about disease control, as much as it did from the disease itself" (109).

is rapidly becoming a city of have-a-lots and have-nots, with the working-class and lower-middle-class population being pushed out. Class (although not race) diversity is disappearing; it has become hard to find niches where idiosyncratic residential, commercial, and cultural life can flourish, and segregation by neighborhoods, classes, and races is increasing.[26]

Like the disappearance of gay institutions of interclass contact that coincides with Newsom's promotion of the institution of gay marriage, the survival of San Francisco's racial diversity camouflages the loss of its class diversity. Before his decision to issue same-sex marriage licenses, Newsom had generated controversy with his inhumane proposals for reducing the city's homeless population. The festival of gay weddings early in 2004 made getting married feel like an act of civil disobedience, as if privatizing intimacy via government-sanctioned nuptials heralded the birth of a new civil rights movement. Media images of all those joyful newlyweds bamboozled liberals everywhere into seeing nothing but sexual progress in Newsom's San Francisco. However, the price of these weddings will not be Newsom's political career but erotic diversity, relational possibilities, and a whole social fabric of interclass contact that, as I have tried to suggest, makes urban life worth living. Ironically, Democrat Newsom illustrates Warner's thesis in *The Trouble with Normal* better even than does Republican Giuliani.

TOWARD AN ETHICS OF CONTACT

Drawing on critiques of urban redevelopment in New York City, this chapter has outlined connections among the following sociopolitical shifts in San Francisco: the promotion of marriage in place of cruising, the reduction of cruising in public space to cruising online, the privatization of public life, the reconception of urban existence on the model of the small town, and the conversion of contact space into network space. Following Delany, I have suggested that these retrograde developments all are motivated by anxieties about interclass contact or, more basically, by fear of the unfamiliar. Our fear of strangers involves a fear of strange*ness* that is only inflamed by the rhetoric of safety and domestic security pervading official political discourse. To the extent that this rhetoric of safety—including discourses of "safe sex"—deters contact with strangers, it should be subject to ethical critique. And insofar as bareback subculture has generated its own critique of the rhetoric of safety, it

---

26. Hartman, *City for Sale*, 2–3.

remains consonant with the ethical argument that I'm advancing here. Engagement with otherness is never completely safe; contact with the unfamiliar, the strange, always entails risk. The remainder of this chapter contends that the ethical imperative to engage otherness becomes more compelling once we grasp how its risks often yield pleasure.

Openness to contact with the other gives rise to an ethics not of self-sacrifice but of pleasure. Foucault pursued his history of sexuality by returning to the Greeks, in part because they developed such an elaborate ethics around the question of pleasure—an ethics that antedates more familiar ethical systems centered on sacrifice (such as that of Christianity). What interested Foucault was how classical civilization, in contrast to modernity, articulated its concern with *aphrodisia* without reference to laws or norms. Now, it is not a matter of extrapolating from classical culture an ethical system directly applicable to our own but, rather, of acknowledging the difficulty and complexity of pleasure. "Pleasure is a very difficult behavior," Foucault noted in an interview. Freud registered a similar difficulty: "Everything relating to the problem of pleasure and unpleasure touches upon one of the sorest spots of present-day psychology."[27]

Reminders about the difficulty of pleasure are necessary in light of what might seem to be this chapter's contradictory claims regarding the pleasures of contact. On one hand, I have pointed to a pervasive anxiety generated by encountering strangers, an anxiety that Delany characterizes as the "wholly provincial and absolutely small-town terror of cross-class contact." On the other hand, also following Delany, I have endeavored to show how interclass contact yields distinctive pleasures that include, while remaining irreducible to, erotic pleasure. The apparent inconsistency between these strands of my argument may be resolved by appealing to a psychoanalytic account of the relationship between pleasure and anxiety, or by demonstrating how the pleasure of contact exists in tension with the pleasure of homeostasis. The quality of pleasure achieved through risk taking differs from that attained by staying safe. I want to develop the ethical implications of Delany's distinction between modes of sociality by redescribing it in psychoanalytic terms; this entails acknowledging that psychoanalysis offers not only a therapy and

27. Michel Foucault, "An Interview by Stephen Riggins," in vol. 1 of *Essential Works*, 129. Freud, *Three Essays*, 209. Earlier in this work, Freud cautions, "Psychology is still so much in the dark in questions of pleasure and unpleasure that the most cautious assumption is the one most to be recommended" (183).

a hermeneutic but also an ethics, a particular philosophy and practice of relating to alterity.

Because it encompasses the whole spectrum of conceivable relations between self and other, the ethics of psychoanalysis concerns far more than a doctor's treatment of his or her patients. As does cruising, the clinical encounter provides an arena in which to explore possible relations with strangers and, indeed, with strangeness. In psychoanalysis (as in cruising) one gets involved with an unknown other, a perfect stranger, by means of whom one encounters his or her own otherness. Encountering a stranger brings one into contact with the unconscious. For this reason, not only for reasons of social class, the encounter with strangers can be both terrifying and exciting. It is also for this reason that the tendency to shun contact with strangers is so pronounced, even in some practices of cruising. From a psychoanalytic perspective, Delany underestimates the extent to which it is possible to have sex with a stranger without making contact with him or her—that is, without allowing the stranger's otherness to have any impact on oneself. Sometimes physiological contact, whether with a stranger or with one's husband, hardly qualifies as *contact* at all.

Here it may be possible to specify further what I mean by contact with the other. Earlier in this chapter, I suggested that, contrary to the claims of certain feminist theorists, the ethical encounter with the other should not be understood primarily in terms of sexual difference, since collapsing otherness with difference in this way privileges heterosexuality as the paradigm of ethical relationality. But I want to insist also that the ethical encounter with the other should not be understood exclusively in terms of class difference either; such a move, although it has the virtue of extending ethics beyond the domestic sphere of family and home, reproduces the same problem by dissolving otherness into merely another axis of difference.[28] The solution to the problem lies not in struggling to account for all possible axes of difference—gender, sexuality, race, class, ethnicity, age, nationality, and so on—under the rubric of otherness but in maintaining the conceptual distinction between otherness and difference.

This distinction also helps to clarify the issue of power in scenes of contact with the other. The account of cross-class contact as motivated not by altruism but by pleasure raises questions about the power differentials involved and

28. In differentiating what I mean by contact from Delany's usage of the concept, I note that he is not proposing interclass contact as the paradigm of ethical relationality as such. Delany's salutary Marxist commitment to class analysis accounts both for his subsuming of racial difference under the rubric of class difference and for his materialist assumption (correct, in my view) that homosexuality does not in itself constitute a class category.

whether pleasure in such encounters is derived at anyone's expense. When discussing contact with the other in public space, I would not want to mislead readers for whom this phraseology might evoke the notion of "contact zones" that has proved to be so productive in postcolonial studies.[29] Although power relations doubtless circumscribe any contact scenario, the kind of contact that I have in mind is not one in which it is possible—much less desirable— to *instrumentalize* the other. It is always possible to instrumentalize another person; but while one may engage the otherness of the unconscious, he or she cannot instrumentalize it. Psychoanalysis entails an ethics because the otherness of the unconscious resists both domination and self-sacrifice. Relative to this other, one may assume the position of neither master nor slave.

Contact with the alterity of the unconscious requires the mediation—we might say, the *provocation*—of another person who may or may not be a stranger and who may or may not inhabit a different social register from oneself. This species of contact should be regarded as ethical insofar as it is not initiated in a purposive, goal-oriented manner; instead, one simply remains open to it. (Here it may be useful to recall both Delany's characterization of networking as more "motive-driven" than contact and John Lindell's claim, quoted in the introduction, that sex-club architecture promotes "an aimless, 'let's see what happens' frame of mind.") What one opens him- or herself to by means of this nonpurposive disposition is the incalculable impact of the other—an impact that psychoanalytic theory has tended to characterize in predominantly negative terms, as disruptive or traumatic, but that may be redescribed in terms of the specific quality of pleasure that it produces. *Times Square Red, Times Square Blue* enables us better to appreciate how the unpredictable pleasures of contact need not be generated at anyone's expense.

CRUISING WITH LAPLANCHE

Originally our opening to the other was not a matter of choice. The significance of a psychoanalytic theory of the unconscious lies in its supposition that the other precedes and thus constitutes the self. It is not a matter of subjects discursively creating others at the expense of whom they define themselves, as if subjectivity were in itself ethically dubious, but rather of what Laplanche calls "the primacy of the other" in the creation of subjectivity. There is no subjectivity

29. In *Imperial Eyes: Travel Writing and Transculturation* (London: Routledge, 1992), Mary Louise Pratt defines contact zones as "social spaces where disparate cultures meet, clash, and grapple with each other, often in highly asymmetrical relations of domination and subordination—like colonialism, slavery, or their aftermaths as they are lived out across the globe today" (4).

without the other, and therefore no subject whose identity remains uncompromised by the unconscious. For Laplanche, our most intimate caretakers, typically but not necessarily the parents, qualify as strangers from the very beginning, thanks to their unwittingly confronting us with indecipherable communications that lodge in the infant body. These indecipherable communications, which Laplanche classifies under the rubric of "the enigmatic signifier," impact not the child's consciousness but its defenseless corporeal form.

A consequence of neither the infant's underdeveloped cognitive skills nor the adult's imperfect parenting skills, this situation results from the existence of an unconscious, that is, from an adult's opacity to him- or herself. In handling the body of a child, an adult communicates unconscious signals to the child regardless of his or her best intentions. These signals remain enigmatic to their infant recipient because they are enigmatic to their adult sender. Laplanche calls this process "generalized seduction": the child is seduced into intersubjectivity by its efforts to fathom unintelligible messages from a stranger—a stranger who may happen to be its mother. Seduction is thus first and foremost inadvertent rather than deliberate, general rather than particular. As he puts it, "the enigma is in itself a seduction and its mechanisms are unconscious."[30]

It follows from this account that one's virginity always is lost to a stranger, even when seduction occurs within the domestic sphere. To rephrase the matter in more explicitly Freudian terms, we might say that the loss of virginity is always a re-losing of it. If seduction occurs through an involuntary making strange of parents to their children, then it is less a question of keeping strangers out of the home or neighborhood than of acknowledging that the stranger is already there, lurking unseen. It is a mistake to devote so many resources to protecting children from strangers, because we cannot protect them from ourselves. Rather than protection from strangers, adults and children need to learn how to live with them. As Julia Kristeva's useful meditation on the political history of the stranger argues, "we know that we are foreigners [*l'étrangers*] to ourselves, and it is with the help of that sole support that we can attempt to live with others."[31]

---

30. Jean Laplanche, *New Foundations for Psychoanalysis*, trans. David Macey (Oxford: Blackwell, 1989), 128. My summary of the theory of generalized seduction draws on this work, as well as on Laplanche's *Essays on Otherness*, ed. John Fletcher (London: Routledge, 1999). New scholarship on seduction and on Laplanche's theory of sexuality appeared recently as a special issue of *New Formations*. See John Fletcher, ed., "Jean Laplanche and the Theory of Seduction," special issue, *New Formations* 48 (2002–2003).

31. Julia Kristeva, *Strangers to Ourselves*, trans. Leon Roudiez (New York: Columbia University Press, 1991), 170. The French noun *l'étranger* is translatable as either *stranger* or *foreigner*; it refers to

This account of the primacy of the other in the genesis of subjectivity and, specifically, Laplanche's description of seduction via an enigmatic signifier bears a striking resemblance to Foucault's account of the genesis of modern sexual subjectivity via what he calls "the perverse implantation." In both cases, sexuality is produced not from inside but from outside the self: it originates in an alien other whose intrusion eroticizes the body helplessly laid open before it. In well-known passages from *The History of Sexuality*, Foucault sketches a picture of what also might be called generalized seduction. Memorably describing how, during the nineteenth century, "all around the child, indefinite *lines of penetration* were disposed," he contends that "the whole machinery of power ... was implanted in bodies":

> The power which thus took charge of sexuality set about contacting bodies, caressing them with its eyes, intensifying areas, electrifying surfaces, dramatizing troubled moments. It wrapped the sexual body in its embrace.[32]

Here power—specifically, *biopower*—sexualizes bodies in a manner akin to how, in Laplanche's account, sexuality is implanted in a child by the enigmatic messages transmitted from the unconscious of its adult caretaker. Sexuality is alien because it comes from the outside, that is, from a stranger.

The difference between Foucault's and Laplanche's accounts of the production of sexuality lies in the latter's insistence on the enigmatic quality of what is implanted in the child. Originating from outside the body, sexuality arrives in the form not of meaning but of impenetrable opacity; in contrast to the cultural discourses anatomized by Foucault, it has no determinate content. Laplanche argues that Freud's theory of the Oedipus complex is mistaken because it too readily translates the enigma into sense. In place of a meaning, figure, or story, there is a hole in meaning that provokes a desiring hole in the human body: the body's apertures are sexualized by the enigmas of the other's unconscious. It is because the other has an unconscious that I have a sexuality. Laplanche's emphasis on the enigma makes this psychoanalytic explanation of sexuality resolutely antiessentialist.

Far from being a one-time event, the opening of the self to the enigma of the other's unconscious is perpetually reactivated in moments of what, following Jacobs and Delany, I have been calling contact. Primal seduction installs

---

a juridical as well as an existential category of being. Kristeva's psychoanalytic account of strangeness, although not pursued in a Laplanchean mode, has influenced considerably my argument in this chapter.

32. Foucault, *History of Sexuality*, vol. 1, 42, 44, emphasis in the original.

an enigma that contingent circumstances subsequently offer opportunities for attempting to translate or retranslate. Delany's account of sexual activity in the Times Square porn theaters helps us to see how contact with the other exemplifies an opportunity for opening to the other; everyday seduction reactivates the scene of primal seduction. Delany also makes clear how the alien intrusion of the other's enigma is capable of becoming a source of pleasure, not only of traumatic disruption. There is pleasure and satisfaction in risking the self by opening it to alterity—pleasure and satisfaction quite distinct from those to be found in securing the self around its familiar coordinates. The pleasure of risk is not identical to that of unprotected sex, although barebacking often gives physical form to what should be understood as an ethical disposition of vulnerability to the other. Therein lie its interest and its ethical value.

When contact is considered in light of Laplanche's seduction theory, we see that cruising may be characterized as seduction in public. This redescription of cruising bears the proviso that, with the interposition of the unconscious, seduction is conceived of as contingent. There is no question here of what Freud at one point imagines as the "clever seducer"; rather, unintentional seduction precedes and consistently shadows deliberate seduction. Delany's distinction between contact and networking—in which the former's unpredictability contrasts with the latter's "motive-driven" aspect—helps to illuminate this ostensibly paradoxical notion of unintentional seduction. What I find interesting about certain practices of cruising is their aimlessness, their encouraging a centrifugal openness to the other without the necessity of having a particular object of seduction in mind. This would be cruising in the Kantian mode of "purposiveness without purpose." It is what Delany is advocating when he argues on behalf of institutions that facilitate our openness to contact with strangers in public space, and it is destroyed when cruising narrows its horizon to the seduction of a particular person or type, or when it focuses compulsively on the accomplishment of a single sexual act. The exigencies of online cruising eliminate what is most interesting and ethically exemplary about cruising.[33]

Cruising as I have redescribed it here involves not just hunting for sex but opening oneself to the world. The distinction between purposive and aimless

---

33. Here my argument overlaps with Bersani's characterization of cruising as "a form of relationality uncontaminated by desire." Drawing on Georg Simmel's modernist account of sociability as a mode of intercourse unmotivated by particular interests, Bersani argues that the deliberate avoidance of *relationships* in cruising "might be crucial in initiating, or at least clearing the ground for, a new relationality." See Leo Bersani, "Sociability and Cruising," *Umbr(a)*, 2002, 9–23.

cruising points to a difference not merely in degree but in kind: aimless cruising entails a centrifugal openness, whereas cruising as a single-minded quest insulates the self from alterity by centripetally narrowing the attention, often to crotch level. Cruising of the single-minded, centripetal sort is not remedied by monogamy (as some commentators argue) but, in fact, duplicates its limitations. From the perspective that I've advanced here, monogamy emerges as an ethical problem to which cruising of the centrifugal sort offers a potential solution. This solution entails acknowledging that cruising as a way of life remains irreducible to sexual cruising.[34]

The distinction between centrifugal and centripetal cruising also enables us to differentiate among manifestations of impersonality in cruising. For psychoanalyst Christopher Bollas, the impersonal relations characteristic of cruising are a problem because they reduce the other to an object; instrumentalizing others subordinates them to the self in ways that are ethically as well as clinically troubling. Yet by acknowledging that "the other may seem to embody strangeness itself," Bollas suggests, almost in spite of himself, how impersonal intimacy offers an opportunity for experiencing the other as greater or more encompassing than the self.[35] Needless to say, the notion of intimacy at stake in one barebacker's characterization of his erotic practice as "unlimited intimacy" cannot be anything but impersonal. This perspective on erotic impersonality qualifies as ethical by virtue of its registering the primacy not of the self but of the other, and by its willingness to engage intimacy less as a source of comfort than of risk.

The risks of intimacy are more profound than the risks of disease, although we tend to use the latter as an alibi for shunning the former. In its refusal of the pernicious ideology of safety, bareback subculture infers that the pleasures of intimacy may be worth the risks. As with certain forms of cruising, bareback sex often involves intimacy with strangers without predicating that intimacy on knowledge or understanding of the other—that is, without the subtle violence that usually accompanies epistemological relations. Throughout this book, I have tried to explore how we may relate to others and even become intimately engaged with them without needing to know or identify with them. When identification fails and one no longer recognizes anything

---

34. I have in mind the psychoanalytic critiques of monogamy advanced differently by Adam Phillips and Leo Bersani, the latter of whom draws on Laplanche. See Phillips, *Monogamy*; and Bersani, "Against Monogamy," *Oxford Literary Review* 20, no. 1-2 (1998): 3–21.

35. Christopher Bollas, "Cruising in the Homosexual Arena," in *Being a Character: Psychoanalysis and Self Experience* (New York: Hill and Wang, 1994), 149.

of him- or herself in the other, ethical conduct becomes paramount. Bareback subculture provokes my argument about impersonalist ethics not only because it involves cruising and impersonal sex but also because the subculture challenges recognition. We may not necessarily see ourselves in it. A psychoanalytic approach to this phenomenon suggests that identities of whatever sort remain incompatible with openness to alterity, and thus identity may be understood as not merely illusory but also, in this sense, as unethical. Contrary to the Christian ethic of viewing the other as a neighbor and loving him or her "as thyself," the psychoanalytic ethic insists that the other's strangeness be preserved rather than annihilated through identification. The question thus emerges in its full resonance: Why should strangers not be lovers and yet remain strangers?

BIBLIOGRAPHY

Achilles, Nancy. "The Development of the Homosexual Bar as an Institution." In *Sexual Deviance*, edited by John Gagnon and William Simon, 228–44. New York: Harper & Row, 1967.

Adams, Parveen. *The Emptiness of the Image: Psychoanalysis and Sexual Differences*. London: Routledge, 1996.

Apter, Emily, and William Pietz, eds. *Fetishism as Cultural Discourse*. Ithaca, NY: Cornell University Press, 1993.

Aydemir, Murat. *Images of Bliss: Ejaculation, Masculinity, Meaning*. Minneapolis: University of Minnesota Press, 2007.

Bad Object-Choices, ed. *How Do I Look? Queer Film and Video*. Seattle: Bay Press, 1991.

Balibar, Étienne. "Violence, Ideality and Cruelty." In *Politics and the Other Scene*, translated by Christine Jones, James Swenson, and Chris Turner, 129–45. London: Verso, 2002.

Bartlett, Neil. *Who Was That Man? A Present for Mr. Oscar Wilde*. London: Serpent's Tail, 1988.

Baudelaire, Charles. *The Painter of Modern Life, and Other Essays*. Translated by Jonathan Mayne. London: Phaidon, 1964.

Baynton, Douglas. *Forbidden Signs: American Culture and the Campaign against Sign Language*. Chicago: University of Chicago Press, 1996.

Bazin, André. "Death Every Afternoon." In *Rites of Realism: Essays on Corporeal Cinema*, edited by Ivone Margulies, translated by Mark A. Cohen, 27–31. Durham, NC: Duke University Press, 2003.

———. *What Is Cinema?* Vol. 1. Translated by Hugh Gray. Berkeley: University of California Press, 1967.

Beck, Ulrich. *Risk Society: Towards a New Modernity*. London: Sage, 1992. First published in German in 1986 by Suhrkamp Verlag.

———. *World Risk Society*. Cambridge: Polity, 1999.

Benveniste, Emile. *Problems in General Linguistics*. Translated by Mary Elizabeth Meek. Coral Gables, FL: University of Miami Press, 1971.

Berlant, Lauren, and Michael Warner. "Sex in Public." In *Intimacy*, edited by Lauren Berlant, 311–30. Chicago: University of Chicago Press, 2000.

Bersani, Leo. "Against Monogamy." *Oxford Literary Review* 20, no. 1-2 (1998): 3–21.

———. "Can Sex Make Us Happy?" *Raritan* 21, no. 4 (2002): 15–30.

———. *The Culture of Redemption*. Cambridge, MA: Harvard University Press, 1990.

———. *The Freudian Body: Psychoanalysis and Art*. New York: Columbia University Press, 1986.

———. *Homos*. Cambridge, MA: Harvard University Press, 1995.

———. "Is the Rectum a Grave?" In Crimp, *AIDS*, 197–222.

———. "Sociability and Cruising." *Umbr(a)*, 2002, 9–23.

Bérubé, Allan. "The History of Gay Bathhouses." In Colter et al., *Policing Public Sex*, 187–220.

Blackwood, Evelyn. "Wedding Bell Blues: Marriage, Missing Men, and Matrifocal Follies." *American Ethnologist* 32, no. 1 (2005): 3–19.

Bollas, Christopher. "Cruising in the Homosexual Arena." In *Being a Character: Psychoanalysis and Self Experience*, 144–64. New York: Hill and Wang, 1994.

Borneman, John. "Until Death Do Us Part: Marriage/Death in Anthropological Discourse." *American Ethnologist* 23, no. 2 (1996): 215–35.

Bourdieu, Pierre. "Marginalia—Some Additional Notes on the Gift." Translated by Richard Nice. In Schrift, *Logic of the Gift*, 231–41.

Boykin, Keith. *Beyond the Down Low: Sex, Lies, and Denial in Black America*. New York: Carroll and Graf, 2005.

Brandt, Allan M. "Behavior, Disease, and Health in the Twentieth-Century United States: The Moral Valence of Individual Risk." In Brandt and Rozin, *Morality and Health*, 53–77.

Brandt, Allan M., and Paul Rozin, eds. *Morality and Health*. New York: Routledge, 1997.

Butler, Judith. *Antigone's Claim: Kinship between Life and Death*. New York: Columbia University Press, 2000.

———. *Bodies That Matter: On the Discursive Limits of "Sex"*. New York: Routledge, 1993.

———. "Is Kinship Always Already Heterosexual?" *Differences* 13, no. 1 (2002): 14–44.

Califia, Pat. *Public Sex: The Culture of Radical Sex*. San Francisco: Cleis, 1994.

Canguilhem, Georges. *The Normal and the Pathological*. Translated by Carolyn R. Fawcett. 1966. Reprint, New York: Zone, 1991.

Carballo-Diéguez, Alex. "HIV, Barebacking, and Gay Men's Sexuality, circa 2001." *Journal of Sex Education and Therapy* 26, no. 3 (2001): 225–33.

Carballo-Diéguez, Alex, and José Bauermeister. "'Barebacking': Intentional Condomless Anal Sex in HIV-Risk Contexts; Reasons For and Against It." *Journal of Homosexuality* 47, no. 1 (2004): 1–16.

Carballo-Diéguez, Alex, Gary W. Dowsett, Ana Ventuneac, Robert H. Remien, Ivan Balan, Curtis Dolezal, Oswaldo Luciano, and Peter Lin. "Cybercartography of Popular Internet Sites Used by New York City MSM Interested in Bareback Sex." *AIDS and Education* 18 (2006): 475–89.

Carsten, Janet. "Substantivism, Antisubstantivism, and Anti-antisubstantivism." In Franklin and McKinnon, *Relative Values*, 29–53.

Cavell, Stanley. *The World Viewed: Reflections on the Ontology of Film*. Cambridge, MA: Harvard University Press, 1979.

Cavnor, B. J. "Dealing with Dick: An Interview with Dick Wadd." *Instigator Magazine*, March 2005, 34–35, 76.

Champagne, John. "'Stop Reading Films!': Film Studies, Close Analysis, and Gay Pornography." *Cinema Journal* 36, no. 4 (1997): 76–97.

Chauncey, George. *Gay New York: Gender, Urban Culture, and the Making of the Gay Male World, 1890–1940*. New York: Basic Books, 1994.

Cheuvront, J. P. "Attaining Meaning in the Face of Sexual Risk-Taking and Risk-Taking Consequences." *Studies in Gender and Sexuality* 8, no. 1 (2007): 69–85.

———. "High-Risk Sexual Behavior in the Treatment of HIV-Negative Patients." *Journal of Gay and Lesbian Psychotherapy* 6, no. 3 (2002): 7–26.

Chisholm, Dianne. *Queer Constellations: Subcultural Space in the Wake of the City*. Minneapolis: University of Minnesota Press, 2005.

Ciccarone, Daniel H., David E. Kanhouse, Rebecca L. Collins, Angela Miu, James L. Chen, Sally C. Morton, and Ron Stall. "Sex without Disclosure of Positive HIV Serostatus in a U.S. Probability Sample of Persons Receiving Medical Care for HIV Infection." *American Journal of Public Health* 93, no. 6 (2003): 949–54.

Clendenning, Alan. "HIV Case Airs Secrets of Porn Industry." *Miami Herald*, April 29, 2004, sec. A:16.

Clifford, James. *The Predicament of Culture: Twentieth-Century Ethnography, Literature, and Art*. Cambridge, MA: Harvard University Press, 1988.

Cohen, Phil. "Subcultural Conflict and Working-Class Community." In Hall et al., *Culture, Media, Language*, 78–87.

Collier, Jane F., and Sylvia J. Yanagisako, eds. *Gender and Kinship: Essays toward a Unified Analysis*. Stanford: Stanford University Press, 1987.

Colter, Ephen Glenn, Wayne Hoffman, Eva Pendleton, Alison Redick, and David Serlin, eds. *Policing Public Sex: Queer Politics and the Future of AIDS Activism*. Boston: South End, 1996.

Comolli, Jean-Louis. "Machines of the Visible." In *The Cinematic Apparatus*, edited by Teresa de Lauretis and Stephen Heath, 121–42. Houndmills, UK: Macmillan, 1980.

Cooper, Dennis. *The Sluts*. New York: Void Books, 2004.

Copjec, Joan. *Imagine There's No Woman: Ethics and Sublimation*. Cambridge, MA: MIT Press, 2002.

———. "Sex and the Euthanasia of Reason." In *Read My Desire: Lacan against the Historicists*, 201–36. Cambridge, MA: MIT Press, 1994.

———. "The Tomb of Perseverance: On *Antigone*." In *Giving Ground: The Politics of Propinquity*, edited by Joan Copjec and Michael Sorkin, 233–66. New York: Verso, 1999.

Copp, David, and Susan Wendell, eds. *Pornography and Censorship*. Buffalo: Prometheus Books, 1983.

Coviello, Peter. *Intimacy in America: Dreams of Affiliation in Antebellum Literature*. Minneapolis: University of Minnesota Press, 2005.

Crawford, Robert. "The Boundaries of the Self and the Unhealthy Other: Reflections on Health, Culture and AIDS." *Social Science and Medicine* 38, no. 10 (1994): 1347–65.

———. "Healthism and the Medicalization of Everyday Life." *International Journal of Health Services* 10, no. 3 (1980): 365–88.

Crimp, Douglas, ed. *AIDS: Cultural Analysis/Cultural Activism*. Cambridge, MA: MIT Press, 1988.

———. "How to Have Promiscuity in an Epidemic." In Crimp, *AIDS*, 237–70.

———. *Melancholia and Moralism: Essays on AIDS and Queer Politics*. Cambridge, MA: MIT Press, 2002.

Crossley, Michele L. "The Perils of Health Promotion and the 'Barebacking' Backlash." *Health* 6, no. 1 (2002): 47–68.

Davis, Mark. "HIV Prevention Rationalities and Serostatus in the Risk Narratives of Gay Men." *Sexualities* 5, no. 3 (2002): 281–99.

Dawidowicz, Lucy. *The Jewish Presence: Essays on Identity and History*. New York: Holt, 1977.

Dawson, Alvin G., Michael W. Ross, Doug Henry, and Anne Freeman. "Evidence of HIV Transmission Risk in Barebacking Men-Who-Have-Sex-With-Men: Cases from the Internet." In Halkitis, Wilton, and Drescher, *Barebacking*, 73–83.

Dean, Carolyn J. "Empathy, Pornography, and Suffering." *Differences* 14, no. 1 (2003): 88–124.

———. *The Frail Social Body: Pornography, Homosexuality, and Other Fantasies in Interwar France*. Berkeley: University of California Press, 2000.

Dean, Tim. *Beyond Sexuality*. Chicago: University of Chicago Press, 2000.

———. "Homosexuality and the Problem of Otherness." In Dean and Lane, *Homosexuality and Psychoanalysis*, 120–43.

———. "Sameness without Identity." *Umbr(a)*, 2002, 25–41.

Dean, Tim, and Christopher Lane, eds. *Homosexuality and Psychoanalysis*. Chicago: University of Chicago Press, 2001.

Dee, Jonathan. "Their Unexpected Adolescence." *New York Times Magazine*, June 26, 2005, 34–41, 54, 60, 63.

Delany, Samuel R. "The Gamble." *Corpus* 3, no. 1 (2005): 140–69.

———. *The Mad Man*. Rev. ed. Ramsey, NJ: Voyant, 2002.

———. "Street Talk/Straight Talk." In *Shorter Views: Queer Thoughts and the Politics of the Paraliterary*, 41–57. Hanover: Wesleyan University Press, 1999.

———. *Times Square Red, Times Square Blue*. New York: New York University Press, 1999.

de Lauretis, Teresa. *The Practice of Love: Lesbian Sexuality and Perverse Desire*. Bloomington: Indiana University Press, 1994.

Derrida, Jacques. *The Gift of Death*. Translated by David Willis. Chicago: University of Chicago Press, 1995.

———. *Given Time: 1. Counterfeit Money*. Translated by Peggy Kamuf. Chicago: University of Chicago Press, 1992.

Derrida, Jacques, and Pierre-Jean Labarrière. *Altérités*. Paris: Osiris, 1986.

Dollimore, Jonathan. "Sexual Disgust." In Dean and Lane, *Homosexuality and Psychoanalysis*, 366–86.

Douglas, Mary. "No Free Gifts." Foreword in Mauss, *The Gift*, vii–xviii.

Duesberg, Peter. *Infectious AIDS: Stretching the Germ Theory beyond Its Limits*. New York: North Atlantic Books, 1996.

————. *Inventing the AIDS Virus*. Washington, DC: Regnery, 1996.

Duggan, Lisa. *The Twilight of Equality? Neoliberalism, Cultural Politics, and the Attack on Democracy*. Boston: Beacon, 2003.

Dworkin, Andrea. *Pornography: Men Possessing Women*. New York: Putnam, 1979.

Dyess, Cynthia, and Tim Dean. "Gender: The Impossibility of Meaning." *Psychoanalytic Dialogues* 10, no. 5 (2000): 735–56.

Eco, Umberto. "How to Recognize a Porn Movie." In *How to Travel with a Salmon, and Other Essays*, translated by William Weaver, 206–10. London: Minerva, 1995.

Eng, David L. *Racial Castration: Managing Masculinity in Asian America*. Durham, NC: Duke University Press, 2001.

Epps, Brad. "The Fetish of Fluidity." In Dean and Lane, *Homosexuality and Psychoanalysis*, 412–31.

Faludi, Susan. "The Money Shot." *New Yorker*, October 30, 1995, 64–87.

Fanon, Frantz. *Black Skin, White Masks*. Translated by Charles Lam Markmann. 1952. Reprint, New York: Grove, 1967.

Faubion, James D., ed. *The Ethics of Kinship: Ethnographic Inquiries*. Lanham, MD: Rowman and Littlefield, 2001.

Feminist Anti-Censorship Taskforce Book Committee, ed. *Caught Looking: Feminism, Pornography, and Censorship*. New York: Caught Looking Press, 1986.

Ferguson, Frances. *Pornography, the Theory: What Utilitarianism Did to Action*. Chicago: University of Chicago Press, 2004.

Fletcher, John, ed. "Jean Laplanche and the Theory of Seduction." Special issue, *New Formations* 48 (2002–03).

Foucault, Michel. *Essential Works of Foucault, 1954–1984*. Vol. 1, *Ethics: Subjectivity and Truth*, edited by Paul Rabinow, translated by Robert Hurley et al. New York: New Press, 1997.

————. "Friendship as a Way of Life." In vol. 1 of *Essential Works*, 135–40.

————. *The History of Sexuality*. Vol. 1, *An Introduction*, translated by Robert Hurley. New York: Random House, 1978.

————. *The History of Sexuality*. Vol. 2, *The Use of Pleasure*, translated by Robert Hurley. New York: Random House, 1985.

————. *The History of Sexuality*. Vol. 3, *The Care of the Self*, translated by Robert Hurley. New York: Random House, 1986.

————. "An Interview by Stephen Riggins." In vol. 1 of *Essential Works*, 121–33.

————. "The Politics of Health in the Eighteenth Century." In *Essential Works of Foucault, 1954–1984*. Vol. 3, *Power*, edited by James D. Faubion, translated by Robert Hurley et al., 90–105. New York: New Press, 2000.

————. "Preface to *The History of Sexuality*, Volume Two." Translated by William Smock. In vol. 1 of *Essential Works*, 199–205.

————. "Sex, Power, and the Politics of Identity." In vol. 1 of *Essential Works*, 163–73.

————. "Sexual Choice, Sexual Act." In vol. 1 of *Essential Works*, 141–56.

————. "The Social Triumph of the Sexual Will." In vol. 1 of *Essential Works*, 157–62.

Franklin, Sarah, and Susan McKinnon, eds. *Relative Values: Reconfiguring Kinship Studies*. Durham, NC: Duke University Press, 2001.

Freeman, Gregory A. "In Search of Death." *Rolling Stone*, February 6, 2003, 44–48.

Freud, Sigmund. "The Antithetical Meaning of Primal Words." In vol. 11 of *Standard Edition*, 153–61.

——. *Beyond the Pleasure Principle.* In vol. 18 of *Standard Edition*, 1–64.

——. *Civilization and Its Discontents.* In vol. 21 of *Standard Edition*, 57–145.

——. *The Complete Letters of Sigmund Freud to Wilhelm Fliess, 1887–1904.* Edited and translated by Jeffrey Moussaieff Masson. Cambridge, MA: Harvard University Press, 1985.

——. "The Dynamics of Transference." In *Papers on Technique*, vol. 12 of *Standard Edition*, 97–108.

——. "Fetishism." In vol. 21 of *Standard Edition*, 149–57.

——. *The Interpretation of Dreams.* Vols. 4 and 5 of *Standard Edition*.

——. "Mourning and Melancholia." In vol. 14 of *Standard Edition*, 237–58.

——. *The Standard Edition of the Complete Psychological Works of Sigmund Freud.* Edited and translated by James Strachey. 24 vols. London: Hogarth, 1953–74.

——. *Three Essays on the Theory of Sexuality.* In vol. 7 of *Standard Edition*, 123–243.

——. *Totem and Taboo.* In vol. 13 of *Standard Edition*, 1–161.

——. "The Unconscious." In *Papers on Metapsychology*, vol. 14 of *Standard Edition*, 159–204.

Frow, John. "Gift and Commodity." In *Time and Commodity Culture: Essays in Cultural Theory and Postmodernity*, 102–217. Oxford: Clarendon, 1997.

Fung, Richard. "Looking for My Penis: The Eroticized Asian in Gay Video Porn." In Bad Object-Choices, *How Do I Look*, 145–68.

Fuss, Diana. "Monsters of Perversion: Jeffrey Dahmer and *The Silence of the Lambs*." In *Media Spectacles*, edited by Marjorie Garber, Jann Matlock, and Rebecca L. Walkowitz, 181–205. New York: Routledge, 1993.

Gadamer, Hans-Georg. *The Enigma of Health: The Art of Healing in a Scientific Age.* Translated by Jason Gaiger and Nicholas Walker. Stanford: Stanford University Press, 1996.

Gaines, Jane M., and Michael Renov, eds. *Collecting Visible Evidence.* Minneapolis: University of Minnesota Press, 1999.

Gallagher, John. "Slipping Up." *Advocate*, July 8, 1997, 33–34.

Gatewood, Charles. *Forbidden Photographs.* San Francisco: Flash Publications, 1995.

Gauthier, DeAnn K., and Craig J. Forsyth. "Bareback Sex, Bug Chasers, and the Gift of Death." *Deviant Behavior* 20, no. 1 (1999): 85–100.

Gavin, James. "Baring the Truth." *Out*, August 2007, 58–62.

Gaylord, Glenn. "Interview with a Barebacker." *Positive Living* (AIDS Project Los Angeles), May 2000. Http://www.thebody.com/apla/may00/barebacker.html.

Gelder, Ken, and Sarah Thornton, eds. *The Subcultures Reader.* London: Routledge, 1997.

Gendin, Stephen. "I Was a Teenage HIV Prevention Activist." In Colter et al., *Policing Public Sex*, 105–14.

Gibson, Pamela Church, and Roma Gibson, eds. *Dirty Looks: Women, Pornography, Power.* London: BFI, 1993.

Gillick, Muriel R. *The Denial of Aging: Perpetual Youth, Eternal Life, and Other Dangerous Fantasies.* Cambridge, MA: Harvard University Press, 2006.

Ginsberg, Allen. *White Shroud: Poems 1980–1985*. New York: Harper & Row, 1987.

Gittler, Ian. *Pornstar*. New York: Simon and Schuster, 1999.

Glenmullen, Joseph. *The Pornographer's Grief, and Other Tales of Human Sexuality*. New York: HarperCollins, 1993.

Goodlad, Lauren M. E., and Michael Bibby, eds. *Goth: Undead Subculture*. Durham, NC: Duke University Press, 2007.

Gordon, Bette. "*Variety*: The Pleasure in Looking." In Vance, *Pleasure and Danger*, 189–203.

Goss, Robert E. *Queering Christ: Beyond Jesus Acted Up*. Cleveland: Pilgrim, 2002.

Gourevitch, Philip. "Behold Now Behemoth: The Holocaust Memorial Museum; One More American Theme Park." *Harper's*, July 1993, 55–62.

Gray, Kevin. "What, Censor Us?" *Details*, December 2003, 132–37.

Gregory, C. A. *Gifts and Commodities*. London: Academic, 1982.

Grmek, Mirko D. *History of AIDS: Emergence and Origin of a Modern Pandemic*. Translated by Russell C. Maulitz and Jacalyn Duffin. Princeton, NJ: Princeton University Press, 1990.

Grosz, Elizabeth. "Lesbian Fetishism?" In *Space, Time, and Perversion: Essays on the Politics of Bodies*, 141–54. New York: Routledge, 1995.

Grov, Christian. "'Make Me Your Death Slave': Men Who Have Sex with Men and Use the Internet to Intentionally Spread HIV." *Deviant Behavior* 25, no. 4 (2003): 329–49.

Guillory, John. *Cultural Capital: The Problem of Literary Canon Formation*. Chicago: University of Chicago Press, 1993.

Habermas, Jürgen. *The Structural Transformation of the Public Sphere: An Inquiry into a Category of Bourgeois Society*. Translated by Thomas Burger. Cambridge, MA: MIT Press, 1989.

Halberstam, Judith. *In a Queer Time and Place: Transgender Bodies, Subcultural Lives*. New York: New York University Press, 2005.

Halkitis, Perry N., Leo Wilton, and Jack Drescher, eds. *Barebacking: Psychosocial and Public Health Approaches*. Binghamton, NY: Haworth Medical, 2005.

Halkitis, Perry N., Leo Wilton, and Paul Galatowitsch. "What's in a Term? How Gay and Bisexual Men Understand Barebacking." In Halkitis, Wilton, and Drescher, *Barebacking*, 35–48.

Halkitis, Perry N., Leo Wilton, Jeffrey T. Parsons, and C. Hoff. "Correlates of Sexual Risk-Taking Behavior among HIV-Positive Gay Men in Seroconcordant Primary Partner Relationships." *Psychology, Health, and Medicine* 19 (2004): 99–113.

Hall, Stuart, Dorothy Hobson, Andrew Lowe, and Paul Willis, eds. *Culture, Media, Language*. London: Hutchinson, 1980.

Hall, Stuart, and Tony Jefferson, eds. *Resistance through Rituals*. London: Routledge, 1993.

Halperin, David M. *What Do Gay Men Want? Sex, Risk, and Subjectivity*. Ann Arbor: University of Michigan Press, 2007.

Hammer, Mark. "Remembering Bob: Final Goodbyes to Poet Robert Creeley." *Artvoice* (Buffalo), April 28, 2005, 13.

Hari, Johann. "The New HIV Threat." *Independent*. November 7, 2005. Http://news .independent.co.uk/uk/health__medical/article325335.ece.

Hart, Lynda. *Fatal Women: Lesbian Sexuality and the Mark of Aggression*. Princeton, NJ: Princeton University Press, 1994.

Hartman, Chester. *City for Sale: The Transformation of San Francisco*. Rev. ed. Berkeley: University of California Press, 2002.

Hebdige, Dick. *Subculture: The Meaning of Style*. London: Methuen, 1979.

Herdt, Gilbert. *Sambia Sexual Culture: Essays from the Field*. Chicago: University of Chicago Press, 1999.

Herring, Scott. *Queering the Underworld: Slumming, Literature, and the Undoing of Lesbian and Gay History*. Chicago: University of Chicago Press, 2007.

Hoang, Nguyen Tan. "The Resurrection of Brandon Lee: The Making of a Gay Asian American Porn Star." In Williams, *Porn Studies*, 223–70.

Hole, Bud. "Fisting: Needing a Hand and Getting One." *Instigator Magazine*, April 2003, 16.

Holmes, Dave, and Dan Warner. "The Anatomy of a Forbidden Desire: Men, Penetration and Semen Exchange." *Nursing Inquiry* 12, no. 1 (2005): 10–20.

Hoover, Jeff. "Big, Bad Media Bugout." *POZ*, May 2005, 6–7.

Hughes, Dave. "Falling on Deaf Ears." *Instigator Magazine*, 2006, 27–29.

Humphreys, Laud. *The Tearoom Trade: Impersonal Sex in Public Places*. Chicago: Aldine, 1970.

Hyde, Lewis. *The Gift: Imagination and the Erotic Life of Property*. New York: Random House, 1983.

Instigator Magazine. Featured Fucko. 2006, 50–54.

Irigaray, Luce. *This Sex Which Is Not One*. Translated by Catherine Porter. Ithaca, NY: Cornell University Press, 1985.

Ivanchikova, Alla. "Sidewalks of Desire: Paradoxes of *Flâneurie* in Contemporary Queer Fiction." PhD diss., University at Buffalo (State University of New York), 2007.

Jacobs, Andrew. "Gays Debate Radical Steps to Curb Unsafe Sex." *New York Times*, February 15, 2005, sec. A:2.

Jacobs, Jane. *The Death and Life of Great American Cities*. New York: Random House, 1961.

Jameson, Fredric. *Signatures of the Visible*. New York: Routledge, 1992.

Juffer, Jane. *At Home with Pornography: Women, Sex, and Everyday Life*. New York: New York University Press, 1998.

Kant, Immanuel. "Perpetual Peace: A Philosophical Sketch." In *Kant: Selections*, edited by Lewis White Beck, 430–57. New York: Macmillan, 1988.

Kappeler, Susanne. *The Pornography of Representation*. London: Polity, 1986.

Kauffman, Linda S. *Bad Girls and Sick Boys: Fantasies in Contemporary Art and Culture*. Berkeley: University of California Press, 1998.

Kim, Richard. "Andrew Sullivan, Overexposed." *Nation*, June 5, 2001. http://www.thenation.com/doc/20010618/kim20010605.

King, J. L. *On the Down Low: A Journey into the Lives of "Straight" Black Men Who Sleep with Men*. New York: Broadway Books, 2004.

Kipnis, Laura. *Bound and Gagged: Pornography and the Politics of Fantasy in America*. New York: Grove, 1996.

Kirsch, Robert H., Brian Mills, and Everett W. Charters. "The Eroticism of Inclusion: A Gay Pornographic New Wave." Paper presented at the World Pornography Conference, Los Angeles, August 8, 1998. http://www.titanmedia.com/wpcpaper.html (accessed November 20, 2000).

Koch, Gertrud. "The Body's Shadow Realm." Translated by Jan-Christopher Horak and Joyce Rheuban. *October*, Fall 1989, 3–29.

Koffler, Kevin. "Life vs. Meth," *POZ*, July/August 2002, 39–42, 52–54.

Kristeva, Julia. *Strangers to Ourselves*. Translated by Leon Roudiez. New York: Columbia University Press, 1991.

Lacan, Jacques. *Écrits: A Selection*. Translated by Alan Sheridan. New York: Norton, 1977.

———. *The Four Fundamental Concepts of Psychoanalysis*. Edited by Jacques-Alain Miller. Translated by Alan Sheridan. Harmondsworth, UK: Penguin, 1979.

———. *Le séminaire, livre III: Les psychoses (1955–1956)*. Edited by Jacques-Alain Miller. Paris: Seuil, 1981.

———. *The Seminar of Jacques Lacan. Book 7, The Ethics of Psychoanalysis, 1959–1960*, edited by Jacques-Alain Miller, translated by Dennis Porter. New York: Norton, 1992.

———. "The Signification of the Phallus." In *Écrits*, 281–91.

———. "The Subversion of the Subject and the Dialectic of Desire in the Freudian Unconscious." In *Écrits*, 292–325.

Lang, Berel. *Holocaust Representation: Art within the Limits of History and Ethics*. Baltimore: Johns Hopkins University Press, 2000.

Laplanche, Jean. *Essays on Otherness*. Edited by John Fletcher. London: Routledge, 1999.

———. *Life and Death in Psychoanalysis*. Translated by Jeffrey Mehlman. Baltimore: Johns Hopkins University Press, 1976.

———. *New Foundations for Psychoanalysis*. Translated by David Macey. Oxford: Blackwell, 1989.

Leap, William L., ed. *Public Sex/Gay Space*. New York: Columbia University Press, 1999.

Leichter, Howard M. "Lifestyle Correctness and the New Secular Morality." In Brandt and Rozin, *Morality and Health*, 359–78.

Lévi-Strauss, Claude. *The Elementary Structures of Kinship*. Translated by James Harle Bell, John Richard von Sturmer, and Rodney Needham. Boston: Beacon, 1969.

———. *Introduction to the Work of Marcel Mauss*. Translated by Felicity Baker. London: Routledge and Kegan Paul, 1987.

Levinas, Emmanuel. *Entre Nous: Thinking-of-the-Other*. Translated by Michael B. Smith and Barbara Harshav. New York: Columbia University Press, 1998.

Lewin, Ellen. *Lesbian Mothers*. Ithaca, NY: Cornell University Press, 1993.

Lewin, Ellen, and William L. Leap, eds. *Out in the Field: Reflections of Lesbian and Gay Anthropologists*. Urbana: University of Illinois Press, 1996.

———, eds. *Out in Theory: The Emergence of Lesbian and Gay Anthropology*. Urbana: University of Illinois Press, 2002.

Lindell, John. "Public Space for Public Sex." In Colter et al., *Policing Public Sex*, 72–80.

Lingis, Alphonso. *Dangerous Emotions*. Berkeley: University of California Press, 2000.

MacKinnon, Catharine A. *Only Words*. Cambridge, MA: Harvard University Press, 1993.

Madigan, Nick. "HIV Cases Shut Down Pornography Film Industry." *New York Times*, April 17, 2004, sec. A:11.

———. "Sex Videos on Pause, and Idled Actors Fret." *New York Times*, April 25, 2004, sec. 9:1.

———. "Voice of Health in a Pornographic World." *New York Times*, May 10, 2004, sec. A:14.

Malloy, Doug. "Body Piercings." In *Modern Primitives*, edited by V. Vale and Andrea Juno, 25–26. San Francisco: Re/Search Publications, 1989.

Mannoni, Octave. *Clefs pour l'imaginaire ou l'autre scène*. Paris: Seuil, 1969.

Marriott, David. *On Black Men*. New York: Columbia University Press, 2000.

Marston, Jayson. "Fucking in the Real World." *Instigator Magazine*, January 2003, 32–33.

———. "White Skinhead Seeks Black Submissives." In *Strategic Sex: Why They Won't Keep It in the Bedroom*, edited by D. Travers Scott, 93–95. New York: Harrington Park, 1999.

Mauss, Marcel. *The Gift: The Form and Reason for Exchange in Archaic Societies*. Translated by W. D. Halls. New York: Norton, 1990.

———. "Gift, Gift." Translated by Koen Decoster. 1924. Reprint in Schrift, *Logic of the Gift*, 28–32.

McBride, Dwight A. "It's a White Man's World: Race in the Gay Marketplace of Desire." In *Why I Hate Abercrombie & Fitch: Essays on Race and Sexuality*, 88–131. New York: New York University Press, 2005.

McCallum, E. L. *Object Lessons: How to Do Things with Fetishism*. Albany: SUNY Press, 1999.

McRuer, Robert. *Crip Theory: Cultural Signs of Queerness and Disability*. New York: New York University Press, 2006.

Menand, Louis. "*Nanook* and Me: *Fahrenheit 9/11* and the Documentary Tradition." *New Yorker*, August 9 and 16, 2004, 90–93, 95–96.

Mercer, Kobena. "Skin Head Sex Thing: Racial Difference and the Homoerotic Imaginary." In Bad Object-Choices, *How Do I Look?* 169–222.

Millet, Catherine. *The Sexual Life of Catherine M*. Translated by Adriana Hunter. New York: Grove, 2002.

Mitchell, Sharon. "How to Put Condoms in the Picture." *New York Times*, May 2, 2004, sec. 4:11.

Mohr, Richard D. *Gay Ideas: Outing and Other Controversies*. Boston: Beacon, 1992.

Moore, Parker. Interview with Dick Wadd. *Unzipped Monthly*, March 2001, 52–54.

Morgan, Robin. "Theory and Practice: Pornography and Rape." In *Take Back the Night: Women on Pornography*, edited by Laura Lederer, 134–40. New York: William Morrow, 1980.

Morin, Stephen F., Karen Vernon, John (Jay) Harcourt, Wayne T. Steward, Jonathan Volk, Thomas H. Riess, Torsten B. Neilands, Marisa McLaughlin, and Thomas J. Coates. "Why HIV Infections Have Increased among Men Who Have Sex with Men and What to Do about It: Findings from California Focus Groups." *AIDS and Behavior* 7, no. 4 (2003): 353–62.

Morris, Paul. "No Limits: Necessary Danger in Male Porn." Paper presented at the World Pornography Conference, Los Angeles, August 8, 1998. http://www.treasureisland media.com/TreasureIslandMedia__2007/paulsPapers.php?article=noLimits (accessed August 2001).

Moss, Donald, and Lynne Zeavin. "The Female Homosexual: C'est Nous." In *That Obscure Subject of Desire: Freud's Female Homosexual Revisited*, edited by Ronnie C. Lesser and Erica Schoenberg, 197–214. New York: Routledge, 1999.

Muggleton, David, and Rupert Weinzierl, eds. *The Post-Subcultures Reader*. Oxford: Berg, 2003.

Murr, Andrew. "A Web of HIV Infections." *Newsweek*, April 26, 2004, 8.

Nardi, Peter M. "Reclaiming the Importance of Laud Humphreys' *Tearoom Trade: Impersonal Sex in Public Places*." In Leap, *Public Sex/Gay Space*, 23–27.

Nietzsche, Friedrich. *Thus Spoke Zarathustra*. Translated by R. J. Hollingdale. Harmondsworth, UK: Penguin, 1961.

Nunokawa, Jeff. "'All the Sad Young Men': AIDS and the Work of Mourning." In *Inside/Out: Lesbian Theories, Gay Theories*, edited by Diana Fuss, 311–23. New York: Routledge, 1991.

Odets, Walt. *In the Shadow of the Epidemic: Being HIV-Negative in the Age of AIDS*. Durham, NC: Duke University Press, 1995.

O'Hara, Scott. *Autopornography: A Memoir of Life in the Lust Lane*. New York: Harrington Park, 1997.

———. "Talking with My Mouth Full." In Colter et al., *Policing Public Sex*, 81–86.

———. "Viral Communion: There's Life beyond Condoms." *POZ*, November 1997, 69.

Olds, Sharon. "More Blessèd." In Schrift, *Logic of the Gift*, xiii.

Padden, Carol, and Tom Humphries. *Inside Deaf Culture*. Cambridge, MA: Harvard University Press, 2005.

Patterson, Orlando. *Slavery and Social Death: A Comparative Study*. Cambridge, MA: Harvard University Press, 1982.

Patton, Cindy. *Fatal Advice: How Safe-Sex Education Went Wrong*. Durham, NC: Duke University Press, 1996.

Phillips, Adam. *Monogamy*. New York: Pantheon, 1996.

———. "Sameness Is All." In *Promises, Promises: Essays on Literature and Psychoanalysis*, 334–41. London: Faber, 2000.

———. *Side Effects*. New York: HarperCollins, 2006.

Pinkerton, Steven D., and Paul R. Abramson. "Is Risky Sex Rational?" *Journal of Sex Research* 29, no. 4 (1992): 561–68.

Povinelli, Elizabeth A. *The Cunning of Recognition: Indigenous Alterities and the Making of Australian Multiculturalism*. Durham, NC: Duke University Press, 2002.

Pratt, Mary Louise. *Imperial Eyes: Travel Writing and Transculturation*. London: Routledge, 1992.

Preston, John. *My Life as a Pornographer and Other Indecent Acts*. New York: Richard Kasak Books, 1993.

Queen, Carol. "Porn HIV Scare May Signal Coming Changes." *Good Vibrations Magazine*, May 12, 2004. Http://www.goodvibes.com/Content.aspx?id=1252&leftMenu=35&lr=y.

Rabinow, Paul. "Artificiality and Enlightenment: From Sociobiology to Biosociality." In *Incorporations*, edited by Jonathan Crary and Sanford Kwinter, 234–52. New York: Zone, 1992.

Raheja, Gloria Goodwin. *The Poison in the Gift: Ritual, Prestation, and the Dominant Caste in a North Indian Village*. Chicago: University of Chicago Press, 1988.

Rakoff, David. "I'm Dying to Meet You in the Next Life." *GQ*, May 2003, 196–201, 213–14.

Rapp, Rayna, Deborah Heath, and Karen-Sue Taussig. "Genealogical Dis-Ease: Where Hereditary Abnormality, Biomedical Explanation, and Family Responsibility Meet." In Franklin and McKinnon, *Relative Values*, 384–409.

Rauch, Jonathan. *Gay Marriage: Why It Is Good for Gays, Good for Straights, and Good for America*. New York: Henry Holt, 2004.

Reid, Colbey Emmerson. "What Pornography Can Teach Religion." *Journal for Cultural and Religious Theory* 6, no. 2 (2005): 109–16.

Relf, Michael V., Bu Huang, Jacquelyn Campbell, and Joe Catania. "Gay Identity, Interpersonal Violence, and HIV Risk Behaviors: An Empirical Test of Theoretical Relationships among a Probability-Based Sample of Urban Men Who Have Sex with Men." *Journal of the Association of Nurses in AIDS Care* 15, no. 2 (2004): 14–26.

Ricco, John Paul. *The Logic of the Lure*. Chicago: University of Chicago Press, 2002.

Richter, Alan. *Sexual Slang: A Compendium of Offbeat Words and Colorful Phrases from Shakespeare to Today*. 3rd ed. New York: HarperCollins, 1995.

Robinson, Paul. *Queer Wars: The New Gay Right and Its Critics*. Chicago: University of Chicago Press, 2005.

Rodgers, Bruce. *Gay Talk: A (Sometimes Outrageous) Dictionary of Gay Slang*. 1972. Reprint, New York: Paragon, 1979.

Rofes, Eric. "Barebacking and the New AIDS Hysteria." *Stranger* (Seattle), April 8, 1999, 15–19.

———. *Dry Bones Breathe: Gay Men Creating Post-AIDS Identities and Cultures*. New York: Harrington Park, 1998.

———. *Reviving the Tribe: Regenerating Gay Men's Sexuality and Culture in the Ongoing Epidemic*. New York: Harrington Park, 1996.

Rose, Nikolas. *The Politics of Life Itself: Biomedicine, Power, and Subjectivity in the Twenty-First Century*. Princeton, NJ: Princeton University Press, 2007.

Rosenberg, Charles. "Banishing Risk: Continuity and Change in the Moral Management of Disease." In Brandt and Rozin, *Morality and Health*, 35–51.

Rosenfeld, Alvin H. "Another Revisionism: Popular Culture and the Changing Image of the Holocaust." In *Bitburg in Moral and Political Perspective*, edited by Geoffrey H. Hartman, 90–113. Indianapolis: Indiana University Press, 1986.

Ross, Scott. "AIM Working to Contain HIV: Search for Second-Generation Continues." *Adult Video News*, April 13, 2004. Http://www.avn.com/video/articles/15719.html.

Rotello, Gabriel, *Sexual Ecology: AIDS and the Destiny of Gay Men*. New York: Dutton, 1997.

Rubin, Gayle. "The Catacombs: A Temple of the Butthole." In *Leatherfolk: Radical Sex, People, Politics, and Practice*, edited by Mark Thompson, 119–41. Boston: Alyson, 1991.

———. "Elegy for the Valley of Kings: AIDS and the Leather Community in San Francisco, 1981–1996." In *In Changing Times: Gay Men and Lesbians Encounter HIV/AIDS*, edited by Martin P. Levine, Peter M. Nardi, and John H. Gagnon, 101–44. Chicago: University of Chicago Press, 1997.

———. "The Miracle Mile: South of Market and Gay Male Leather 1962–1997." In *Reclaiming San Francisco: History, Politics, Culture*, edited by James Brook, Chris Carlsson, and Nancy J. Peters, 247–72. San Francisco: City Lights Books, 1998.

———. "Sexual Traffic." Interview with Judith Butler. *Differences* 6, no. 2-3 (1994): 62–99.

———. "The South of Market Leather History." *San Francisco Frontiers*, September 20, 2001, 20–22.

———. "Thinking Sex: Notes for a Radical Theory of the Politics of Sexuality." In Vance, *Pleasure and Danger*, 267–319.

———. "The Traffic in Women: Notes on the 'Political Economy' of Sex." In *Toward an Anthropology of Women*, edited by Rayna R. Reiter, 157–210. New York: Monthly Review, 1975.

———. "The Valley of the Kings: Leathermen in San Francisco, 1960–1990." PhD diss., University of Michigan, 1994.

Santner, Eric L. *On the Psychotheology of Everyday Life: Reflections on Freud and Rosenzweig.* Chicago: University of Chicago Press, 2001.

Santora, Marc. "Tests Pending in Cases Tied to Fierce HIV." *New York Times*, March 30, 2005, sec. B:5.

Santora, Marc, and Lawrence K. Altman. "Rare and Aggressive HIV Reported in New York." *New York Times*, February 12, 2005, sec. A:3.

Scarce, Michael. "A Ride on the Wild Side: An HIV-Prevention Activist Goes through the Latex Looking Glass to Discover Who's Doing It Raw, and Why," *POZ*, February 1999, 52–55, 70–71.

———. "Something Borrowed, Something Blue: Viagra Use among Gay Men." In *Smearing the Queer: Medical Bias in the Health Care of Gay Men*, 137–53. New York: Harrington Park, 1999.

Schehr, Lawrence R. "Writing Bareback." *Journal of Twentieth-Century/Contemporary French Studies* 6, no. 1 (2002): 181–202.

Schmid, David. *Natural Born Celebrities: Serial Killers in American Culture.* Chicago: University of Chicago Press, 2005.

Schmidt, Casper G. "The Group-Fantasy Origins of AIDS." *Journal of Psychohistory* 12, no. 1 (1984): 37–78.

Schneider, David M. *A Critique of the Study of Kinship.* Ann Arbor: University of Michigan Press, 1984.

Schrift, Alan D., ed. *The Logic of the Gift: Toward an Ethic of Generosity.* New York: Routledge, 1997.

Scott, D. Travers, ed. *Strategic Sex: Why They Won't Keep It in the Bedroom.* New York: Harrington Park, 1999.

Scott, Joan W. "'Experience.'" In *Feminists Theorize the Political*, edited by Judith Butler and Joan W. Scott, 22–40. New York: Routledge, 1992.

Sedgwick, Eve Kosofsky. *Between Men: English Literature and Male Homosocial Desire.* New York: Columbia University Press, 1985.

———. *Epistemology of the Closet.* Berkeley: University of California Press, 1990.

———. *Touching Feeling: Affect, Pedagogy, Performativity.* Durham, NC: Duke University Press, 2003.

Shernoff, Michael. *Without Condoms: Unprotected Sex, Gay Men, and Barebacking.* New York: Routledge, 2006.

Shidlo, Ariel, Huso Yi, and Boaz Dalit. "Attitudes toward Unprotected Anal Intercourse: Assessing HIV-Negative Gay or Bisexual Men." In Halkitis, Wilton, and Drescher, *Barebacking*, 107–28.

Solnit, Rebecca, and Susan Schwartzenberg. *Hollow City: The Siege of San Francisco and the Crisis of American Urbanism.* New York: Verso, 2000.

Somerville, Siobhan B. *Queering the Color Line: Race and the Invention of Homosexuality in American Culture.* Durham, NC: Duke University Press, 2000.

Sontag, Susan. *AIDS and Its Metaphors.* New York: Farrar, Straus, and Giroux, 1989.

Specter, Michael. "Higher Risk: Crystal Meth, the Internet, and Dangerous Choices about AIDS." *New Yorker,* May 23, 2005, 38–45.

Spyer, Patricia, ed. *Border Fetishisms: Material Objects in Unstable Spaces.* New York: Routledge, 1998.

Steiner, George. *In Bluebeard's Castle: Some Notes towards the Redefinition of Culture.* New Haven: Yale University Press, 1971.

Stewart, Susan. "The Marquis de Meese." In *Crimes of Writing: Problems in the Containment of Representation,* 235–72. New York: Oxford University Press, 1991.

Stoler, Ann Laura. *Race and the Education of Desire: Foucault's History of Sexuality and the Colonial Order of Things.* Durham, NC: Duke University Press, 1995.

Strathern, Marilyn. *After Nature: English Kinship in the Late Twentieth Century.* Cambridge: Cambridge University Press, 1992.

———. *The Gender of the Gift: Problems with Women and Problems with Society in Melanesia.* Berkeley: University of California Press, 1988.

———. *Reproducing the Future: Anthropology, Kinship, and the New Reproductive Technologies.* New York: Routledge, 1992.

Strong, Thomas. "Kinship between Judith Butler and Anthropology: A Review Essay." *Ethnos* 67, no. 3 (2002): 401–18.

Suarez, Troy, and Jeffrey Miller. "Negotiating Risks in Context: A Perspective on Unprotected Anal Intercourse and Barebacking among Men Who Have Sex with Men—Where Do We Go from Here?" *Archives of Sexual Behavior* 30, no. 3 (2001): 287–300.

Sullivan, Andrew. "Poz4Poz Saves Lives." *Advocate,* October 11, 2005, 112.

———, ed. *Same-Sex Marriage: Pro and Con.* New York: Vintage, 1997.

———. "Sex- and Death-Crazed Gays Play Viral Russian Roulette!" *Salon,* January 24, 2003. Http://www.salon.com/opinion/sullivan/2003/01/24/rolling/index.html.

———. *Virtually Normal: An Argument about Homosexuality.* New York: Knopf, 1995.

Taormino, Tristan. "Porn Faces Reality: HIV Outbreak in California Porn Industry Highlights Risky Business." *Village Voice,* April 30, 2004. Http://www.villagevoice.com/people/0418,taormino,53111,24.html.

Taylor, Charles. *Multiculturalism and "The Politics of Recognition": An Essay,* edited by Amy Gutmann. Princeton, NJ: Princeton University Press, 1992.

Tewksbury, Richard. "Bareback Sex and the Quest for HIV: Assessing the Relationship in Internet Personal Advertisements of Men Who Have Sex with Men." *Deviant Behavior* 24 (2003): 467–82.

———. "Bathhouse Intercourse: Structural and Behavioral Aspects of an Erotic Oasis." In *Sexual Deviance: A Reader,* edited by Christopher Hensley and Richard Tewksbury, 203–32. Boulder: Lynne Rienner, 2003.

Thorn, Michael. "Barebacking with Jeff Palmer." *Instigator Magazine,* April 2003, 18–24.

———. "Fort Troff." *Instigator Magazine,* January 2003, 17–20.

———. "Fucking Deep into the Core of Reality." *Instigator Magazine*, January 2003, 2.

———. Letter from Our Editor, *Instigator Magazine*, April 2003, 2.

Thornton, Sarah. *Club Cultures: Music, Media, and Subcultural Capital*. Cambridge: Polity, 1995.

Titmuss, Richard M. *The Gift Relationship: From Human Blood to Social Policy*. New York: Pantheon, 1971.

Tomso, Gregory. "Bug Chasing, Barebacking, and the Risks of Care." *Literature and Medicine* 23, no. 1 (2004): 88–111.

Toy. "Biker Bitch Fantasy." *Instigator Magazine*, January 2003, 49–54.

Trask, Michael. *Cruising Modernism: Class and Sexuality in American Literature and Social Thought*. Ithaca, NY: Cornell University Press, 2003.

Treichler, Paula A. *How to Have Theory in an Epidemic: Cultural Chronicles of AIDS*. Durham, NC: Duke University Press, 1999.

Tucker, Scott. "Gender, Fucking, and Utopia: An Essay in Response to John Stoltenberg's *Refusing to Be a Man*." *Social Text* 27 (1990): 3–34.

Tuhkanen, Mikko. "Clones and Breeders: An Introduction to Queer Sameness." *Umbr(a)*, 2002, 4–7.

———. Review of *Antigone's Claim*, by Judith Butler. *Umbr(a)*, 2003, 140–44.

Tuller, David. "Experts Fear a Risky Recipe: Viagra, Drugs and HIV." *New York Times*, October 16, 2001, sec. F:5(L).

Van de Ven, P., S. Kippax, J. Crawford, P. Rawstorne, G. Prestage, A. Grulich, and D. Murphy. "In a Minority of Gay Men, Sexual Risk Practice Indicates Strategic Positioning for Perceived Risk Reduction Rather than Unbridled Sex." *AIDS Care* 14, no. 4 (2002): 471–80.

Vance, Carole S., ed. *Pleasure and Danger: Exploring Female Sexuality*. London: Routledge, 1984.

———. "The Pleasures of Looking: The Attorney General's Commission on Pornography versus Visual Images." In *The Critical Image: Essays on Contemporary Photography*, edited by Carol Squiers, 38–58. Seattle: Bay Press, 1990.

"Visual AIDS: Gay Male Porn and Safer Sex Pedagogy." Roundtable discussion, organized and edited by Nicolas Sheon, Center for AIDS Prevention Studies, University of California, San Francisco, May 28, 1999. Http://hivinsite.ucsf.edu/prevention/prev__contro/2098.4218.html (accessed September 2000).

Wagner, Roy. "Analogic Kinship: A Daribi Example." *American Ethnologist* 4 (1977): 623–42.

Waldby, Catherine, and Robert Mitchell. *Tissue Economies: Blood, Organs, and Cell Lines in Late Capitalism*. Durham, NC: Duke University Press, 2006.

Warner, Michael. *Publics and Counterpublics*. New York: Zone, 2002.

———. *The Trouble with Normal: Sex, Politics, and the Ethics of Queer Life*. New York: Free Press, 1999.

Watney, Simon. *Policing Desire: Pornography, AIDS, and the Media*. London: Methuen, 1987.

Waugh, Thomas. *Hard to Imagine: Gay Male Eroticism in Photography and Film from Their Beginnings to Stonewall*. New York: Columbia University Press, 1996.

Weston, Kath. *Families We Choose: Lesbians, Gays, Kinship*. New York: Columbia University Press, 1991.

Williams, Linda. *Hard Core: Power, Pleasure, and the "Frenzy of the Visible"*. Berkeley: University of California Press, 1989.

———, ed. *Porn Studies*. Durham, NC: Duke University Press, 2004.

———. "Second Thoughts on *Hard Core*: American Obscenity Law and the Scapegoating of Deviance." In Gibson and Gibson, *Dirty Looks*, 46–61.

———. "Skin Flicks on the Racial Border: Pornography, Exploitation, and Interracial Lust." In Williams, *Porn Studies*, 271–308.

Willis, Ellen. "Feminism, Moralism, and Pornography." In *Desire: The Politics of Sexuality*, edited by Ann Snitow, Christine Stansell, and Sharon Thompson, 82–88. London: Virago, 1984.

Willis, Paul. "Notes on Method." In Hall et al., *Culture, Media, Language*. 88–95.

Wilton, Leo, Perry N. Halkitis, Gary English, and Michael Roberson. "An Exploratory Study of Barebacking, Club Drug Use, and Meanings of Sex in Black and Latino Gay and Bisexual Men in the Age of AIDS." In Halkitis, Wilton, and Drescher, *Barebacking*, 49–72.

Winge, Theresa M. "Constructing 'Neo-Tribal' Identities through Dress: Modern Primitives and Body Modifications." In Muggleton and Weinzierl, *The Post-Subcultures Reader*, 119–32.

Winnicott, D. W. *Playing and Reality*. 1971. Reprint, London: Routledge, 1991.

Wyschogrod, Edith, Jean-Joseph Goux, and Eric Boynton, eds. *The Enigma of Gift and Sacrifice*. New York: Fordham University Press, 2002.

Yep, Gust A., Karen E. Lovaas, and Alex V. Pagonis. "The Case of 'Riding Bareback': Sexual Practices and the Paradoxes of Identity in the Era of AIDS." *Journal of Homosexuality* 42, no. 4 (2002): 1–14.

Zeeland, Steven. *Barrack Buddies and Soldier Lovers: Dialogues with Gay Young Men in the U.S. Military*. New York: Harrington Park, 1993.

———. *The Masculine Marine: Homoeroticism in the U.S. Marine Corps*. New York: Harrington Park, 1996.

———. *Military Trade*. New York: Harrington Park, 1999.

———. *Sailors and Sexual Identity: Crossing the Line between "Straight" and "Gay" in the U.S. Navy*. New York: Harrington Park, 1995.

Ziplow, Stephen. *The Film Maker's Guide to Pornography*. New York: Drake, 1977.

Žižek, Slavoj. "The Real of Sexual Difference." In *Reading Seminar XX: Lacan's Major Work on Love, Knowledge, and Feminine Sexuality*, edited by Suzanne Barnard and Bruce Fink, 57–75. Albany: SUNY Press, 2002.

VIDEOGRAPHY

American Porn. Directed by Michael Kirk. Frontline, 2002.

Anal Cum Drippers. Directed by Mysterio. Maximum Xposure, 2004.

Beyond Vanilla. Directed by Claes Lilja. Strand, 2003.

Breed Me. Directed by Paul Morris. Treasure Island Media, 1999.

Breeding Mike O'Neill. Directed by Paul Morris. Treasure Island Media, 2002.

Breeding Season. Directed by Paul Morris. Treasure Island Media, 2006.

Cocktails #2. Directed by Lizzy Borden. Extreme Associates, 2001.

Creampie Milkshakes. Directed by Rob Black. Extreme Associates, 2004.

Forced Entry. Directed by Rob Black. Extreme Associates, 2002.

Fucking Crazy. Directed by Erich Lange. Treasure Island Media, 2003.

The Gift. Directed by Louise Hogarth. Dream Out Loud Productions, 2003.

Knocked Up. Directed by Paul Morris. Treasure Island Media, 2002.

Max Hardcore Extreme. Vol. 7. Directed by Max Hardcore. Max World Entertainment, 2005.

Meat Rack. Directed by Max Sohl. Treasure Island Media, 2005.

Niggas' Revenge. Directed by Dick Wadd. Dick Wadd Productions, 2001.

NYPD. Directed by Dick Wadd. Dick Wadd Productions, 1997.

The Other Side of AIDS. Directed by Robin Scovill. Hazel Wood Pictures, 2004.

Pigs at the Troff. Directed by Dick Wadd. Dick Wadd Productions, 2000.

Plantin' Seed. Directed by Paul Morris. Treasure Island Media, 2004.

Riding Billy Wild. Directed by Paul Morris. Treasure Island Media, 2003.

Some Pigs. Directed by Dick Wadd. Dick Wadd Productions, 1998.

Swallow. Directed by Paul Morris. Treasure Island Media, 2000.

What I Can't See. Directed by Paul Morris. Treasure Island Media, 1999.

WEB SITES

Adult Industry Medical Healthcare Foundation, http://www.aim-med.org.

AIDS Myth Exposed, http://www.aidsmythexposed.com.

Bareback.com home page, http://www.bareback.com.

Bareback Exchange, http://bugshare.net.

BarebackJack.com home page, http://www.barebackjack.com.

Chaps II, Chaps Bar San Francisco home page, http://www.chapsbarsanfrancisco.com.

Dick Wadd Media, http://www.dickwaddfetish.com.

Duesberg on AIDS, Peter Duesberg's HIV/AIDS research site, http://www.duesberg.com.

Gay Shame San Francisco, http://www.gayshamesf.org.

Geek Slut's home page, http://www.geekslut.org.

HIV InSite: University of California, San Francisco, Center for HIV Information, http://hivinsite.ucsf.edu.

Jeff Palmer's home page, http://www.jeffpalmer.net.

Machofucker, http://www.machofucker.com.

Paul Morris/Treasure Island Media, http://www.treasureislandmedia.com.

POZ.com home page, http://www.poz.com.

Rawloads.com home page, http://www.rawloads.com.

The Body: The Complete HIV/AIDS Resource, http://www.thebody.com.

Titan Media/TitanMen.com home page, http://www.titanmen.com.

TitPig's home page, http://www.titpig.net.

VirusMyth: A Rethinking AIDS Web Site, http://www.virusmyth.net.

LEGAL CASES

Lawrence v. Texas, 539 U.S. 558 (2003).

Marvin Miller v. State of California, 413 U.S. 15 (1973).

United States of America v. Extreme Associates, Inc., 352 F.Supp. 2d 578 (W.D. Pa. 2005).

INDEX

Made in the USA
Lexington, KY
01 October 2014